THE TWELVE STEP LIFE RECOVERY™ DEVOTIONAL

DAVID STOOP, Ph.D.
Minirth-Meier-Stoop Clinic
STEPHEN ARTERBURN, M.Ed.
New Life Treatment Centers

Tyndale House Publishers, Inc.
Wheaton, Illinois

Library of Congress Cataloging-in-Publication Data

Arterburn, Stephen, date
The twelve step life recovery devotional : thirty meditations for each step in recovery / Stephen Arterburn, David Stoop.
p. cm.
ISBN 0-8423-4758-5—ISBN 0-8423-4753-4 (pbk.)
1. Twelve-step programs—Religious aspects—Christianity—Meditations. 2. Bible—Meditations. 3. Devotional calendars. I. Stoop, David A. II. Title. III. Title: 12 step life recovery devotional.
BL624.5.A77 1991
242′.4—dc20 91-27979

Printed in the United States of America

97 96 95 94
10 9 8 7 6 5

The Twelve Steps

1. We admitted that we were powerless over our dependencies—that our lives had become unmanageable.
2. We came to believe that a Power greater than ourselves could restore us to sanity.
3. We made a decision to turn our will and our lives over to the care of God as we understood him.
4. We made a searching and fearless moral inventory of ourselves.
5. We admitted to God, to ourselves, and to another human being the exact nature of our wrongs.
6. We were entirely ready to have God remove all these defects of character.
7. We humbly asked him to remove our shortcomings.
8. We made a list of all persons we had harmed and became willing to make amends to them all.
9. We made direct amends to such people wherever possible, except when to do so would injure them or others.
10. We continued to take personal inventory and when we were wrong promptly admitted it.
11. We sought through prayer and meditation to improve our conscious contact with God, as we understood him, praying only for knowledge of his will for us and the power to carry it out.
12. Having had a spiritual awakening as the result of these steps, we tried to carry this message to others, and to practice these principles in all our affairs.

The Twelve Steps in this devotional book have been adapted from the Twelve Steps of Alcoholics Anonymous.

The Twelve Steps of Alcoholics Anonymous

(1) We admitted we were powerless over alcohol—that our lives had become unmanageable. (2) Came to believe that a Power greater than ourselves could restore us to sanity. (3) Made a decision to turn our will and our lives over to the care of God *as we understood Him.* (4) Made a searching and fearless moral inventory of ourselves. (5) Admitted to God, to ourselves and to another human being the exact nature of our wrongs. (6) Were entirely ready to have God remove all these defects of character. (7) Humbly asked Him to remove our shortcomings. (8) Made a list of all persons we had harmed, and became willing to make amends to them all. (9) Made direct amends to such people wherever possible, except when to do so would injure them or others. (10) Continued to take personal inventory and when we were wrong promptly admitted it. (11) Sought through prayer and meditation to improve our conscious contact with God, *as we understood Him*, praying only for knowledge of His will for us and the power to carry that out. (12) Having had a spiritual awakening as the result of these steps, we tried to carry this message to alcoholics, and to practice these principles in all our affairs.

Acknowledgments

A lot of people have played a part in the creation of this devotional, but we want to especially thank Connie Neal, for letting us draw from her own recovery, and Mark Norton, at Tyndale House Publishers, for bringing it all together.

Introduction

It's impossible to go through life without experiencing hurt, especially in the invisible world of our thoughts and emotions. We all respond differently to these hurts. Some of us try to avoid feeling the pain by turning to harmful behaviors or addictive substances—hoping to numb the hurts within. Others of us try to distance ourselves from the pain by throwing ourselves into more noble pursuits—hoping to stay busy enough to silence the painful memories from our past.

Over the years, millions have found help and hope by working through the Twelve Steps of Alcoholics Anonymous. More recently, many who have not been addicted to alcohol or other addictive chemicals also have found healing through these steps. *The Twelve Step Life Recovery Devotional* has been designed for all of us whose lives have in some way been touched by addictions or other compulsive behaviors.

All of the Twelve Steps are rooted in spiritual principles that are displayed prominently in God's Word. And each meditation in this book is based upon biblical truths that will lead us to freedom from the prisons of our addictions and compulsions. This fits with our desire to bring recovery back to the Bible.

These biblical meditations have been written and edited by people who are in recovery. Some of them are focused more toward those of us struggling with addictions; others deal with issues common among those living alongside those with addictions and compulsions. Although we may go about dealing with our problems in very different ways, we're all trying to deal with the pain of growing up in a broken world. Reading these meditations will help us understand the struggles that are common to all of us in recovery. Sharing the truths we encounter will encourage our growth and lead us out of our isolation and loneliness.

This book contains thirty meditations for each of the Twelve Steps, plus five additional meditations to use when starting over after a relapse. There are no wrong ways to use this book (unless it is used to point a finger at someone else!). Some of us may choose to read one meditation each day for a year, progressing a step each month. Others may find it more helpful to read through the meditations for a single step several times before progressing to the next. Our recovery is the goal; use the book with this in mind! And this devotional will be helpful whether or not we're active in Twelve Step groups.

Working through the Twelve Steps will unite us with millions of others who are working through their programs. Looking for help in God's Word will unite us with God and the power he offers for our healing. He longs to bring us good news, to heal our broken hearts, to comfort those of us who mourn, and to free us from the bondage of our past. "For I know the plans I have for you, says the Lord. They are plans for good and not for evil, to give you a future and a hope" (Jeremiah 29:11).

STEP ONE

We admitted that we were powerless over our dependencies— that our lives had become unmanageable.

Jesus said, "I tell you as seriously as I know how that anyone who refuses to come to God as a little child will never be allowed into his Kingdom" **(Mark 10:15).**

STEP ONE

DAY 1 Like Little Children

Bible Reading: Mark 10:13-16

We admitted that we were powerless over our dependencies—that our lives had become unmanageable.

For many of us in recovery, memories of childhood are memories of the terrors associated with being powerless. If we were raised in families that were out of control, where we were neglected, abused, or exposed to domestic violence and family dysfunction, the thought of being powerless might be unreasonably frightening. We may have silently vowed never again to feel as vulnerable as we did when we were children.

Jesus tells us that the first step into the kingdom of God is to become like a little child, and this involves being powerless. He said, "I tell you as seriously as I know how that anyone who refuses to come to God as a little child will never be allowed into his Kingdom" (Mark 10:15).

In any society, children are the most dependent members. They have no inherent power for self-protection; no means to insure that their lives will be safe, comfortable, or fulfilling. Little children are singularly reliant on the love, care, and nurture of others for their most basic needs. They *must* cry out even though they may not know exactly what they need. They *must* trust their lives to someone who is more powerful than they, and hopefully, they will be heard and lovingly cared for.

We, too, must dare to admit that we are truly powerless if our lives are to become healthy. This doesn't mean we have to become victims again. Admitting our powerlessness is an honest appraisal of our situation in life and a positive step toward recovery.

Discovering our powerlessness is the first step toward wholeness.

DAY 2 A Humble Beginning

Bible Reading:
2 Kings 5:1-15

We admitted that we were powerless over our dependencies—that our lives had become unmanageable.

It can be very humiliating to admit that we are powerless, especially if we are used to being in control. We may be powerful in some areas of our lives, but out of control in terms of our addictive/compulsive behaviors. If we refuse to admit our powerlessness, we may lose everything. That one unmanageable part of our lives may infect and soon destroy everything else.

The experiences of a man named Naaman illustrate how this is true (2 Kings 5:1-15). He was a powerful military and political figure, a man of wealth, position, and power. He also had leprosy, which promised to bring about the loss of everything he held dear. Lepers were made outcasts from their families and society. Ultimately, they faced a slow, painful, and disgraceful death.

Naaman heard that there was a prophet in Israel who could heal him. He found the prophet and was told that in order to be healed he needed to dip himself seven times in the Jordan River. He went away outraged, having expected his power to buy him an instant and easy cure. In the end, however, he acknowledged his powerlessness, followed the instructions, and recovered completely.

Our "disease" is as life threatening as the leprosy in Naaman's day. It slowly separates us from our families and leads toward the destruction of everything important to us. There is no instant or easy cure. The only answer is to admit our powerlessness, humble ourselves, and submit to the process that will eventually bring us recovery.

We must let go in order to hold on to the things dear to us.

DAY 3 A Haunting Weakness

Bible Reading: Romans 7:15-20

We admitted that we were powerless over our dependencies—that our lives had become unmanageable.

A key to recovery is breaking through our denial and admitting our powerlessness. We may want to pretend that all of our struggles are in the past, especially after we begin to "understand the problem." If we are going to maintain our sobriety, however, we need to continually work the first step, remembering that powerlessness is a part of the human condition.

The apostle Paul expressed some thoughts that probably sound like something we might have written ourselves. He says, "I don't understand myself at all, for I really want to do what is right, but I can't. I do what I don't want to—what I hate. I know perfectly well that what I am doing is wrong, and my bad conscience proves that I agree with these laws I am breaking. But I can't help myself, because I'm no longer doing it. It is sin inside me that is stronger than I am that makes me do these evil things. I know I am rotten through and through so far as my old sinful nature is concerned. No matter which way I turn I can't make myself do right. I want to but I can't. When I want to do good, I don't; and when I try not to do wrong, I do it anyway. Now if I am doing what I don't want to, it is plain where the trouble is: sin still has me in its evil grasp" (Romans 7:15-20).

The apostle Paul spoke in the present tense about his own condition. And he spoke for all of us. We will never escape the struggle of being human and susceptible to the pull of our lower nature. Admitting this is the first step toward wholeness.

Powerlessness is part of what it means to be human.

DAY 4 Dangerous Self-Deception

Bible Reading: Judges 16:1-31

We admitted that we were powerless over our dependencies—that our lives had become unmanageable.

When we refuse to admit our powerlessness we are only deceiving ourselves. The lies we tell ourselves and others are familiar: "I could stop any time I want to." "I'm in control; this *one* won't hurt anything." And all the while, we are inching closer to disaster.

Samson was one of Israel's judges. As a child, he had been dedicated to God, and God had gifted him with supernatural strength. But Samson had a lifelong weakness; it had to do with the way he related to women. Samson was especially blinded to the dangers he faced in his relationship with Delilah. His enemies were paying her to discover the secret of his strength. Three times she begged him to let her in on his secret. Each time she set him up and tried to hand him over to the enemy. Three times Samson lied to her and was able to escape. But each time he got closer to telling her the truth. In the end, Samson revealed his secret, was taken captive, and died a slave in enemy hands (Judges 14–16).

Samson's real problem can be found in the lies he told himself. By not admitting his powerlessness, he remained blind to the obvious danger his addiction was leading him into. This caused him to gradually inch his way toward an untimely death.

We need to be careful not to fall into the same trap. As we learn to acknowledge our powerlessness over our addictive/compulsive tendencies on a daily basis, we will become more aware of behaviors that will likely lead to our downfall.

When we lie to ourselves, a dangerous blindness begins to grow within us.

DAY 5 The Paradox of Powerlessness

Bible Reading:
2 Corinthians 4:7-10

We admitted that we were powerless over our dependencies—that our lives had become unmanageable.

We may be afraid to admit that we are powerless and that our lives are unmanageable. If we admit that we are powerless, won't we be tempted to give up completely in the struggle against our addiction? It doesn't seem to make sense that we can admit powerlessness and still find the power to go on. This paradox will be dealt with as we go on to Steps Two and Three.

Life is full of paradoxes. The apostle Paul tells us, "This precious treasure—this light and power that now shine within us—is held in a perishable container, that is, in our weak bodies. Everyone can see that the glorious power within must come from God and is not our own. We are pressed on every side by troubles, but not crushed and broken. (2 Corinthians 4:7-8).

The picture here presents a contrast between a precious treasure and the simple clay pot in which the treasure is stored. The living power poured into our lives from above is the treasure. Our human lives, with all the everyday pressures and problems, are represented by the clay pot, the earthen container. As human beings, we have inherent weaknesses.

Once we recognize the paradox of powerlessness it can be quite a relief. We don't have to always be strong or pretend to be perfect. We can live a real life, with daily struggles, in a human body beset with weakness, and still find the power from above to keep going without being crushed and broken.

Our powerlessness displays the magnificent power of God.

DAY 6 Difficult Losses

Bible Reading: John 15:1-8

We admitted that we were powerless over our dependencies—that our lives had become unmanageable.

Some of us have seen everything we have produced in life go up in smoke because of our addictions. If it hasn't happened to us, surely we've seen others who have lost all that they have worked for: home, career, family, health, finances, and friendships. During the times when life becomes unmanageable, we are faced with the fact that we are not self-sufficient. Sometimes our losses (or even potential losses) can act to spur us on toward taking the first step on the road to recovery.

All of us have times of weakness; none of us are self-sufficient. Jesus recognized this when he said, "Yes, I am the Vine; you are the branches. Whoever lives in me and I in him shall produce a large crop of fruit. For apart from me you can't do a thing. If anyone separates from me, he is thrown away like a useless branch, withers, and is gathered into a pile with all the others, and burned" (John 15:5-6).

Some of us have already lost many of the good things our lives produced. For us it is a matter of facing the losses, admitting that we can't make it on our own, and starting to grow again. For others of us, things may still look rewarding, but if we don't deal honestly with the effects of our addictions we risk seeing the fruits of our lives burned up. It's hard to give up our pride and admit that on our own we "can't do a thing." Perhaps, by considering the possible losses and the value of our previous investments, we will be able to "hit bottom" before we lose everything.

Apart from God, our efforts cannot bear fruit.

DAY 7 The End of Ourselves

Bible Reading:
Psalm 116:1-19

We admitted that we were powerless over our dependencies—that our lives had become unmanageable.

For some of us, we have to stare death in the face before we can admit our need for help. We may experience a crisis where we literally come close to death. Or we may be overwhelmed by depression, suicidal tendencies, and self-destructive behaviors. Sometimes it is our hopelessness and despair that act as a springboard, driving us into recovery. When we realize that we are at the end of ourselves, we may find the humility to reach out and accept the help we need.

King David, whom God loved dearly, felt this way, too. He once said, "The pangs of death encompassed me, and the pangs of Sheol laid hold of me; I found trouble and sorrow. Then I called upon the name of the Lord: 'O Lord, I implore You, deliver my soul!' . . . What shall I render to the Lord for all His benefits toward me? I will take up the cup of salvation, and call upon the name of the Lord" (Psalm 116:3-4, 12-13, NKJV). David had hit bottom. He had finally come to the point of realizing that he had nothing to offer except an empty cup, a life in need of salvation. What did he have left to offer? All he had was "a sacrifice of thanksgiving."

When we have reached our darkest hour and feel that all hope is lost, we may be closer to the help we need than ever before. When death stares us in the face and we realize that our cup is empty, we can lift up our empty cup by admitting our powerlessness, and thus, open up to salvation. In time, we, too, will be able to be thankful once again.

Staring death in the face can be a starting point for recovery.

DAY 8 No-Win Situations

Bible Reading: Genesis 16:1-15

We admitted that we were powerless over our dependencies—that our lives had become unmanageable.

Sometimes we are powerless because of our station in life. We may be in a situation where other people have power over our lives. We may feel that we're trapped by the demands of others, and that there's no way to please them all. It's a double bind: to please one is to disappoint another. Sometimes when we feel stuck and frustrated with our relationships, we look for a measure of control by escaping through our addictive behaviors.

Hagar is a picture of powerlessness. She had no rights. As a girl, she was a slave to Sarai and Abram. When they were upset because Sarai could not bear children, she was given to Abram as a surrogate. When she did become pregnant, as they had wanted, Sarai was so jealous that she beat the girl and she ran away. All alone, out in the wilderness, she was met by an angel who told her, "Return to your mistress and act as you should, for I will make you into a great nation. Yes, you are pregnant and your baby will be a son, and you are to name him Ishmael ('God hears'), because God has heard your woes" (Genesis 16:10-11).

When we are caught in no-win situations, it's tempting to run away through our addictive/compulsive escape hatches. At times like these, God is there and he is listening to our woes. We need to learn to express our pain to God, instead of just trying to escape. He hears our woes and is willing to give us hope for the future.

It is wise to turn and face our problems, accepting God's promise of help.

DAY 9 Promises for Children

Bible Reading: Genesis 21:1-21

We admitted that we were powerless over our dependencies—that our lives had become unmanageable.

There is a special kind of powerlessness experienced when we're unable to take care of the needs of our children or others who are dependent on us. For those of us raised in dysfunctional families, there is grief and fear associated with watching our children suffer, as the effects of our own past fall upon them.

With God's help, Hagar had faced her life with Abraham and Sarah. When Sarah was finally able to give birth to her own son, she demanded that Hagar and Ishmael be thrown out of the family. In response, Abraham "strapped a canteen of water to Hagar's shoulders and sent her away with their son. She walked out into the wilderness of Beersheba, wandering aimlessly. When the water was gone she left the youth in the shade of a bush and went off and sat down a hundred yards or so away. 'I don't want to watch him die,' she said, and burst into tears, sobbing wildly. Then God heard the boy crying, and the Angel of God called to Hagar from the sky, 'Hagar, what's wrong? Don't be afraid! For God has heard the lad's cries as he is lying there. Go and get him and comfort him, for I will make a great nation from his descendants.' Then God opened her eyes and she saw a well; so she refilled the canteen and gave the lad a drink" (Genesis 21:14-19).

God doesn't forget his promises toward us or our children. When we are powerless to help them, God is listening to their cries and ours. We can expect God's help when we are powerless to help our children. He loves them even more than we do.

Our problems won't seem so impossible if we let God handle them.

DAY 10 Hope amidst Suffering

Bible Reading:
Job 6:2-13

We admitted we were powerless over our dependencies—that our lives had become unmanageable.

There are times when we are so confused and overwhelmed by the pain in our lives that we wish we could die. No matter what we do, we are powerless to change things for the better. The weight of the sadness seems too heavy to bear. We can't see why our heart just doesn't break and allow death to free us.

Job felt that way. He'd lost everything, even though he had always done what was right. His ten children were dead. He had lost his business, his riches, and his health. And all this happened in a matter of days! He was left with a sharp-tongued wife and three friends who blamed him for his own misfortune. Job cried out, "Oh, that my sadness and troubles were weighed. . . . Oh, that God would grant the thing I long for most—to die beneath his hand, and be freed from his painful grip. . . . Oh, why does my strength sustain me? How can I be patient till I die? Am I unfeeling, like stone? Is my flesh made of brass? For I am utterly helpless, without any hope" (Job 6: 2-3, 8-9, 11-13).

Job didn't know that the end of his life would be even better than it had been at the beginning. God restored everything he had lost, and then some. "Then at last he died, an old, old man, after living a long, good life" (Job 42:17). Even when we're pressed to the point of death, there is still hope that our lives will change. Our recovery could be so complete that the final line written about us might read: "At last they died, after living a long, good life." We must remember: life can be good again!

Trusting God in difficult times will stretch our faith.

DAY 11 A Time to Choose

Bible Reading: Acts 9:1-9

We admitted we were powerless over our dependencies—that our lives had become unmanageable.

There are important moments in life that can bring about changes in our very destiny. These are often times when we are confronted with how powerless we really are over our own lives. These moments can either destroy us or forever set the course of our lives in a much better direction.

Saul had such a moment. After Jesus' ascension, Saul took it upon himself to rid the world of Christians. As he took off on his quest, "suddenly a brilliant light from heaven spotted down upon him! He fell to the ground and heard a voice saying to him, 'Paul! Paul! [God changed his name.] Why are you persecuting me? . . . I am Jesus, the one you are persecuting! Now, get up and go into the city and await my further instructions.' . . . [Paul] found that he was blind. He had to be led into Damascus and was there three days, blind, going without food and water all that time" (Acts 9:3-6, 8).

Paul was suddenly confronted with the fact that his life wasn't as perfect as he thought. Self-righteousness had been his trademark. By letting go of his illusions of power, however, he soon became one of the most powerful men ever: the apostle Paul. When we're confronted with the fact that our lives aren't in our control, we have a choice. We can continue in denial and self-righteousness, or we can face the fact that we have been blind to some important issues. If we become willing to be led into recovery and a whole new way of life, we will find true power.

Moments of crisis present us with opportunities for great change.

DAY 12 Desperate for Love

Bible Reading: Genesis 29:16-35

We admitted we were powerless over our dependencies—that our lives had become unmanageable.

We'll do almost anything to gain the love we need (which may have been denied us as children or in our marriage). Maybe the pain and sadness over our powerlessness to attract the love we desperately need drives us to find a way to deaden the pain.

Leah was a plain girl with a beautiful younger sister and a scheming father. Her father tricked Jacob into marrying Leah. He then allowed Jacob also to have her sister, Rachel. "So Jacob slept with Rachel, too, and he loved her more than Leah . . . but because Jacob was slighting Leah, Jehovah let her have a child, while Rachel was barren. So Leah became pregnant and had a son, Reuben . . . for she said, 'Jehovah has noticed my trouble—now my husband will love me.' She soon became pregnant again and had another son and named him Simeon (meaning 'Jehovah heard'), for she said, 'Jehovah heard that I was unloved, and so he has given me another son.' Again she became pregnant and had a son, and named him Levi (meaning 'Attachment'), for she said, 'Surely now my husband will feel affection for me, since I have given him three sons!'" (Genesis 29:30-34).

We may be powerless to make someone love us, spending our lives trying to produce something to make us worthy of their love. This need might gnaw away at us and lead to relapse when the pain becomes overwhelming. When people won't love us, we can learn to draw upon the love of God. He loves us as we are.

Drawing on God's unconditional love and grace can fill our need to be wanted.

DAY 13 Emotional Time Bombs

Bible Reading:
2 Samuel 13:1-24

We admitted that we were powerless over our dependencies—that our lives had become unmanageable.

There are times when we become deeply upset by the injustices of life, the abuses kept as family secrets, the feelings buried alive, and our vows to get even. In such times, we often become powerless over the strength of our inner turmoil. All we can feel is the resolve to act out our hatred. We can't control feelings.

Absalom became powerless over his hatred and rage. It ultimately controlled his life to the point that he fought to overthrow his father's rule. He was outraged when his half brother raped his sister, Tamar. When King David did nothing to avenge his daughter, Absalom vowed revenge in his heart. He waited until the time was right and murdered the guilty brother. This sequence of abuse, family secrecy, denial, unprocessed feelings, and revenge destroyed Absalom's relationship with his father. He never forgave David and died in a military rebellion against him (2 Samuel 13:1–18:33).

We may use our addictive/compulsive behaviors to distract us from the deep, unresolved family issues that cut us to the heart. There may be so many strong emotions, which we don't know how to process appropriately, that we simply try to stuff them down inside. Eventually these feelings are expressed in some way. We need to confront the family secrets, express our feelings, convict the guilty, and work through forgiveness. If we try to ignore them, we will be controlled by these explosive hidden emotions.

Hatred leads to disaster; accepting our powerlessness leads to recovery and wholeness.

DAY 14 Destructive Pride

Bible Reading: Acts 8:9-23

We admitted that we were powerless over our dependencies—that our lives had become unmanageable.

For many of us, personal power is used as the foundation for our self-esteem. We become used to getting things our way, through whatever influences we have at our disposal (money, power, sex, love, etc.). It can be very unsettling to arrive at a place in life where we can't buy the power we need. For those of us who use power to bolster our self-esteem, admitting powerlessness will require a foundational change.

"A man named Simon had formerly been a sorcerer . . . he was a very influential, proud man because of the amazing things he could do. . . . Then Simon himself believed [that Jesus was the Messiah]. . . . When Simon saw this—that the Holy Spirit was given when the apostles placed their hands upon people's heads—he offered money to buy this power. . . . But Peter replied, 'Your money perish with you for thinking God's gift can be bought! You can have no part in this, for your heart is not right before God. Turn from this great wickedness and pray. Perhaps, God will yet forgive your evil thoughts—for I can see that there is jealousy and sin in your heart'" (Acts 8:9-10, 13, 18-23).

Simon realized he was powerless in this situation. He admitted his pride and powerlessness and was able to change. We need to be aware of how pride can hinder us. We can't buy our way out of addiction. No matter how "powerful" we are in worldly terms, our recovery will come by working a program, day by day.

Our recovery can only begin as we "give up" our efforts and our pride.

DAY 15 Serenity despite Powerlessness

Bible Reading: Luke 1:26-56

We admitted that we were powerless over our dependencies—that our lives had become unmanageable.

There are times in life when we are powerless over the circumstances around us. We're not in the driver's seat. We have to do things someone else's way. And often, the whole experience is uncomfortable and frightening. During these times we can find hope and serenity in the promises of God.

Mary was in her early teens when destiny took her by the hand. She was greeted by an angel who announced that she had been chosen by God to be the mother of the Messiah. She found herself pregnant, much to the confusion of her fiancé, family, friends, and neighbors. After the angel returned to visit her fiancé, he believed Mary's story and married her. When the time came to give birth, she and Joseph were required to travel the long, difficult journey to Bethlehem. There, in a smelly stable carved out of the side of a rocky hill, she delivered the baby. No one but her husband was there to attend Jesus' birth (Luke 1:26–2:20).

What power did she have over her circumstances? She was powerless under the will of God, the decree of the state, the limitations of their financial poverty, and the demands of her body. And yet, by holding on to the promises God had given her, she found serenity in her powerlessness and gave birth to the Savior. When we are powerless, we can find serenity by holding on to the promises of God. When we do this, we will find new life and salvation being born again into our lives.

No matter what our circumstances, God meets us there with his grace.

DAY 16 Self-Control versus Willpower

Bible Reading: Galatians 5:16-23

We admitted that we were powerless over our dependencies—that our lives had become unmanageable.

There's a struggle going on inside of us—a fight for control. Our willpower fails us repeatedly. Where can we turn when we realize that we can't control ourselves?

The apostle Paul says, "I advise you to obey only the Holy Spirit's instructions. He will tell you where to go and what to do, and then you won't always be doing the wrong things your evil nature wants you to. For we naturally love to do evil things that are just the opposite from the things that the Holy Spirit tells us to do; and the good things we want to do when the Spirit has his way with us are just the opposite of our natural desires. These two forces within us are constantly fighting each other to win control over us, and our wishes are never free from their pressures. . . . But when the Holy Spirit controls our lives he will produce this kind of fruit in us: love, joy, peace, patience, kindness, goodness, faithfulness, gentleness and self-control" (Galatians 5:16-17, 22-23).

Self-control is not willpower. It's not something we get by gritting our teeth and forcing ourselves to "just say no." Self-control is called a fruit. Fruit doesn't instantly pop out on the tree. As the tree grows and seasons pass, the fruit naturally develops. As we continue to follow God's guidance, taking one step at a time, our self-control will naturally grow. Our job is to stay connected to God. It's the Holy Spirit's job to produce the fruit of self-control.

As God takes control of our lives, self-control will be the natural result.

DAY 17 Victim or Victor?

Bible Reading:
1 Samuel
17:20-49

We admitted that we were powerless over our dependencies—that our lives had become unmanageable.

There will be times in life when right and wrong stand in stark contrast. Even when we know what's right and how things should be changed, the power may seem to be on the wrong side. We may feel powerless even though we know we are standing for what is right. But even when this is true, we still shouldn't give up. Sometimes situations where we feel powerless can prompt action that changes everything for the better.

David "saw Goliath the giant step out from the Philistine troops and shout his challenge to the army of Israel. As soon as they saw him the Israeli army began to run away in fright. 'Have you seen the giant?' the soldiers were asking. 'He has insulted the entire army of Israel.'" David convinced the king to let him fight the giant his own way. He shouted to Goliath, "'You come to me with a sword and a spear, but I come to you in the name of the Lord of the armies of heaven and of Israel—the very God whom you have defied. Today the Lord will conquer you'" (1 Samuel 17:23-25, 45-46).

The army saw themselves as helpless victims. Their powerlessness paralyzed them so they just stood there and took the abuse. David took courageous action to recover their dignity. There are times when we need courage and God's help to fight against the tendency to remain a victim. We need to stand up for our human dignity and respond in new ways if we are to claim our recovery.

With God by our side there is no need to wait; we can move forward into our recovery.

DAY 18 Painful Abandonment

Bible Reading: Isaiah 54:1-8

We admitted that we were powerless over our dependencies—that our lives had become unmanageable.

Many of us know the deep sorrow and shame that come from being abandoned. Those we should have been able to depend on weren't there for us. We may have lost them through an untimely death; or perhaps they were there in body but out of our reach emotionally because of their own addictions. We know the deep, unspeakable fear that can reach up and grab hold of us at any moment. We may have used our own compulsive behaviors to find comfort and distance from our feelings of abandonment.

Here's the Lord's message to those who have experienced the loss of an important relationship: "Sing, O childless woman! . . . For she who was abandoned has more blessings now than she whose husband stayed! . . . Fear not; you will no longer live in shame. The shame of your youth and the sorrows of widowhood will be remembered no more, for your Creator will be your 'husband.' The Lord Almighty is his name; he is your Redeemer, the Holy One of Israel, the God of all the earth. For the Lord has called you back from your grief" (Isaiah 54:1, 4-6).

God wants to give us such confidence in our relationship with him that we can be free of the fear of abandonment and overcome its scars. He can make up to us all that we have missed in our past relationships. He can fill the shoes of the one who isn't there for us. There is a season for grieving the losses, but the Lord can call us back from grief and give us renewed joy.

God delivers us from shame and abandonment, welcoming us to the joy of recovery.

DAY 19 God's Power

Bible Reading: Isaiah 42:21-25

We admitted that we were powerless over our dependencies—that our lives had become unmanageable.

Many of us believe that God's law is good and that it provides helpful moral standards. We may try hard to be perfect, but find ourselves frustrated. Some of us may be troubled by this, and we probably avoid thinking about it. We try not to feel the shame and guilt that come with violating these values that we've taken as our own. We may pretend that everything is fine with us and focus on another person's addiction to avoid our own inner conflict.

Isaiah tells us, "The Lord has magnified his law and made it truly glorious. . . . But what a sight his people are—these who were to demonstrate to all the world the glory of his law; for they are robbed, enslaved, imprisoned, trapped, fair game for all. They will not understand the reason why—that it is God, wanting them to repent" (Isaiah 42:21-22, 25). The words translated *repent* literally mean "take it to heart." God wanted his people to take his law to the depth of their being. This is the part of us where we feel, think, and choose.

The law of God is designed to magnify God's righteousness, not ours! "We are all infected and impure with sin. When we put on our prized robes of righteousness, we find they are but filthy rags" (Isaiah 64:6). When we are powerless over sin to the point where we become enslaved and unprotected, God wants us to "take it to heart." When we allow ourselves to feel and think and choose in response to our own powerlessness, we are on our way to finding God's power, the only power that leads to freedom.

Our powerlessness leads us directly to God's power.

DAY 20 Our Limitations

Bible Reading: Galatians 3:19-26

We admitted that we were powerless over our dependencies—that our lives had become unmanageable.

Many of us begin our recovery by seeing that we've been powerless to measure up to God's laws. Some of us, however, expect that once we're well on the road to recovery we'll start keeping the laws of God. And we hope that this will guarantee our standing with God on the basis of our good works. We start with a recognition of our powerlessness, but hope for the day when we will no longer be powerless. Surely our standing before God must be somewhat dependent upon our keeping of the law! Otherwise, why would he have given us his laws in the first place?

The apostle Paul answers by saying, "Well then, why were the laws given? They were added after the promise [of salvation through faith] was given, to show men how guilty they are of breaking God's laws. . . . If we could be saved by his laws, then God would not have had to give us a different way to get out of the grip of sin—for the Scriptures insist we are all its prisoners. The only way out is through faith in Jesus Christ; the way of escape is open to all who believe him. . . . The Jewish laws were our teacher and guide until Christ came to give us right standing with God through our faith" (Galatians 3:19, 22, 24).

The law of God is an eternal reminder of our true powerlessness—our ongoing need for a Savior and for the power of God. Our failures should point us back to the only One able to help us recover.

God sets us free from our failures and places us on the path toward recovery.

DAY 21 Powerless and Abused

Bible Reading: Judges 19:12-30

We admitted that we were powerless over our dependencies—that our lives had become unmanageable.

There are societal forces beyond our control. We live in times when sexual abuse is commonplace and security in relationships is hard to find. We may know the agony of being sexually abused or bear the shame of allowing someone else to be victimized when we were in a position to protect them. A deep sense of powerlessness is experienced in this kind of situation.

Before Israel had a king, there was no law and order; "every man did whatever he thought was right" (Judges 21:25). A horrifying story is told of a young woman who was brutally gang-raped. Her husband had allowed her to be taken by a group of men who had been trying to attack and rape him. "The girl's husband pushed her out to them, and they abused her all night. . . . When her husband opened the door to be on his way, he found her there, fallen down in front of the door with her hands digging into the threshold" (Judges 19:25-27). The girl died there on the doorstep. Her death became a rallying cry for reform, but she had been lost. Her husband was left with terrible shame and guilt. The man and his young wife were both victims, suffering the pain of powerlessness in a crime-filled society.

If we have been victims of sexual abuse, we must begin by acknowledging that we were powerless. Although we suffered the abuse, we were not the cause of it. This realization is an important key to our recovery.

Recovery from being a victim begins by recognizing our powerlessness.

DAY 22 Secure Love

Bible Reading:
Song of Solomon 5:1-8

We admitted that we were powerless over our dependencies—that our lives had become unmanageable.

The search for love and permanent security in relationships is deep within all of us. Even though we may be in a relationship where we are loved, we may deeply fear the loss of that love. This is especially true if we've been abandoned in the past or had our love betrayed.

The Song of Solomon is a love poem dedicated to the girl Solomon loved. He describes a nightmare she had, "I opened to my beloved, but he was gone. My heart stopped. I searched for him but couldn't find him anywhere. . . . I adjure you, O women of Jerusalem, if you find my beloved one, tell him that I am sick with love" (Song of Solomon 5:6, 8). The fear of separation darkened the girl's joy at being deeply loved. At the end of the poem she says, "Seal me in your heart with permanent betrothal, for love is strong as death and jealousy is as cruel as Sheol [the grave]" (Song of Solomon 8:6).

We are all haunted by a deep need for a "permanent betrothal," a secure love that won't escape us. When we lose a close and intimate relationship, we become lovesick. We feel powerless over the forces driving us in search of permanent and true love. No matter how much a person loves us, our needs seem deeper. Perfect love that never leaves can only be found in the one who is *Love.* When we are powerless over the forces of love or over our own obsessions, we need to look to God to satisfy our deepest longings so that fear and dissatisfaction don't become a trap.

God can—and will—satisfy our deepest longings.

DAY 23 Breaking the Cycle

Bible Reading: Ecclesiastes 1:1-18

We admitted that we were powerless over our dependencies—that our lives had become unmanageable.

Human existence consists of a series of patterns. Our world goes around the sun in an unending orbit; it spins on its axis with tireless regularity. Dysfunctional family patterns seem to resurface generation after generation in a wearying march of repetitious pain. We may grow tired and wonder if there's really any escape from the merry-go-round of addictive behavior and suffering.

King Solomon examined life and was discouraged by some of his observations. "Generations come and go but it makes no difference. The sun rises and sets and hurries around to rise again. The wind blows south and north, here and there, twisting back and forth, getting nowhere. The rivers run into the sea but the sea is never full, and the water returns again to the rivers . . . everything is unutterably weary and tiresome. No matter . . . how much we hear, we are not content" (Ecclesiastes 1:3-8).

Life can seem like one meaningless, wearying cycle after another. Solomon observed that our lives can be spent without ever going anywhere. He also wrote these instructions, "Follow the steps of the godly instead, and stay on the right path" (Proverbs 2:20). Throughout the Bible we see that life can be linear, leading somewhere. Even though we are powerless to stop all the destructive cycles around us, we can take our own steps in the direction of recovery and a new way of life.

Our efforts just add to the destructive cycles in life; only God can break them.

DAY 24 Starting with Ourselves

Bible Reading: Ecclesiastes 3:15–4:3

We admitted that we were powerless over our dependencies—that our lives had become unmanageable.

Some of us avoid or cope with our own pain by trying to fix the world. We try to right every wrong, heal every wound, point out every injustice. We spend our time demanding that the world system reform. We may also dedicate ourselves to rescuing and reforming those we love. Our zealousness to set the world aright can be a means of denying that we are powerless to do so.

Solomon said, "Throughout the earth justice is giving way to crime and even the police courts are corrupt. I said to myself, 'In due season God will judge everything man does.' . . . I observed all the oppression and sadness throughout the earth—the tears of the oppressed, and no one helping them, while on the side of their oppressors were powerful allies" (Ecclesiastes 3:16-17; 4:1). He saw that the world was not as it should be. He also recognized that it was God's job to judge and overcome the injustices in our world.

When we set out to save the world we err by taking on a role that belongs to God. What we gain by taking on such a massive task is the guarantee that we'll always be busy. Then we'll never have the time or energy to face our own issues. The Bible makes it clear that the world will never be right until Jesus Christ returns to make it so. We need to accept the fact that we are powerless to do his job. However, when we focus on our own recovery, fixing ourselves instead of everyone else, we will then be able to be more effective in helping others, too.

If we try to fix the world before fixing ourselves, we'll do both badly.

DAY 25 Magical Thinking

Bible Reading:
Ecclesiastes
5:10-12

We admitted that we were powerless over our dependencies—that our lives had become unmanageable.

This is one of the rules that governs a dysfunctional family: Always blame someone or something whenever things get out of control. We might say, "If only I weren't poor, then I could handle life." We might dream of how all our problems would be resolved if only we were rich. But by blaming our lack of wealth, we fail to take responsibility for coping with life.

Solomon was one of the richest men who ever lived. He had this to say on the subject, "He who loves money shall never have enough. The foolishness of thinking that wealth brings happiness! The more you have, the more you spend, right up to the limits of your income. So what is the advantage of wealth—except perhaps to watch it as it runs through your fingers! The man who works hard sleeps well whether he eats little or much, but the rich must worry and suffer insomnia" (Ecclesiastes 5:10-12).

Solomon, along with many affluent people of our day, is living proof that riches don't solve our problems or guarantee happiness. Wealthy people are just as powerless over their lives and addictions as poor people. Accepting this reality can help us to face the fact that it is not anything external that keeps us from recovery. We don't need to wait until we have more money to begin coping with our lives and our compulsive behaviors. The sooner we stop all the blaming and begin to acknowledge the true powerlessness of the human condition, the sooner we'll recover.

No matter how much or how little we have, it will never be "enough."

DAY 26 Chasing the Wind

Bible Reading: Ecclesiastes 2:1-11

We admitted that we were powerless over our dependencies—that our lives had become unmanageable.

We may have gotten involved in our addictive behavior on an experimental basis at first. We wanted to taste life's pleasures and find the fun and excitement. For a while the "partying" makes us feel good; but when we pull back to look at our lives we realize that we're not really getting any closer to fulfillment.

Solomon set out to taste all of life's pleasures, and he had the means to do so without limit. He writes, "I said to myself, 'Come now, be merry, enjoy yourself to the full.' But I found that this, too, was futile. For it is silly to be laughing all the time; what good does it do?'" Solomon systematically explored drinking, looking for wisdom, toying with folly, trying to find fulfillment through public works projects and empire building, collecting slaves, silver and gold, enhancing his sense of power, involvement in the cultural arts and vast sexual exploits. He then explains, "Anything I wanted, I took, and did not restrain myself from any joy. I even found great pleasure in hard work. This pleasure was, indeed, my only reward for all my labors. But as I looked at everything I had tried, it was all so useless, a chasing of the wind, and there was nothing really worthwhile anywhere" (Ecclesiastes 2:1-2, 10-11).

Like Solomon, we, too, may be chasing after the wind and getting nowhere. The futility of being driven to excess in our "chasing around," whether in work or play, can cause us to miss the true purpose of our existence and the fulfillment we seek.

Our addictions are like the wind: we may feel them as they pass, but we can never hold on to them.

DAY 27 A Balanced Life

Bible Reading: Ecclesiastes 7:14-17

We admitted that we were powerless over our dependencies—that our lives had become unmanageable.

For those of us raised in chaotic situations our response may be to try to maintain control of something . . . anything! We may become rigid and controlling of our children, or insist on having control in our homes or work relationships. Perhaps we focus on our eating habits or develop rituals for living that give us the feeling of being in control of our own lives.

King Solomon tells us, "Enjoy prosperity whenever you can, and when hard times strike, realize that God gives one as well as the other—so that everyone will realize that nothing is certain in this life. In this silly life I have seen everything, including the fact that some of the good die young and some of the wicked live on and on. . . . Yes, there is a time and a way for everything, though man's trouble lies heavy upon him; for how can he avoid what he doesn't know is going to happen?" (Ecclesiastes 7:14-15; 8:6-7).

It's understandable that we would want to develop a security system to protect our lives in response to our past powerlessness and the pain it brought. Maintaining control can serve to make us feel safer in an uncertain world. However, it can also pose a trap for us, if we must always have control in order to cope. We need to balance our understanding of life to realize that life is uncertain. We will not always be in situations where we have the power and control we need to make us feel safe. This balance can keep us on track, even when an unexpected loss of power occurs.

If we must always be in control, we're out of control.

DAY 28 Powerless over Death

Bible Reading:
Ecclesiastes 7:1-4

We admitted that we were powerless over our dependencies—that our lives had become unmanageable.

From the moment of birth, we all are living under the sentence of death. For some of us there is the added burden of knowing we are going to die as the result of previous risky behavior related to our addictions. Others of us realize that our addictions could kill us if they are not brought under control. We are all powerless over death. The understanding of this can actually be beneficial for us.

King Solomon wisely noted, "The day one dies is better than the day he is born! It is better to spend your time at funerals than at festivals. For you are going to die and it is a good thing to think about it while there is still time. Sorrow is better than laughter, for sadness has a refining influence on us. Yes, a wise man thinks much of death, while the fool thinks only of having a good time now. . . . No one can hold back his spirit from departing; no one has the power to prevent his day of death, for there is no discharge from that obligation and that dark battle" (Ecclesiastes 7:1-4; 8:8).

Realizing that we are powerless over the inevitable approach of death should have a sobering effect on us all. Death has a way of revealing our powerlessness and uncovering hidden sorrow as nothing else can. Thinking about the end of life, however, should also help us realize how precious each day of life actually is. The sorrow of approaching death can help us by revealing what is really important in life and by strengthening our commitment to recovery.

We all live under the sentence of death; we should make the most of each and every day.

DAY 29 When Heroes Lose

Bible Reading: Ecclesiastes 9:11-12

We admitted that we were powerless over our dependencies—that our lives had become unmanageable.

Some of us who grew up in dysfunctional families vowed to escape their downward pull. We may have become the "family hero," the one who "was going to make it." We set out believing in some formula for success, maybe even based on scriptural principles. We have told ourselves, "If I only do thus and such, I will have to be successful." It feels very safe as long as our beliefs match with our experience.

Solomon relates, "Again I looked throughout the earth and saw that the swiftest person does not always win the race, nor the strongest man the battle, and that wise men are often poor, and skillful men are not necessarily famous; but it is all by chance, by happening to be at the right place at the right time. A man never knows when he is going to run into bad luck. He is like a fish caught in a net, or a bird caught in a snare" (Ecclesiastes 9:11-12).

Life doesn't always follow our rules or any other set of rules that might help us predict how things will happen. Even the truth of the Bible leaves room for a struggle between the forces of good and evil. There are times when we do our best, try our hardest to be good, and apply ourselves completely. But life still doesn't work out the way we think it should. Our lives are interwoven with the lives of others in a world that isn't always fair. Regardless of how hard we try, we cannot predict with certainty or guarantee the exact journey we will take through life.

This world grants only one guarantee—our powerlessness.

DAY 30 Powerless to Understand

Bible Reading: Lamentations 5:7-22

We admitted that we were powerless over our dependencies—that our lives had become unmanageable.

When the bottom falls out of our world, we grapple with confusion. We try to understand what is happening and why it's happening to us. Is it our fault? What did we do wrong? We look for someone to blame. We search for meaning in the madness. We stagger in our attempt to make some sense of it all.

After the destruction of Jerusalem the prophet Jeremiah poured out his heart to God. He described the horrifying conditions that fell upon the people he loved. He cried out, "Our fathers sinned but died before the hand of judgment fell. We have borne the blow that they deserved! . . . Our glory is gone. . . . O Lord, forever you remain the same! Your throne continues from generation to generation. Why do you forget us forever? Why do you forsake us for so long? Turn us around and bring us back to you again! That is our only hope! Give us back the joys we used to have! *Or have you utterly rejected us? Are you angry with us still?*" (Lamentations 5:7, 16-17, 19-22).

Even this great prophet of God was often powerless to understand the meaning of the troubling events in his life. Whose fault was it? Why did this have to happen to us and our loved ones? When we are powerless to understand, it is wise to follow Jeremiah's example and turn to God. God is always there. He understands when we can't. He has promised that "he will listen to the prayers of the destitute" (Psalm 102:17).

Though we can't always understand the events of life, we can know that God does.

STEP TWO

We came to believe that a Power greater than ourselves could restore us to sanity.

"What is faith? It is the confident assurance that something we want is going to happen" **(Hebrews 11:1).**

STEP TWO

DAY 1 Grandiose Thinking

Bible Reading: Daniel 4:19-33

We came to believe that a Power greater than ourselves could restore us to sanity.

When we're caught up in our addiction, it's common for us to deceive ourselves with grandiose thinking. We may believe that we're above it all, a god unto ourselves, accountable to no one.

In his day, Nebuchadnezzar, king of ancient Babylon, was the most powerful ruler on earth. He believed himself to be a god and demanded worship as such. God said to him, "The Most High God has decreed . . . that your people will chase you from your palace, and you will live in the fields like an animal. . . . This will be your life, until you learn that the Most High God dominates the kingdoms of men, and gives power to anyone he chooses" (Daniel 4:24-25).

All this happened just as predicted. At the end of the king's time in exile, he said, "I . . . looked up to heaven, and my sanity returned, and I praised and worshiped the Most High God and honored him who lives forever. . . . When my mind returned to me, so did my honor and glory and kingdom . . . with even greater honor than before. Now I, Nebuchadnezzar, praise and glorify and honor the King of Heaven, the Judge of all, whose every act is right and good; for he is able to take those who walk proudly and push them into the dust!" (Daniel 4:34, 36-37).

We must remember that we are not God. We're accountable to a higher Power who can remedy our "madness" and restore our lives to be even better than before our season of insanity.

God is not going to shape our lives until we acknowledge him as God.

DAY 2 Healing Faith

Bible Reading: Luke 8:43-48

We came to believe that a Power greater than ourselves could restore us to sanity.

Faith is a key to successfully working the second step. For some of us faith comes easily. For others, especially if we have experienced betrayal, it may be more difficult. Sometimes we must exhaust all of our own resources in trying to overcome our addictive "disease" before we will risk believing in a higher Power.

When Jesus was on earth he was renowned for his healing power. Crowds of sick people constantly pressed in on him. One day "a woman who wanted to be healed came up behind and touched him, for she had been slowly bleeding for twelve years, and could find no cure. . . . But the instant she touched the edge of his robe, the bleeding stopped." Jesus realized that someone had deliberately touched him because he felt the healing power go out from him. When the woman confessed that she was the one who had been healed, Jesus said, "Your faith has healed you. Go in peace" (Luke 8:43-48).

In order to recover we need to follow the example of this woman. We cannot afford to stand back, hoping for a "cure," and avoid deliberate action because of our lack of faith. We may have lived with our condition for many years, spending our resources on promising "cures" without success. When we can come to believe in a Power greater than ourselves and have the faith to take hold of our own recovery, we will find the healing power we've been looking for.

What a difference between knowing about Jesus and reaching out to touch him!

DAY 3 Restoration

Bible Reading: Luke 15:11-24

We came to believe that a Power greater than ourselves could restore us to sanity.

In the natural progression of addiction our lives necessarily degenerate. In one way or another, many of us wake up one day to realize that we are living like animals. How this is true depends on the nature of our addiction. Some of us may be living like animals in terms of our physical surroundings. Others of us may be slaves to our animal passions—powerful emotions that dehumanize us.

A young man took an early inheritance and wandered away from home. When the money was spent, the women just a memory, and the "high" long gone, he resorted to slopping pigs to earn a meager living. When he became so hungry that he was eyeing the pig's slop with envy, he realized he had a problem. "When he finally came to his senses, he said to himself, 'At home even the hired men have food enough and to spare, and here I am, dying of hunger! I will go home to my father. . . .' So he returned home to his father. And while he was still a long distance away, his father saw him coming, and was filled with loving pity and ran and embraced him and kissed him" (Luke 15:17-18, 20).

The fact that we are able to recognize our lives as degenerate or insane proves that there is hope for a better way of life. We are reminded of a time when life was good and we long to have it restored. When we turn in the direction of One who is more powerful, who represents the memory of something better, we will find the Power that can restore us to sanity.

God doesn't force us to come to him; he simply waits for us to come to our senses.

DAY 4 Hope in Faith

Bible Reading: Hebrews 11:1-10

We came to believe that a Power greater than ourselves could restore us to sanity.

Step Two is often referred to as "the hope step." In coming to believe that a Power greater than ourselves can restore us to sanity, we must remember what it was like to live sanely, and have the faith to hope that sanity can return.

"What is faith?" the Bible asks. "It is the confident assurance that something we want is going to happen. It is the certainty that what we hope for is waiting for us, even though we cannot see it up ahead" (Hebrews 11:1). How can we be confident that something we want is going to happen, especially if all of our hopes have been dashed? How can we risk believing that the life we hope for is waiting for us around the bend?

The Bible tells us that the key is in the nature of the higher Power we look to. We are told, "Anyone who wants to come to God must believe that there is a God and that he rewards those who sincerely look for him" (Hebrews 11:6). If we see God as one waiting to reward us, we will be more eager to look for him. If our faith has not matured to that point yet, we can ask for help. There was one man who came to Jesus and asked him to help his young son who was afflicted by a demon. He said to Jesus, "'Oh, have mercy on us and do something if you can.' 'If I can?' Jesus asked. '*Anything* is possible if you have faith.' The father instantly replied, 'I *do* have faith; oh, help me to have *more!*'" (Mark 9:22-24). We can start by asking God to help us to have more faith. Then we can ask him for the courage to hope for a better future.

Faith starts when we believe God is who he is.

DAY 5 Internal Bondage

Bible Reading: Mark 5:1-13

We came to believe that a Power greater than ourselves could restore us to sanity.

When we are under the influence of our addiction, it may feel like its hold has supernatural force. We may give up on living, throwing ourselves into self-destructive behaviors with wild abandonment. People also may give up on us. They may divorce themselves from us, as though we were already dead. Whether our "insanity" is self-induced or even if it has a more sinister origin, there is power to restore us to sanity.

Jesus helped a man who was known to be acting insanely. "This man lived among the gravestones, and had such strength that whenever he was put into handcuffs and shackles—as he often was—he snapped the handcuffs from his wrists and smashed the shackles and walked away. No one was strong enough to control him. All day long and through the night he would wander among the tombs and in the wild hills, screaming and cutting himself with sharp pieces of stone" (Mark 5:3-5). Jesus went into the graveyard and assessed the situation. He dealt with the forces of darkness that were afflicting him and restored the man to sanity. He then sent him home to his friends and family.

We may be so far gone that we have broken all restraints. We struggle to be free from the control of society and loved ones. Then we discover that our bondage doesn't come from outside sources. All hope seems lost; but if there is still life there is still hope. God can come into our "graveyard," too, and restore us to sanity.

Only a Power greater than ourselves can free us from our bondage.

DAY 6 Filling the Emptiness

Bible Reading: Luke 8:35-39

We came to believe that a Power greater than ourselves could restore us to sanity.

Some of us enter recovery because of the intervention of those who love us. We are confronted and persuaded to break from our addiction. Perhaps, we have received spiritual help and been delivered from demonic influences as well. Intervention can be a very helpful starting place but we cannot afford to stop there.

With the demon-possessed man who lived among the tombs, Jesus came into his territory and confronted him. There is no record that the man was seeking help before this "intervention." After the encounter, the crowd "saw the man . . . sitting quietly at Jesus' feet, clothed and sane!" (Luke 8:35).

Most of us would stop right there, but if we did, we would probably end up in worse shape than before. Jesus explains, "When a demon is cast out of a man, it goes to the deserts, searching there for rest; but finding none, it returns to the person it left, and finds that its former home is all swept and clean, but empty. . . . Then it goes and gets seven other demons more evil than itself, and they all enter the man. And so the poor fellow is . . . worse off than he was before" (Luke 11:24-26).

If we are to remain free, we must go beyond just accepting deliverance. It's not enough to just let Christ clean us up. We must use our season of sobriety to go back and deal with filling up the empty, broken places in our hearts and lives.

Recovery is a beginning of restoration; but to be in recovery, we need to continue what we begin.

DAY 7 Finding Support

Bible Reading:
Galatians 6:1-5

We came to believe that a Power greater than ourselves could restore us to sanity.

For some of us the higher Power we turn to first is the power of something we can see and feel. When we find a group of supportive people, who understand our struggle and care about our recovery, we can turn to them to help us on the road toward restoration.

The apostle Paul wrote about the value of people helping people. He instructed, if someone "is overcome by some sin, you who are godly should gently and humbly help him back onto the right path, remembering that next time it might be one of you who is in the wrong" (Galatians 6:1). Some versions say, "restore such a one in a spirit of gentleness" (NKJV). In the original biblical language, the word *restore* means to allow a broken bone to set and heal properly. Paul was calling to mind a picture of people lifting up and carrying a person who had been injured. It implies that they will continue to uphold the suffering person until the injury has had time to heal.

We can't recover all alone any more than someone with a broken leg can heal properly while walking around without any support. We need support from people who are willing to gently bear us up and walk beside us until we've had time to heal.

The verse warns those giving the support that they should remember their own capacity for falling. It is important for us to turn to people who have some understanding of their own brokenness, who will be able to act in a "spirit of gentleness."

No one is ever independent enough to not need help from others.

DAY 8 Coming to Believe

Bible Reading: Romans 1:18-20

We came to believe that a Power greater than ourselves could restore us to sanity.

To say that we "came to believe" in anything describes a process. Belief is the result of consideration, doubt, reasoning, and concluding. Forming beliefs shows the mark of God's image in our lives. It involves emotion and logic. It leads to action. What's the process that leads to solid belief, which leads us to change our lives?

We start with our own experience. We see what doesn't work. Looking at the condition of our life, we realize that there isn't enough power in ourselves to restore us to sanity. We try with all our might, but to no avail. When we're quiet enough to listen, we hear that little voice inside us saying, "There is a God and he's extremely powerful." The apostle Paul said it this way, "For the truth about God is known to them [all people] instinctively; God has put this knowledge in their hearts" (Romans 1:19).

After looking at our internal weakness, we then need to look outside ourselves. We need to see that there are others who have struggled with addictions and recovered. We can see that they, too, were unable to heal themselves, yet they are able to live free of the addictive behavior. We conclude that there must be a greater Power that helped them. Since we can see the similarities between their struggle and our own, we come to believe that there must be a Power greater than ourselves that can restore us to sanity also. This is where many people are when they get to Step Two; and it's a good place to be on the way to recovery.

God has put knowledge about himself inside each of us, but sometimes we can see him best in others.

DAY 9 God's Character

Bible Reading: Romans 1:21-23

We came to believe that a Power greater than ourselves could restore us to sanity.

Most of us who have lived with addictions struggle with inner guilt. We may conclude that God is against us, and/or that we are against him. Our fear of rejection, coupled with the fear of having to give up an addiction that helps us cope, can cause us to distance ourselves from God. When this happens, our minds become confused. We concoct a long list of all the things we need to do in order to come to God. This list usually describes our version of what it means to be "good enough." And in our minds, it often disqualifies us from the hope of having a loving relationship with God.

The apostle Paul once wrote, "Yes, they knew about him [God] all right, but they wouldn't admit it or worship him or even thank him for all his daily care. And after awhile they began to think up silly ideas of what God was like and what he wanted them to do. The result was that their foolish minds became dark and confused. Claiming themselves to be wise without God, they became utter fools instead" (Romans 1:21-22).

If we have negative feelings toward God, we need to look carefully at the reasoning behind our conclusions. We may have concluded that we don't want, or can't accept, God. If we examine these conclusions and compare them with what the Bible really says about God, we may be happy to find that God is far more loving and accepting than we might have believed possible.

Addictions begin when we reject what we know about God; recovery begins when we rediscover it.

DAY 10 Persistent Seeking

Bible Reading:
Job 14:1-6

We came to believe that a Power greater than ourselves could restore us to sanity.

One thing that may make it hard to believe in God is that life often seems unfair to us. We didn't ask to be born into a dysfunctional family! We didn't have any say over the abuses and injustices we suffered! We didn't choose our predisposition toward addiction! And yet we're held accountable over something we can't control on our own! This makes it hard to initially turn to God, as the Power to restore our sanity. He seems unreasonable in his demands!

Job understood these feelings. In the midst of his suffering he said, "How frail is man, how few his days, how full of trouble! He blossoms for a moment like a flower—and withers; as the shadow of a passing cloud, he quickly disappears. Must you be so harsh with frail men, and demand an accounting from them? How can you demand purity in one born impure?" (Job 14:1-4).

That's a good question—one which most people, especially addicts, have asked themselves in one form or another. Job persisted in his questioning because deep inside he believed God to be good and fair, even though life wasn't. He was honest with his emotions and questions, but he never stopped seeking God.

There's a good answer to the question posed by Job, one which will satisfy both our hearts and our minds. It will only be found, however, by those who are willing to work through the pain and unfairness of life, and still seek God. Those who seek him will find him, and the answers they seek as well.

No matter how unfair life may seem, God can offer hope in its darkest hours.

DAY 11 God's Solution

Bible Reading: Romans 3:21-26

We came to believe that a Power greater than ourselves could restore us to sanity.

Even though life may seem unfair to us, we also may feel justifiably guilty for all the pain we've caused others. We may struggle with a desire for fairness in life, but also feel that if everything were as it should be, we'd deserve God's anger and punishment. When we fear punishment from God, we'll probably hesitate to approach him to ask for the power we need to recover.

There's a solution to the problem of needing God's power, but feeling that we don't deserve it. "Now God has shown us a different way to heaven—not by 'being good enough' and trying to keep his laws, but by a new way. . . . God declares us 'not guilty' of offending him if we trust in Jesus Christ, who in his kindness freely takes away our sins. For God sent Christ Jesus to take the punishment for our sins and to end all God's anger against us. He used Christ's blood and our faith as the means of saving us from his wrath. In this way he was being entirely fair. . . . But isn't this unfair for God to let criminals go free, and say that they are innocent? No, for he does it on the basis of their trust in Jesus who took away their sins" (Romans 3:21, 24-26).

God figured out a way to remain just in an unfair world. He found a way to punish our sins without having to destroy our lives as the penalty. When we can accept that Jesus' death was payment for our sins, not his own, it solves the problem for us. It also gives us access to the greatest Power there is: God himself.

God's solution is available to each of us, regardless of our failures.

DAY 12 Never Hopeless

Bible Reading: John 11:37-45

We came to believe that a Power greater than ourselves could restore us to sanity.

As much as we want to believe that a Power greater than ourselves can restore us to sanity, we may have to deal with nagging doubts. We may see other people who have recovered from their addictions and still wonder if we will be able to recover as they did. We may fear that our lives are "too far gone."

If anyone was too far gone to recover from anything, it was Lazarus, a friend of Jesus. Lazarus had been dead and buried (without embalming) for four days when Jesus finally arrived on the scene. "Then they came to the tomb. It was a cave with a heavy stone rolled across its door. 'Roll the stone aside,' Jesus told them. But Martha, the dead man's sister, said, 'By now the smell will be terrible, for he has been dead four days.' 'But didn't I tell you that you will see a wonderful miracle from God if you believe?' Jesus asked her. So they rolled the stone aside. Then Jesus looked up to heaven and said, 'Father, thank you for hearing me. (You always hear me, of course, but I said it because of all these people standing here, so that they will believe you sent me.)' Then he shouted, 'Lazarus, come out!' And Lazarus came—bound up in the gravecloth, his face muffled in a head swath. Jesus told them, 'Unwrap him and let him go!'" (John 11:38-44).

When we feel like our lives are too far gone we can remember Lazarus. Jesus wanted everyone to know that when God is in the picture, no one is ever too far gone.

Because of God's power, no one is beyond recovery.

DAY 13 Beyond Insanity

Bible Reading: *1 Samuel 21:10-15*	**We came to believe that a Power greater than ourselves could restore us to sanity.**

There are times in life when our "insanity" is useful to keep us alive or help us cope with a particularly difficult set of circumstances. We may have begun using our addictive/compulsive behavior as a survival mechanism. Maybe now we're stuck with the "craziness" just because it's familiar, even though its usefulness has long since passed. We may feel more comfortable with chaos than with "sanity" because it's all we've known.

Young David was fleeing from King Saul, who was trying to kill him to prevent him from taking over his throne. "David hurried on, for he was fearful of Saul, and went to King Achish of Gath. But Achish's officers weren't happy about his being there. 'Isn't he the top leader of Israel?' they asked. 'Isn't he the one the people honor at their dances, singing, "Saul has slain his thousands and David his ten thousands"?' David heard these comments and was afraid of what King Achish might do to him, so he pretended to be insane! He scratched on doors and let his spittle flow down his beard, until finally King Achish said to his men, 'Must you bring me a madman? We already have enough of them around here! Should such a fellow as this be my guest?' So David left Gath and escaped" (1 Samuel 21:10–22:1).

If David had continued to act insane after he was out of danger, he never would have become king or gone on to great victories. We, too, need to let go of the "insanity" that helped us cope in the past, and move on toward our own victories.

Our insanity can end as soon as our recovery begins.

DAY 14 Power from God

Bible Reading:
Acts 2:1-18

We came to believe that a Power greater than ourselves could restore us to sanity.

Maybe we've traveled this route before. This isn't the first time for us to begin recovery. We found courage once before, only to fail when the going got rough. Now we're starting over, but it's even harder than at first because we feel like a failure.

There is plenty of power, even for those who have failed on a grand scale. Peter didn't want to follow Jesus in the first place. Peter told Jesus to go away because Peter was aware of his own sinfulness. But Jesus wouldn't let him go. So Peter followed him, cautiously at first, then with bold confidence. When Jesus was arrested, Peter disappointed himself by denying that he even knew Jesus. Peter was afraid that he would be arrested, too.

After Jesus rose from the dead, he tried to help Peter feel better by reaffirming his love; but Peter's confidence was still sorely shaken. Then something happened that renewed Peter with power from on high. "As the believers met together that day, suddenly there was a sound like the roaring of a mighty windstorm in the skies above them and it filled the house where they were meeting. . . . And everyone present was filled with the Holy Spirit. . . . Then Peter stepped forward with the eleven apostles, and shouted to the crowd" (Acts 2:1-2, 4, 14). Peter found the power to stand tall that day, and three thousand people found new life as a result.

Although we may have failed in the past, Peter is proof that there is no limit to the forgiveness and power available from God!

God's power brings stability and hope to our lives of fear and uncertainty.

DAY 15 Honest Grieving

Bible Reading:
1 Samuel 1:2-18

We came to believe that a Power greater than ourselves could restore us to sanity.

Circumstances in life can be overwhelming. Yet at times, the grief we feel is misunderstood by those who observe us going through it. They may despise us, look down on us for our "weakness," or think we're losing our grasp on reality. On the contrary, when the pain of living becomes overwhelming, we aren't crazy to grieve. It would be crazy for us not to!

God looks on our heart and has compassion for us in our times of grief, even when those around us don't understand. Hannah was overwhelmed by grief in response to a troubling family situation. "One evening . . . Hannah went over to the Tabernacle. Eli the priest was sitting at his customary place beside the entrance. She was in deep anguish and was crying bitterly as she prayed to the Lord. . . . Eli noticed her mouth moving as she was praying silently and, hearing no sound, thought she had been drinking. 'Must you come here drunk?' he demanded. 'Throw away your bottle.' 'Oh no, sir!' she replied, 'I'm not drunk! But I am very sad and I was pouring out my heart to the Lord. Please don't think that I am just some drunken bum!' 'In that case,' Eli said, 'cheer up! May the Lord of Israel grant you your petition, whatever it is!'" (1 Samuel 1:9-10, 12-17).

Sometimes what people see as insane behavior is really grief being expressed. At these times we need loving support to acknowledge our pain.

As we turn to face our pain and grief, we will discover that God is there with us.

DAY 16 An Overwhelming Struggle

Bible Reading: Romans 8:35-39

We came to believe that a Power greater than ourselves could restore us to sanity.

Sometimes we may feel like giving up the struggle. We try, only to fall once again. We take two steps forward, but then stumble backwards. We feel condemned, and fear that even God may give up on us. At times there are so many difficulties, so many issues to work through, so many patterns in our lives that have to be changed, we begin to feel like we're going crazy.

God acknowledges the difficulties we may face, but he also promises us victory in the end. The apostle Paul once wrote, "Overwhelming victory is ours through Christ who loved us enough to die for us. For I am convinced that nothing can ever separate us from his [Christ's] love. Death can't, and life can't. The angels won't, and all the powers of hell itself cannot keep God's love away. . . . Nothing will ever be able to separate us from the love of God demonstrated by our Lord Jesus Christ when he died for us" (Romans 8:37-39). Paul also said, "I am sure that God who began the good work within you will keep right on helping you grow in his grace until his task within you is finally finished on that day when Jesus Christ returns" (Philippians 1:6).

When we feel like we're going crazy and don't think that we can handle life, God is there. He is determined not to give up on us. We can rely on his persistent love. God has promised to keep working on us until we are whole. There will still be crazy times, but with his help we can handle life, one day at a time.

Nothing can remove us from God's presence.

DAY 17 A Little Faith

Bible Reading:
Luke 17:5-6

We came to believe that a Power greater than ourselves could restore us to sanity.

How many times have we wished that we could overcome the addictions and compulsions that keep us in bondage? We know what it is to struggle with the effects of addiction, and the craziness this brings to our lives. We may feel despair and wonder if there really is any way out of the insanity of our current circumstances. Maybe our plight is impossible, at least without God's help, but faith can make even the impossible happen.

"One day the apostles said to the Lord, 'We need more faith; tell us how to get it.' 'If your faith were only the size of a mustard seed,' Jesus answered, 'it would be large enough to uproot that mulberry tree over there and send it hurtling into the sea! Your command would bring immediate results!'" (Luke 17:5-6). Matthew also recorded Jesus' words, "For if you had faith even as small as a tiny mustard seed you could say to this mountain, 'Move!' and it would go far away. Nothing would be impossible" (Matthew 17:20).

Faith is a mysterious commodity. Jesus says that if we have faith, real faith, it only takes a small amount to make a big difference. We may be exercising faith without even realizing it. It takes faith to believe that a Power greater than ourselves could restore us to sanity. It takes faith to work through the steps of a recovery program. It's comforting to know that God only needs a tiny bit of faith in order to work in powerful ways to restore our sanity.

Just a little faith can take root and grow, first underground and then visibly.

DAY 18 Worthy Promises

Bible Reading: Hebrews 6:12-18

We came to believe that a Power greater than ourselves could restore us to sanity.

We may believe that a Power greater than ourselves can restore our sanity, but still wonder how long it's going to take. Over time, we may grow discouraged at the length of the process. We may have our spirits dampened by the chaos we can't seem to escape. Some people report instant release from their addictions and the accompanying craziness. But for most of us, it will take patience to inherit the promise of a sane new life.

The book of Hebrews tells us: "You will be anxious to follow the example of those who receive all that God has promised them because of their strong faith and patience. For instance, there was God's promise to Abraham: God took an oath in his own name, . . . that he would bless Abraham again and again, and give him a son and make him the father of a great nation of people. Then Abraham waited patiently until finally God gave him a son, Isaac, just as he had promised" (Hebrews 6:12-15). (The entire story of Abraham's life can be found in Genesis 11–25.)

The key point to consider here is that Abraham had to wait twenty-five years to see God's promise fulfilled. There were times he took matters into his own hands, times he probably wondered if he had really received the promise at all, and times he laughed in disbelief to think that the promise would ever come true. In the end, "Abraham was . . . a very old man, and God blessed him in every way" (Genesis 24:1). Just because our restoration takes time doesn't mean our faith is in vain. Let's keep holding on!

Since God is Truth, we can rest securely in his promises.

DAY 19 A Desperate Faith

Bible Reading: Matthew 15:22-28

We came to believe that a Power greater than ourselves could restore us to sanity.

Sometimes the insanity of living with our own addictions or with someone who is acting in bizarre ways can cause us to become desperate for help.

Jesus dealt with a woman who was driven to him out of desperation. "A woman from Canaan who was living there came to him [Jesus], pleading, 'Have mercy on me, O Lord, King David's Son! For my daughter has a demon within her, and it torments her constantly.' But Jesus gave her no reply—not even a word. Then his disciples urged him to send her away. . . . Then he said to the woman, 'I was sent to help the Jews—the lost sheep of Israel—not the Gentiles.' But she came and worshiped him and pled again, 'Sir, help me!' 'It doesn't seem right to take bread from the children and throw it to the dogs,' he said. 'Yes, it is!' she replied, 'for even the puppies beneath the table are permitted to eat the crumbs that fall.' 'Woman,' Jesus told her, 'your faith is large, and your request is granted.' And her daughter was healed right then" (Matthew 15:22-28).

It took a lot of courage for this woman to even speak to Jesus, because of the racism of their time. She was despised and ridiculed for seeking an end to her family's torment, but she didn't give up. She believed God was the only one who could help her and would not be deterred. Our own desperation can lead to a sincere faith that can be a tremendous help in recovery.

When we realize that God is the only One who can help, nothing can block our recovery.

DAY 20 God's Wisdom

Bible Reading: James 3:13-18

We came to believe that a Power greater than ourselves could restore us to sanity.

When we get caught up in catering to our addictions, it's almost like we're a different person. It's like there are two of us tied up together. The Bible recognizes this dual nature in all of us. One part yearns for good and the other part of us is drawn toward corrupt desires and animal passions. The Bible describes a kind of "worldly" wisdom that justifies destructive behavior and leads to disorder, instability, and confusion.

We need to beware of this type of wisdom, which is characterized by jealousy and selfishness. James wrote, "For jealousy and selfishness are not God's kind of wisdom. Such things are earthly, unspiritual, inspired by the devil. For wherever there is jealousy or selfish ambition, there will be disorder and every other kind of evil" (James 3:15-16).

This kind of thinking causes us to focus on what others are and have. It makes us want the same things for ourselves to the point where we are always dissatisfied. It is easy to become so consumed with our own desires that we become inconsiderate of others, often hurting the ones we love. This type of wisdom is inspired by the devil, and will lead to our ultimate destruction; his "purpose is to steal, kill and destroy" (John 10:10).

If we see that our thoughts are still dominated by these characteristics, we need to ask God to replace our "wisdom" with his wisdom. We can trust him to change our minds and our lives.

True wisdom restores our sanity and leads us to peace and wholeness.

DAY 21 A Loving Father

Bible Reading: Proverbs 4:1-10

We came to believe that a Power greater than ourselves could restore us to sanity.

Some people grow up in families where wisdom is modeled and taught by their parents. They have the privilege of receiving wise advice at home. Many of us grew up in families that were crazy. Our parents didn't provide wise guidance for us. This deprivation can leave us wondering how we can fill up the void of what we missed. We may feel like the rest of the human race has passed us by. Some of us feel anger, resentment, and a sense of shame because we never learned how to make wise choices. We may ask ourselves, *Shouldn't someone have shown me the way?*

Ideally, all of us should have had wise and godly instruction. The book of Proverbs records a father instructing his son in the way God intended. "For I, too, was once a son, tenderly loved by my mother . . . and a companion of my father. He told me never to forget his words. . . . *'Learn to be wise,'* he said, *'and develop good judgment and common sense! I cannot overemphasize this point.'* Cling to wisdom—she will protect you. Love her—she will guard you" (Proverbs 4:3-6).

For those of us who were left unprotected and unguarded because of our parent's insane ways, it's not too late. We have a Father in heaven who is eager to give us the wisdom we need. James once wrote, "If you want to know what God wants you to do, ask him, and he will gladly tell you" (James 1:5). God loves us tenderly, as a parent should. He is always there for us, waiting to give us the wisdom we need whenever we ask.

God wants to encourage us with his love and compassion.

DAY 22 Daring to Believe

Bible Reading: Joshua 1:1-9

We came to believe that a Power greater than ourselves could restore us to sanity.

There must have been a time when we had high hopes for a promising life—before those hopes were dashed. But then, through the crazy and chaotic circumstances of growing up, we learned to settle for a life that was far less than what we had once hoped for. We may have come to the conclusion that a sane, good life is reserved for people better or stronger than ourselves.

God led the nation of Israel out of bondage in Egypt, through the wilderness, and to the edge of the Promised Land. But as they stood on the border, looking into the fruitful and prosperous land of Canaan, they lacked the faith and courage to go in. Joshua was one of the few who had the faith to enter, but because of the others, he was held back. Forty years later the chance came again. Just before he entered the land, the Lord told him, "Yes, be bold and strong! Banish fear and doubt! For remember, the Lord your God is with you wherever you go" (Joshua 1:9).

There is a Promised Land for each one of us. Jeremiah tells us, "For I know the plans I have for you, says the Lord. They are plans for good and not for evil, to give you a future and a hope" (Jeremiah 29:11). We need to be courageous. We need to believe that there can be good things in life for us. We, too, can be encouraged that regardless of the failures in our families and our past, we can start again. We can find our way out of the chaos of the wilderness, into the Promised Land of sane and healthy living.

We may not succeed by the world's standards, but we can by God's standards, and his opinion lasts forever.

DAY 23 Common Temptations

Bible Reading:
1 Corinthians
10:12-13

We came to believe that a Power greater than ourselves could restore us to sanity.

Entertaining belief in an addiction's magical cure often hinders recovery. One of the most common such beliefs is that someday we will finally be beyond the reach of temptation. Unfortunately, temptation is a permanent part of our world and of human experience. The Bible says, "The wrong desires that come into your life aren't anything new and different. Many others have faced exactly the same problems before you" (1 Corinthians 10:13). Not only is temptation all around us, it's within us as well. "Temptation is the pull of man's own evil thoughts and wishes" (James 1:14). Even if we could rid ourselves of all external temptations, we'd still have to live with the destructive desires within our secret selves.

Even Jesus Christ himself faced temptation; and yet, he never sinned. Before he was tempted, he spent an extended period of time alone in the wilderness, and during that time he went without food. We are usually tempted the most during the times when we're lonely and hungry.

Facing temptation is a part of accepting reality. We need to accept that we will always be susceptible to temptation in our areas of weakness and predisposition. It is unrealistic to believe that our sinful nature will ever get better. When we put away the magical belief that temptation will disappear, we will be more aware and better able to avoid falling under temptation's power. We need to prayerfully seek God's help in dealing with this reality of life.

Temptations touch everyone; facing this fact is an important step in recovery.

DAY 24 A Day at a Time

Bible Reading: Matthew 6:25-34

We came to believe that a Power greater than ourselves could restore us to sanity.

Living one day at a time is a discipline we all have to focus on when we're in recovery. It's easy to slip back into letting ourselves focus on worries about tomorrow, the "what ifs" and the "if onlys." Each day brings with it a host of things we cannot change. We face the continual reality of momentary circumstances beyond our control. There is also the reality of who we are, human beings confined within the slice of life we call today. It is tempting to deny the present, but escaping reality is part of the insanity of our addictive way of life.

Jesus once said, "Will all your worries add a single moment to your life? . . . God will take care of your tomorrow too. Live one day at a time" (Matthew 6:27, 34). The prophet Jeremiah said, "It is only the Lord's mercies that have kept us from complete destruction. Great is his faithfulness; his loving-kindness begins afresh each day" (Lamentations 3:22-23). Since God's grace comes in daily doses, that's the best way to face life.

We need to ask ourselves at every turn, Am I accepting this present moment or am I pretending, trying to escape into the past or the future? For each day, there is something to find joy in, and there is strength promised for the troubles of that day. The psalmist wrote, "This is the day that the Lord has made. We will rejoice and be glad in it!" (Psalm 118:24). We, too, can choose to find joy, strength, and sanity when we accept today's realities.

Our days can be filled with worry and anxiety or joy and anticipation; it's our choice.

DAY 25 A Worthy Friend

Bible Reading:
Job 33:23-32

We came to believe that a Power greater than ourselves could restore us to sanity.

We may find ourselves in a pit of depression. We may be hiding in the dark, unable to work effectively, sick in body and mind, unable to cope, unable to pray, confused, and misunderstood.

Job's young friend Elihu noted how God can help one who is in this condition: "If a messenger from heaven is there to intercede for him as a friend, to show him what is right, then God pities him and says, 'Set him free. Do not make him die, for I have found a substitute.' Then his body will become as healthy as a child's, firm and youthful again. And when he prays to God, God will hear and answer and receive him with joy, and return him to his duties. And he will declare to his friends, 'I sinned, but God let me go. He did not let me die. I will go on living in the realm of light.' Yes, God often does these things for man—brings back his soul from the pit, so that he may live in the light of the living" (Job 33:23-30).

When we are so drugged and/or depressed that we can't function, we have a friend to intercede for us before God. He made himself our substitute so that we don't have to die when life becomes overwhelming. God is in the business of restoring health to our bodies, reviving our darkened spiritual lives, renewing prayer, restoring us to our jobs, and making it so that we can face the light of day. When we're in the pit of depression we can be assured that God can bring us out because he has successfully done it for many others.

God is in the business of restoring lives, and he starts right where we are.

DAY 26 Bringing Order to Chaos

Bible Reading: Isaiah 40:25-31

We came to believe that a Power greater than ourselves could restore us to sanity.

We may be worn out by the overwhelming feelings that dominate our lives and the chaos that wearies us. We probably feel the need for someone who has the power to bring order into our lives.

God leaves us this reminder, "'With whom will you compare me? Who is my equal?' asks the Holy One. Look up into the heavens! Who created all these stars? As a shepherd leads his sheep, calling each by its pet name, and counts them to see that none are lost or strayed, so God does with stars and planets! O Jacob, O Israel, how can you say that the Lord doesn't see your troubles and isn't being fair? Don't you yet understand? Don't you know by now that the everlasting God, the Creator of the farthest parts of the earth, never grows faint or weary? No one can fathom the depths of his understanding. He gives power to the tired and worn out, and strength to the weak" (Isaiah 40:25-29).

Take a moment to ponder the vastness of the universe, the innumerable stars and planets that all continue to move in perfect order. Scientists marvel at how predictable and consistent the universe remains. Doesn't it make sense that the One who made the universe and keeps every star in place can also have the power to bring order into the chaos of our lives? He knows the weariness that comes with disorder. He understands our need for safe, predictable patterns in life. He, who made us, can bring order to our lives, too.

Even the strongest people get tired, but God's strength never diminishes.

DAY 27 Risky Decisions

Bible Reading: Jonah 1:3-12

We came to believe that a Power greater than ourselves could restore us to sanity.

We may do crazy things when we're caught up in stormy circumstances resulting from our own "out of control" behavior. We take risks that can have terrible consequences, but find that we've lost the power to choose otherwise.

Jonah made a risky decision that seems crazy by any definition! Let's try to learn something from his experience. Jonah was running away from God. He boarded a ship going the opposite direction from where God told him to go. "Suddenly the Lord flung a terrific wind over the sea, causing a great storm that threatened to send them to the bottom." The sailors identified Jonah as the cause of the storm. "Then he [Jonah] told them that he was running away from the Lord. The men were terribly frightened when they heard this. 'Oh, why did you do it?' they shouted. 'What should we do to you to stop the storm?' . . . 'Throw me out into the sea,' he said, 'and it will become calm again.' . . . Then they picked up Jonah and threw him overboard into the raging sea—and the storm stopped!" (Jonah 1:4, 10-12, 15).

When we follow our own ways, God may allow us to get caught up in a "storm." He often does this to help us face the insanity of the risks we take. Jonah was rescued and taken back to where God had intended him to go. God can rescue us out of our personal storms as well. He can take us back to a place where the available choices aren't life threatening or dangerous.

Even when we go our own way, God is there with us, ready to restore us.

DAY 28 Seasons of Darkness

Bible Reading: Psalm 6:1-10

We came to believe that a Power greater than ourselves could restore us to sanity.

At times we get so caught up in our pain that we forget that life comes in seasons. No one is happy all the time. We may be paranoid and gloomy today, but that can change. Being upset and disturbed doesn't have to be forever.

When David was a young boy he lived a relatively carefree life, tending his father's sheep. He believed in his own goodness and expected the best. Later he realized his own frailties and faced many enemies. These pressures darkened his life. He cried out to God, "No, Lord! Don't punish me in the heat of your anger. Pity me, O Lord, for I am weak. Heal me, for my body is sick, and I am upset and disturbed. My mind is filled with apprehension and with gloom. Oh, restore me soon. Come, O Lord and make me well. In your kindness save me. For if I die I cannot give you glory by praising you before my friends. I am worn out with pain; every night my pillow is wet with tears" (Psalm 6:1-6). David did come out of this dark season of life, and was able to share his experience, strength, and hope with others. He says of God, "He fulfills the desires of those who reverence and trust him; he hears their cries for help and rescues them" (Psalm 145:19).

If we're in a season of mental anguish, we need to remember that we haven't always felt this way and we won't always feel this way. We can cry out for help and expect God to rescue us. Someday we will share our experience and hope with others.

When we are at the end of ourselves, God creates a new beginning.

DAY 29 Life from Death

Bible Reading:
Ezekiel 37:1-14

We came to believe that a Power greater than ourselves could restore us to sanity.

It may be that our families have been governed by the craziness of addiction for a long time. It may be that we have lost hope of ever recovering; our hope may be just a skeleton, long dead.

God has demonstrated his power to restore in even the most hopeless of situations. Consider this vision given to the prophet Ezekiel. "I was carried away by the Spirit of the Lord to a valley full of old, dry bones that were scattered everywhere across the ground. He led me around among them. . . . Then he told me to speak to the bones and say: 'O dry bones, listen to the words of God for the Lord God says, "See! I am going to make you live and breathe again! I will replace the flesh and muscles on you and cover you with skin. I will put breath into you, and you shall live and know I am the Lord."'" Ezekiel saw these bones come to life. The Lord explained, "These bones . . . represent all the people of Israel. They say: 'We have become a heap of dried-out bones—all hope is gone.' But tell them . . . 'My people, I will open your graves of exile and cause you to rise again and return to the land of Israel'" (Ezekiel 37:1-2, 4-6, 11-12).

Israel is the only nation in history that has been nearly destroyed, the people exiled throughout the world, and then, centuries later, reborn as a nation. If God was able to restore the nation of Israel, surely he can restore our lives as well!

If God can give life to scattered bones, he can restore our shattered lives.

DAY 30 Confidence in God

Bible Reading: Amos 4:9-13

We came to believe that a Power greater than ourselves could restore us to sanity.

Many of us began recovery experiencing one disaster after another. We probably wondered whether Someone was trying to tell us something. But as we came to believe that God's power could reach into our world in positive ways, we also received hope. We were able to exchange our fear of punishment for confidence in the power of God to restore us to sanity.

The Lord had allowed many disasters to befall the people of Israel, in hopes that they would return to him. God warned them of the evils that would result from continuing to resist his help, but they wouldn't listen. Finally, he said, "Therefore I will bring upon you all these further evils I have spoken of. Prepare to meet your God in judgment, Israel. For you are dealing with the One who . . . knows your every thought . . . Jehovah, the Lord, the Lord Almighty, is his name" (Amos 4:12-13).

Ignoring the fact that God has power over our lives can be disastrous. He may try to get our attention by allowing us to experience the consequences of our wrong behaviors. We need to realize that God's ultimate goal is to lead us back to himself. Even the pain God allows us to suffer is designed to bring about our healing. His power is for our good; it isn't there to destroy us. Considering the mighty power of God, even in the natural realm, can encourage us. The one strong enough to form the mountains and the winds is willing to use his power to restore us to sanity.

Even our greatest failures can be a means for God to make us his own.

We made a decision to turn our will and our lives over to the care of God as we understood him.

Jesus said, "Come to me and I will give you rest—all of you who work so hard beneath a heavy yoke" **(Matthew 11:28).**

STEP THREE

DAY 1 Submission and Rest

Bible Reading: Matthew 11:27-30

We made a decision to turn our will and our lives over to the care of God as we understood him.

When our burdens become heavy and we see that our way of life is leading us toward death, we may finally become willing to let someone else do the driving. We've probably worked hard at trying to get our lives on the right track, but still feel like we always end up on a dead-end street.

Proverbs tells us, "Before every man there lies a wide and pleasant road that seems right but ends in death" (Proverbs 14:12). When we began our addictive behaviors we were probably seeking a way to find pleasure or to overcome the pain of living. The way seemed right at first, but it became clear that we were on the wrong track. But then we were unable to turn around on our own. Jesus said, "Come to me and I will give you rest—all of you who work so hard beneath a heavy yoke. Wear my yoke—for it fits perfectly—and let me teach you; for I am gentle and humble, and you shall find rest for your souls" (Matthew 11:28-30).

To take on a yoke implies being united to another in order to work together. Those who are yoked together must go in the same direction, but by doing so, their work is made considerably easier. Jesus is saying that when we finally decide to submit our lives and our will to his direction, our burdens will become manageable. When we let him do the driving, we will be able to "find rest" for our souls. He knows the way and has the strength to turn us around and get us on the road toward life.

We all wear a yoke on our shoulders; the trick is in finding the right master.

DAY 2 Releasing Worry

Bible Reading: Matthew 6:25-34

We made a decision to turn our will and our lives over to the care of God as we understood him.

It is often our worries about the small details of life that lead to our undoing. Life's daily demands can be overwhelming. Perhaps, our "acting out" is a way of escaping. When we are sober, we are once again faced with the pressures of life. Learning to manage these in a new way is a key to maintaining our sobriety.

Jesus said, "Don't worry about *things*—food, drink, and clothes. For you already have life and a body—and they are far more important than what to eat and wear. Look at the birds! They don't worry about what to eat . . . your heavenly Father feeds them. And you are far more valuable to him than they are. Will all your worries add a single moment to your life?

"And why worry about your clothes? Look at the field lilies! They don't worry about theirs. . . . And if God cares so wonderfully for flowers that are here today and gone tomorrow, won't he more surely care for you? . . .

"So don't worry at all about having enough food and clothing. . . . Your heavenly Father already knows perfectly well that you need them, and he will give them to you if you give him first place in your life and live as he wants you to. So don't be anxious about tomorrow. God will take care of your tomorrow too. Live one day at a time" (Matthew 6:25-34).

Since God cares deeply for us, we can choose to live one day at a time and turn the details of our lives over to him.

God calls us to live one day at a time.

DAY 3 Discovering God

Bible Reading: Acts 17:23-28

We made a decision to turn our will and our lives over to the care of God as we understood him.

Before we can turn our lives over to God, we need to have an accurate understanding of who he is. It's crucial that our lives be turned over to the God who loves us, and not the "god" of this world who seeks only to deceive and destroy. The apostle Paul described the deceiver this way: "Satan, who is the god of this evil world, has made him [the deceived person] blind, unable to see the glorious light of the Gospel that is shining upon him, or to understand the amazing message we preach about the glory of Christ, who is God" (2 Corinthians 4:4). Has Satan deceived us? How can we be sure that we have a true understanding of God?

When Paul addressed the men of Athens he said, "I saw your many altars, and one of them had this inscription on it—'To the Unknown God.' You have been worshiping him without knowing who he is, and now I wish to tell you about him. . . . His purpose in all of this is that they [all people] should seek after God, and perhaps feel their way toward him and find him—though he is not far from any one of us. For in him we live and move and are!" (Acts 17:23, 27-28).

Even though God may be unknown to us, he is near and willing to reveal himself. God has promised, "You will find me when you seek me, if you look for me in earnest" (Jeremiah 29:13). Turning over our will involves becoming willing to accept God as he is, instead of insisting on creating him in our own image. When we seek God with an open heart and mind, we will find him.

As we seek God, he makes himself known to us.

DAY 4 Belonging to God

Bible Reading: Daniel 3:14-27

We made a decision to turn our will and our lives over to the care of God as we understood him.

Our decision to turn our will and our lives over to God will be tested. By making this decision we set our lives at odds with the crowd. This will include most of our old friends and maybe even members of our family. We should expect some heat and not be shocked when it comes. But God will be with us in the fire, to preserve us and to bring us through.

In the book of Daniel we meet three young Jewish men who were taken captive and relocated to a strange land. They entrusted their lives to God and refused to worship the idols of Babylon. Their resolve was so strong that when they were threatened with death by fire they replied, "If we are thrown into the flaming furnace, our God is able to deliver us; and he will deliver us. . . . But if he doesn't, please understand, sir, that even then we will never under any circumstance serve your gods." They were promptly bound with ropes and thrown into the furnace. The king was amazed at what he saw then. "Look!" Nebuchadnezzar shouted, "I see *four* men, *unbound*, walking around in the fire, and they aren't even hurt by the flames! And the fourth looks like a god!" (Daniel 3:17-18, 25).

God was right there, taking the heat with them. The only thing they lost by turning their will and their lives over to him was the ropes that had bound them. Those were burned up in the flames. When we're challenged because of our decision to turn our lives over to God, we can expect God to be there for us, too.

Nothing can bind us when God wants us to be free.

DAY 5 An Open Hand

Bible Reading: Matthew 16:24-28

We made a decision to turn our will and our lives over to the care of God as we understood him.

Many of us who struggle with addictions have spent much of our strength just trying to hold on to our lives. Maybe we fear loosening our grip to let someone else take care of us. We may be doing a lousy job of caring for our own life, but we still hesitate about letting go. Perhaps, we're afraid that if we do let go, no one will be there to take hold of us.

In the Old Testament we often hear about people being "consecrated" to God. This meant that they were making a decision to turn the remainder of their lives over to God for whatever purpose he desired. The root of this word literally means "an open hand" as opposed to a closed one. They had a ceremony to let go of what they were holding on to for their own lives, and to proclaim that God was welcome to take hold of them. Jesus told us, "For anyone who keeps his life for himself shall lose it; and anyone who loses his life for me shall find it again" (Matthew 16:25-26). By now we probably recognize that we were losing our lives anyway, no matter how hard we tried to hang on.

Once we decide to let go of the control of our will and our lives, something wonderful is promised. Jesus says of those who turn their lives over to him: "I give them eternal life and they shall never perish. No one shall snatch them away from me" (John 10:28). When we finally find the courage to let go, God is waiting to grasp our lives firmly and hold them securely for all eternity.

Holding on, we lose what we have; letting go, we receive even more.

DAY 6 Trusting God

Bible Reading: Numbers 23:18-24

We made a decision to turn our will and our lives over to the care of God as we understood him.

It is not uncommon to link our perceptions about God to our childhood experiences with people who played powerful roles in our lives. If we have been victimized in the past by people who were capricious, abusive, distant, uncaring, or incompetent, we may now anticipate these qualities in God.

Just because God is a power greater than we are, and the people who victimized us represented a power greater than we were, it does not mean that God will harm us if we entrust our lives to him. Even Jesus tells us that he didn't entrust himself to men because he knew what was in their hearts. Nevertheless, he voluntarily turned his life over to the will of God the Father. "It is better to trust the Lord than to put confidence in men" (Psalm 118:8).

We may have learned that when we place our confidence in people, our lives can be devastated by disappointment. We can't let this keep us from ever trusting again. In working Step Three we can make a healthy decision to turn our will and our lives over to the only one who is worthy of being trusted. The Bible tells us, "God is not a man, that he should lie; he doesn't change his mind like humans do" (Numbers 23:19). And God has said, "I will never, *never* fail you nor forsake you" (Hebrews 13:5).

We realize that we can't make it all alone. This time we can stop being the victim. We can turn our lives over to someone who is really able to care for our needs.

We trust in many things, but it is best to trust in the only One worthy of our trust—God himself.

DAY 7 Giving up Control

Bible Reading: Psalm 61:1-8

We made a decision to turn our will and our lives over to the care of God as we understood him.

The thought of turning our will and our lives over can be attractive. When we give in to our addictions aren't we giving control of ourselves over to another power? Aren't we, in some way, giving up personal responsibility for our lives? When we are overwhelmed or wanting to escape, our addictions can make us feel strong or safe, attractive, powerful, or happy. So, in a sense, we are very comfortable with the thought of giving up control of our will and our lives.

We can simply change our focus and turn our lives over to God instead of the sources we have turned to in the past. The apostle Paul touched on this contrast when he said, "Don't drink too much wine, for many evils lie along that path; be filled instead with the Holy Spirit, and controlled by him" (Ephesians 5:18).

When we are overwhelmed and in need of some kind of escape, we have a new place to turn. King David declared, "All who are oppressed may come to him [God]. He is a refuge for them in their times of trouble. All those who know your mercy, Lord, will count on you for help. For you have never yet forsaken those who trust in you" (Psalm 9:9-10).

David also wrote, "For wherever I am, though far away at the ends of the earth, I will cry to you for help. When my heart is faint and overwhelmed, lead me to the mighty, towering Rock of safety. For you are my refuge, a high tower where my enemies can never reach me" (Psalm 61:2-3).

God never changes; he is always present with us.

DAY 8 Free to Choose

Bible Reading: Deuteronomy 30:15-20

We made a decision to turn our will and our lives over to the care of God as we understood him.

Everyone has a life or death decision to make. We've been created with the supreme privilege of free will, the ability to choose. Even when we are in the bondage of our addiction we still have choices confronting us. When we are in recovery, we face the nagging lure of choosing to fall back into our addiction. The freedom to choose brings with it the burden of the results of our choices. And these choices affect our lives and the lives of our children. Free will is our blessing and our responsibility!

God spoke through Moses, saying, "Look, today I have set before you life and death, depending on whether you obey or disobey. I have commanded you today to love the Lord your God and to follow his paths and to keep his laws, so that you will live . . . and so that the Lord your God will bless you. . . . But if your hearts turn away and you won't listen . . . then I declare to you this day that you shall surely perish. . . . I call heaven and earth to witness against you that today I have set before you life or death, blessing or curse. Oh, that you would choose life; that you and your children might live! Choose to love the Lord your God and to obey him and to cling to him, for he is your life and the length of your days" (Deuteronomy 30:15-20).

Although we may feel out of control with respect to our addiction, we can choose to set our hearts in the direction of life. We can choose to love God and begin to follow his paths.

God doesn't force his will on us, but he is there if we decide to put ourselves in his hands.

DAY 9 Single-Minded Devotion

Bible Reading: James 4:7-10

We made a decision to turn our will and our lives over to the care of God as we understood him.

We may already have chosen to follow God's way, letting his paths define the overall direction for our lives. But even so, many of us still keep a part of our heart hidden away from God. We have devoted this part of ourselves to gratifying our addictions, to doing things that are contrary to the will of God. This sets us up for living a double life, which can fill us with guilt, shame, and instability.

Even for those of us who have made the decision to give our hearts to God, we face new moments of decision every day. James was addressing Christians when he wrote, "So give yourselves humbly to God. Resist the devil and he will flee from you. And when you draw close to God, God will draw close to you. Wash your hands, you sinners, and let your hearts be filled with God alone to make them pure and true to him" (James 4:7-8).

When we choose to live the double life, it is easy to become doubtful that God hears us at all. James wrote, "For a doubtful mind will be as unsettled as a wave of the sea that is driven and tossed by the wind; and every decision you then make will be uncertain, as you turn first this way, and then that" (James 1:6-8).

When we resist the devil at every turn and choose to draw close to God, he will draw close to us. When we open up our hidden hearts and begin to make choices in favor of recovery, we will soon grow confident that God desires to help us.

God has already defeated the devil; all we need to do is choose the winning side.

DAY 10 Redeeming the Past

Bible Reading: Isaiah 54:4-8

We made a decision to turn our will and our lives over to the care of God as we understood him.

We all come to God with a past. In turning our lives over to him, we need to give him our past with all its losses and shame. We need to hand over every moment of disgrace, every tear we've ever cried, every word we wish we could take back, all the broken promises, the loneliness, all the dreams that died, the dashed hopes, the broken relationships, our successes and failures, all of our yesterdays and the scars they've left in our lives.

Under Old Testament law, if someone lost freedom, property, or spouse because of a disaster or a debt, the next of kin was looked to as a "redeemer." If property had been lost because of an inability to pay, the redeemer would pay for it and return it to the original owner. If a woman lost her husband, the redeemer would marry her, providing her with protection and love. God tells us, "Fear not; you will no longer live in shame. The shame of your youth and the sorrows of widowhood will be remembered no more, for your Creator will be your 'husband.' The Lord Almighty is his name; he is your Redeemer. . . . For the Lord has called you back from your grief" (Isaiah 54:4-6).

God is our redeemer, the restorer of our losses. We need to make him Lord of all, even of the days and dreams in our past. When we give God our past, he can make up for all that we've lost. He can rid us of the shame. He can fill the empty places in our hearts.

We sell ourselves into slavery; God removes our shame and buys us back.

DAY 11 The Deal of a Lifetime

Bible Reading: Philippians 3:4-11

We made a decision to turn our will and our lives over to the care of God as we understood him.

When we think of turning our lives over to God, it's not unusual to try to polish up our credentials as best we can before presenting them to him. We look at all the worthwhile things we've done, how we've tried to be good, whatever we feel we have to offer. We don't really need to sort out the good from the bad. God doesn't care what's in the mix, as long as we give him the whole package.

Before Paul became a Christian he kept careful count of his "good deeds" and took pride in his ancestry. When he finally decided to turn his life over to the care of God, this is what he said, "But all these things that I once thought very worthwhile--now I've thrown them all away so that I can put my trust and hope in Christ alone. Yes, everything else is worthless when compared with the priceless gain of knowing Christ Jesus my Lord. I have put aside all else, counting it worth less than nothing, in order that I can have Christ, and become one with him" (Philippians 3:7-9).

When we've made the decision to turn our will and our lives over to God, we need to give him our whole life with all its assets and liabilities. We can't earn his love by the "good stuff" in our lives any more than we can discourage his love by all the "bad stuff." It's a straight trade-in. We give him our whole life and being. He gives us complete forgiveness, love, redemption, and acceptance in the person of Jesus Christ. When we see what God is offering us and the little we have to offer him, it's clear that we're getting quite a deal!

God offers us far more than anyone could ever give in return.

DAY 12 A Bright Future

Bible Reading: Luke 23:32-43

We made a decision to turn our will and our lives over to the care of God as we understood him.

Perhaps we've become so disappointed that we've given up hope for the future altogether. We don't know what the future holds, but when we give our lives to God, he can be trusted with our future. Regardless of how bad our lives might be at the moment, we can still trust him to bring about glorious good in our lives.

Here's a story of a man who dared to trust God with his future. And he trusted God when it looked like he didn't even have a future to look forward to. "Two others, criminals, were led out to be executed with him [Jesus] at a place called 'The Skull.' There all three were crucified—Jesus on the center cross, and the two criminals on either side. . . . One of the criminals hanging beside him scoffed, 'So, you're the Messiah, are you? Prove it by saving yourself—and us, too, while you're at it!' But the other criminal protested. 'Don't you even fear God when you are dying? We deserve to die for our evil deeds, but this man hasn't done one thing wrong.' Then he said, 'Jesus, remember me when you come into your Kingdom.' And Jesus replied, 'Today you will be with me in Paradise. This is a solemn promise'" (Luke 23:32-33, 39-43).

No matter what dire straits we may find ourselves in presently, we can give God our future and be assured that eternal life in Paradise will far outweigh the sufferings of this present life. He can also transform our lives right now, making our future down here as bright as the heavenly one!

Even when everything seems dark and hopeless, God promises us a bright, new future.

DAY 13 Never Lost

Bible Reading: Deuteronomy 8:1-18

We made a decision to turn our will and our lives over to the care of God as we understood him.

The road that leads to recovery is often uncharted and dangerous. We may have been born into a family that was lost in a maze of dysfunction and we have had to look for the way out. There are times of need, times of fear, times when we wonder if there is a God out there who cares at all.

The Israelites who were born in the wilderness must have experienced similar feelings. Their parents had sinned and were left to wander in the wilderness for forty years. The new generation had spent much of their lives going nowhere, and for no fault of their own. When the Israelites were about to enter the Promised Land, Moses showed how even there, God's care was present. He said, "Beware that you don't forget the God who led you through the great and terrible wilderness with the dangerous snakes and scorpions, where it was so hot and dry. He gave you water from the rock! He fed you with manna in the wilderness . . . so that you would become humble and so that your trust in him would grow, and he could do you good" (Deuteronomy 8:4, 15-16).

Even when we seem lost, God is watching over us to protect our lives until we can get to a better place. He does take care of us in ways we may take for granted. Peter tells us, "Let him have all your worries and cares, for he is always thinking about you and watching everything that concerns you" (1 Peter 5:7). Just being alive and in recovery shows that God cares for our lives!

When lost in our personal deserts, we can be sure God is never far away.

DAY 14 No One Is Worthless

Bible Reading: Matthew 25:14-30

We made a decision to turn our will and our lives over to the care of God as we understood him.

When we've come out of a difficult season of life, we tend to think of our lives as a mess. But we need to realize that there is more in our lives than pain and problems; there is more to us than our addictions. If we've been treated as worthless, we may overlook our many assets—our talents, resources, and abilities. God wants these turned over to him, too.

Jesus told a story about a man who went away on a long trip. He left some "talents" to three of his servants to invest while he was away. (A talent was a unit of currency used in biblical times.) They were given differing amounts of money to invest in keeping with each of their abilities. Two of the servants used their money profitably. The third was afraid to try and buried his in the ground. When the master returned he was very pleased with the first two servants and rewarded them. He was very angry with the servant who just hid the money away, failing to make a return on it. The master had expected him to make the most of what he had been given (Matthew 25:14-30).

When we turn our lives over to God, that includes all the gifts he has entrusted to us. To say that we have no talents or abilities, is an insult to the One who gave them to us. We're not worthless! We may have to dig around a bit to find those talents that have been buried while we were consumed by our craziness, but God expects us to find them and use them. This will improve our self-esteem and help in our recovery.

God wants all of us because he loves all of us.

STEP THREE

DAY 15 Filled with Joy

Bible Reading: Acts 3:2-8

We made a decision to turn our will and our lives over to the care of God as we understood him.

As we travel the road to recovery, we may feel like we've been reduced to begging for help. Our lives have been crippled by our own addictions and the addictions of others. We approach God's door, with heads down, because we feel desperate for the help he promises to give. But even though we come to God with our heads down, that's not how it has to stay.

Listen to this story about Peter and John's encounter with a man who felt this way: "They saw a man lame from birth carried along the street and laid beside the Temple gate . . . as was his custom every day. As Peter and John were passing by, he asked them for some money. They looked at him intently, and then Peter said, 'Look here!' The lame man looked at them eagerly, expecting a gift. But Peter said, 'We don't have any money for you! But I'll give you something else! I command you in the name of Jesus Christ of Nazareth, *walk!*' Then Peter took the lame man by the hand and pulled him to his feet. And as he did, the man's feet and ankle-bones were healed and strengthened . . . and [he] began walking! Then, walking, leaping, and praising God, he went into the Temple with them" (Acts 3:2-8).

We may turn to God hoping for a meager handout to keep us going. But he has much more for us! He wants to give us such a full recovery that we are healed and transformed. He wants to take us from being the beggar at God's door, to being so full of joy that we can't keep from leaping and praising God.

When we ask God for help, he gives us what we really need.

DAY 16 An Unfair World

Bible Reading: Genesis 39:1-23

We made a decision to turn our will and our lives over to the care of God as we understood him.

There are times when life treats us unfairly. We may protest the injustices, fall victim to self-pity, give in to a why-even-try kind of mentality, or sink into depression. We are invited to leave the injustices we experience in the hands of God.

If there's anyone in history who can complain of unfair treatment, it's Joseph. He was one of eleven brothers, the favorite of his father. In their jealousy, the ten older brothers sold Joseph as a slave into Egypt. Once a slave, Joseph devoted himself to doing a good job for his master and was quickly promoted. He was then propositioned by his master's wife, and when he refused her, was falsely accused of rape by this vindictive woman. Thrown into prison with no hope of release, he again did his best. He was soon running the administration of the whole prison. In the end, Joseph was freed and promoted to be Prime Minister of Egypt. In this position he was able to confront and forgive the brothers who had sold him into slavery so many years before (Genesis 37–45).

It takes courage and wisdom to maintain a healthy attitude when life isn't fair. This comes from trusting that God will take up our cause and vindicate us, as he has promised. We can't change the fact that we live in an imperfect world, where things aren't as they should be. Turning these matters over to God can help us change our response to the injustices of life and continue to focus on our recovery rather than remaining a victim.

Looking at circumstances brings despair; looking to God brings hope for recovery.

DAY 17 Unexpected Problems

Bible Reading:
2 Samuel 15:13-26

We made a decision to turn our will and our lives over to the care of God as we understood him.

There are times in recovery when it seems like we've made it. We reach a place where we feel like we can relax and stop living one day at a time. Then life surprises us with an unexpected problem.

King David had reached a pinnacle of success. He had conquered giants, won many battles, captured the hearts of his people, and overcome enemies on every side. While he was in this comfortable position, life surprised him with a rebellion led by his own son. Here's what happened: "A messenger soon arrived in Jerusalem to tell King David, 'All Israel has joined Absalom in a conspiracy against you!' 'Then we must flee at once or it will be too late!' was David's instant response to his men. 'If we get out of the city before he arrives, both we and the city of Jerusalem will be saved. . . . If the Lord sees fit,' David said, 'he will bring me back to see the Ark and the Tabernacle again. But if he is through with me, well, let him do what seems best to him'" (2 Samuel 15:13-14, 26).

King David wisely accepted what was happening and responded to reality, not to what he wished were true. It seems that David had gotten out of the habit of relying on God, day by day, but he quickly placed his life back in God's hands. God did protect him and returned him to the throne in Jerusalem. When life hits us with unexpected threats, we, too, can let that be a reminder to turn our lives back over to God.

When we think we've arrived, it's time to begin again.

DAY 18 Doing God's Will

Bible Reading:
1 Samuel 24:1-11

We made a decision to turn our will and our lives over to the care of God as we understood him.

Sometimes it's hard to tell the difference between the right thing to do and just an opportune moment. When we are working to make changes in our lives and relationships, we may be uncertain of what to do at times. When this happens, we need to rely on God's wisdom to help us make our decisions.

The jealousy and abuse of King Saul made young David's life miserable. Saul knew that God had chosen David to be king instead of him. Although David was a loyal subject, Saul tried to kill him. Once, when David was hiding in a cave, King Saul came in without knowing David was there. "'Now's your time!' David's men whispered to him. 'Today is the day the Lord was talking about when he said, "I will certainly put Saul into your power, to do with as you wish"!' Then David crept forward and quietly slit off the bottom of Saul's robe! But then his conscience began bothering him. 'I shouldn't have done it,' he said to his men. 'It is a serious sin to attack God's chosen king in any way.' These words of David persuaded his men not to kill Saul" (1 Samuel 24:4-8).

David knew what God expected of him in this situation and he chose to go along with God's will. In trying to give our will to God, it is important to know what his will is in a given situation. When we aren't sure what to do, we can look to see if the Bible gives us any guidance on similar situations. Then we will have a clear view of what it means to turn our will over to God.

When we've turned our lives over to God, we can rest assured that he is with us.

DAY 19 Self-Control

Bible Reading:
2 Peter 1:2-9

We made a decision to turn our will and our lives over to the care of God as we understood him.

We would love to have self-control! But trying to find it within ourselves can become as much of an obsession as our primary addiction.

According to Peter, self-control is one step in the middle of a larger progression. He said, "Do you want more and more of God's kindness and peace? Then learn to know him better and better. For as you know him better, he will give you, through his great power, everything you need for living a truly good life: he even shares his own glory and his own goodness with us! And by that same mighty power he has given us all the other rich and wonderful blessings he promised; for instance, the promise to save us from the lust and rottenness all around us, and to give us his own character. But to obtain these gifts, you need more than faith; you must also work hard to be good, and even that is not enough. For then you must learn to know God better and discover what he wants you to do. Next, learn to put aside your own desires [*self-control*] so that you will become patient and godly, gladly letting God have his way with you. This will make possible the next step, which is for you to enjoy other people and to like them, and finally you will grow to love them deeply" (2 Peter 1:2-7).

Self-control is something that comes as we grow progressively closer to God. Taking one step at a time, one day at a time, God will give us his own character, including self-control.

Our self-control increases as we give increasing control over to God.

DAY 20 Freedom in Forgiveness

Bible Reading: Matthew 6:9-15

We made a decision to turn our will and our lives over to the care of God as we understood him.

We can sometimes get so focused on ourselves during recovery that we don't spend much time dealing with the way others have sinned against us. Or maybe we're totally focused on the way we've been mistreated, as an excuse for our behavior. This leaves us with emotional baggage that will hinder our progress. Forgiving others is an important key to turning our will over to God.

Jesus taught his disciples, "Pray along these lines: 'Our Father in heaven, we honor your holy name. We ask that your kingdom will come now. May your will be done here on earth, just as it is in heaven. Give us our food again today, as usual, and forgive us our sins, just as we have forgiven those who have sinned against us. Don't bring us into temptation, but deliver us from the Evil One. Amen.' Your heavenly Father will forgive you if you forgive those who sin against you; but if *you* refuse to forgive *them, he* will not forgive *you*'" (Matthew 6:9-15).

Forgiveness is a choice of our will. Just as our forgiveness was not based on excusing the wrongs we've done, neither does our forgiveness of others call for us to excuse what they've done. We must first convict the offender in our minds, then turn the matter of vengeance over to God. This helps us face the truth about our own pain. It also frees us from any excuse to continue our compulsive behavior because of what's been done to us.

Forgiveness begins as a choice but becomes a process that opens us to God's love and forgiveness.

DAY 21 Learning to Trust

Bible Reading:
Jeremiah 9:4-9

We made a decision to turn our will and our lives over to the care of God as we understood him.

Most of us know the pain caused by deceit, both for the deceiver and for the one who has been betrayed. We may be trying to learn to trust again after living in situations where we haven't been given any reason to trust.

David cried, "Lord! Help! Godly men are fast disappearing. Where in all the world can dependable men be found? Everyone deceives and flatters and lies. There is no sincerity left. But the Lord will not deal gently with . . . those proud liars who say, 'We will lie to our hearts' content. Our lips are our own; who can stop us?'" (Psalm 12:1-4).

Jeremiah prophesied, "Beware of your neighbor! Beware of your brother! All take advantage of one another and spread their slanderous lies. With practiced tongues they fool and defraud each other; they wear themselves out with all their sinning. 'They pile evil upon evil, lie upon lie, and utterly refuse to come to me,' says the Lord. Therefore the Lord Almighty says this: 'See, I will melt them in a crucible of affliction. I will refine them and test them like metal.'" (Jeremiah 9:4-8).

When we turn our lives over to God, we should try to give him our trust as well. He understands that this will be hard. Our trust in God can be absolute. Trust in people should be cautious; it should only be placed in those who have proven themselves trustworthy.

Trust is only as worthy as its object; trust in God is always a wise bet.

DAY 22 Hope in God

Bible Reading: Jeremiah 17:5-8

We made a decision to turn our will and our lives over to the care of God as we understood him.

We may have learned a long time ago that hoping only brings disappointment. Our hopes were dashed. The promises we believed were broken. We were left feeling like fools for ever hoping in the first place. But perhaps we were devastated because we put our hope in the wrong place.

"The Lord says: Cursed is the man who puts his trust in mortal man and turns his heart away from God. He is like a stunted shrub in the desert, with no hope for the future; he lives on the salt-encrusted plains in the barren wilderness; good times pass him by forever. But blessed is the man who trusts in the Lord and has made the Lord his hope and confidence. He is like a tree planted along a riverbank, with its roots reaching deep into the water—a tree not bothered by the heat nor worried by long months of drought. Its leaves stay green and it goes right on producing all its luscious fruit" (Jeremiah 17:5-8).

Turning our lives over to God includes placing our hope in him, even if people have disappointed us. When we place *all* of our hope in other people, it's like expecting a tree to flourish in a barren desert. Our thirst continues, and they are unable to satisfy our deepest needs. Placing our hope in God changes everything. Jesus said "The water I give them . . . becomes a perpetual spring within them, watering them forever with eternal life" (John 4:14). When our hope is in God, and our lives in his care, we are sustained when we otherwise would be devastated.

If we put our trust and hope in God, we will never be let down.

DAY 23 God's Faithfulness

Bible Reading: Lamentations 3:17-26

We made a decision to turn our will and our lives over to the care of God as we understood him.

Perhaps we're brokenhearted because of the bitter suffering in our family. Maybe our once-good reputations have been ruined and now we're ashamed. Our lives have been taken captive and destroyed before the watchful eyes of friend and foe alike.

Jeremiah watched this happen to his beloved nation, Israel. It's no wonder he's known as the weeping prophet. The people of God refused to listen to Jeremiah's warnings and were taken captive by a heathen nation as a result. Lamentations is a record of Jeremiah's lament over the shameful fate of God's people. He weeps, "O Lord, all peace and all prosperity have long since gone, for you have taken them away. I have forgotten what enjoyment is. All hope is gone; my strength has turned to water, for the Lord has left me. Oh, remember the bitterness and suffering you have dealt to me! For I can never forget these awful years; always my soul will live in utter shame. *Yet there is one ray of hope: his compassion never ends*. It is only the Lord's mercies that have kept us from complete destruction. Great is his faithfulness; his loving-kindness begins afresh each day. My soul claims the Lord as my inheritance; therefore I will hope in him. It is good both to hope and to wait quietly for the salvation of the Lord" (Lamentations 3:17-26).

Turning our lives over to God includes giving him our pain and suffering. God is strong and loving enough to lift our burdens and mend our broken hearts.

When all hope is gone, we can entrust ourselves to God, remembering his neverending compassion.

DAY 24 Glorious Victory

Bible Reading:
Zechariah 9:9-12

We made a decision to turn our will and our lives over to the care of God as we understood him.

Our lives may be a battlefield. We may have been taken captive in the ongoing war between good and evil. When we turn our lives over to God, will he rescue us and keep us safe?

Five hundred years before the birth of Jesus, the prophet Zechariah wrote these words: "Rejoice greatly, O my people! Shout with joy! For look—your King is coming! He is the Righteous One, the Victor! Yet he is lowly, riding on a donkey's colt! [This prophecy was fulfilled by the coming of Jesus (see Matthew 21:4-11).] I will disarm all peoples of the earth, including my people in Israel, and he shall bring peace among the nations. His realm shall stretch from sea to sea, from the river to the ends of the earth. I have delivered you from death in a waterless pit because of the covenant I made with you, sealed with blood. Come to the place of safety, all you prisoners, for there is yet hope! I promise right now, I will repay you two mercies for each of your woes!" (Zechariah 9:9-12).

Jesus fulfilled part of these prophecies when he came the first time. He did deliver us from death by shedding his own blood to seal our pardon. When he comes again, as he promised, he will bring peace on earth. For now, we can take cover in Jesus as our refuge. When the war is over and Jesus is crowned King of kings, he will repay all those who are his, two mercies for every woe suffered in the war! In the battles of life we can turn our lives over to God and have a strong, sure hope.

When we give ourselves to God, he always gives back more than we gave.

DAY 25 Promised Joy

Bible Reading:
1 Peter 1:3-6

We made a decision to turn our will and our lives over to the care of God as we understood him.

Life is rough. We must constantly struggle against the sin inherent in our mortal bodies. We live with the realities of pain, sickness, and death. We live in a world that is constantly decaying. Even if we turn our lives over to God, what is there to look forward to?

Peter tells us, "Now we live in the hope of eternal life because Christ rose again from the dead. And God has reserved for his children the priceless gift of eternal life; it is kept in heaven for you. . . . And God, in his mighty power, will make sure that you get there safely to receive it, because you are trusting him. It will be yours in that coming last day for all to see. So be truly glad! There is wonderful joy ahead, even though the going is rough for a while down here" (1 Peter 1:3-6).

Paul encourages us with this, "And since we are his children, we will share his treasures—for all God gives to his Son Jesus is now ours too. But if we are to share his glory, we must also share his suffering. Yet what we suffer now is nothing compared to the glory he will give us later. For all creation is waiting patiently and hopefully for that future day when God will resurrect his children. For on that day thorns and thistles, sin, death, and decay—the things that overcame the world against its will at God's command—will all disappear, and the world around us will share in the glorious freedom from sin which God's children enjoy" (Romans 8:17-21). These promises are for us!

Our trust in God's work on our behalf allows us to live in hope and joy.

DAY 26 Hungry Hearts

Bible Reading:
Ruth 1–4

We made a decision to turn our will and our lives over to the care of God as we understood him.

"Please love me!" Isn't this the whispered cry of our hearts? We may be afraid to admit it for fear of rejection, but we are all hungry for love. Some of us are starving because of previous losses. We find ourselves gathering whatever crumbs we can find to fill that hunger deep inside.

Ruth was a young woman who had known loss and hunger. Her husband died, leaving her without any means of emotional or physical sustenance. She followed her mother-in-law, Naomi, to a foreign land and was forced to gather leftover grain from the harvested fields just to stay alive. The man who owned the fields was a relative who could, if he so chose, marry Ruth and fulfill her needs for love and protection. Naomi told her to go to the threshing floor where this man, Boaz, was sleeping and curl up at his feet. Culturally, this displayed a request to be taken care of. Boaz was quite happy to find Ruth there and married her, providing the love and provision she had lost and now longed for (Ruth 1–4).

In turning our lives over to God we need to venture toward developing healthy love relationships with people and with God. It's scary to say "please love me," but it's worth the risk. If we don't fill our hunger for love in a legitimate way, we'll be driven back toward our addictive/compulsive behaviors. We can be sure that when we "curl up" at the feet of Jesus, he will be glad to find us there. He will provide for us, protect us, and love us.

When we risk reaching out to God, he fills the deep longings of our souls.

DAY 27 Unconditional Love

Bible Reading:
1 John 4:7-10

We made a decision to turn our will and our lives over to the care of God as we understood him.

Real love brings security into our lives. For many of us, feelings of insecurity contribute to the power of our addictions. Trusting that love can bring lasting security is hard for those of us who've been abandoned. Maybe someone we loved betrayed our trust. Perhaps someone turned away from us when we betrayed theirs. It could be that someone we needed died, leaving us permanently.

Jesus promised, "I will not abandon you or leave you as orphans in the storm—I will come to you" (John 14:18). We may ask, "How can I trust in God's love when it feels like all I've ever known is love that disappoints?" Here's the difference: Jesus is the only one who entered our lives through the "one way" door of death. "God showed how much he loved us by sending his only Son into this wicked world to bring to us eternal life through his death. In this act we see what real love is: it is not our love for God, but his love for us when he sent his Son to satisfy God's anger against our sins" (1 John 4:9-10). The psalmist wrote, "For he [God] knows we are but dust, and that our days are few and brief. . . . But the loving-kindness of the Lord is from everlasting to everlasting to those who reverence him" (Psalm 103:14-17).

God's love is unconditional and always waiting for us. Turning our lives over to God involves opening the door of our hearts to his love. Filling up on God's love helps us to avoid relapse. It meets us at our deepest need and eases our most powerful insecurities.

As we give our lives over to God's care, he brings healing and love to our hurts and pain.

DAY 28 Rest and Peace

Bible Reading: Philippians 4:4-7

We made a decision to turn our will and our lives over to the care of God as we understood him.

The world doesn't get any better just because we're in recovery! We still have to pay our bills, deal with people, and face the stressful changes that recovery can bring. There are pressures outside of our control that will tend to wear us down if we aren't careful to protect ourselves from the world's onslaught of anxiety.

The apostle Paul gave us a strategy to help guard against the troubles of daily life. He wrote, "Don't worry about anything; instead, pray about everything; tell God your needs, and don't forget to thank him for his answers. If you do this you will experience God's peace, which is far more wonderful than the human mind can understand. His peace will keep your thoughts and your hearts quiet and at rest as you trust in Christ Jesus" (Philippians 4:6-7).

The word translated "keep" is a military term that means to keep under guard, like one protected by a sentry. The image is one of a guard marching around the border of our hearts and minds to keep out the pressing anxieties of life. This is only promised if we routinely turn every worry and need over to God and develop an attitude of gratitude. When we turn our worries over to the care of God, we will discover the protection of inner peace that passes all understanding.

The key to God's peace is found in continually turning our lives over to him.

DAY 29 Declared "Not Guilty"

Bible Reading: Romans 4:1-5

We made a decision to turn our will and our lives over to the care of God as we understood him.

When our addictive patterns represent "sinful" behavior, it's common to feel awkward about getting close to God. We may feel ineligible to receive God's love; instead, we may expect anger. We might feel guilty, and be afraid that God will reject us. Secretly, we may wish that we could have a loving relationship with God and the assurance of a place in heaven, but we feel that we will never be good enough.

The apostle Paul has shown us that we can have the love and acceptance we desire. He wrote, "For the Scriptures tell us Abraham *believed God*, and that is why God canceled his sins and declared him 'not guilty.' . . . Being saved is a gift; if a person could earn it by being good, then it wouldn't be free—but it is! It is *given* to those who do *not* work for it. For God declares sinners to be good in his sight if they have faith in Christ to save them from God's wrath. . . . God will accept us in the same way he accepted Abraham—when we believe the promises of God who brought back Jesus our Lord from the dead. He died for our sins and rose again to make us right with God" (Romans 4:3-5, 24-25).

There's a free gift waiting for us that could help in our recovery. It's God's forgiveness, acceptance, and support. It's a notice that we're "not guilty." It's a special home in heaven with our name on it. There's no need for us to do anything but accept this free gift. This is the best reward of turning our lives over to God!

We begin our recovery burdened with guilt and shame; God encourages our recovery with the burden's release.

DAY 30 True Wisdom

Bible Reading: Matthew 7:24-27

We made a decision to turn our will and our lives over to the care of God as we understood him.

When we lack wisdom, the storms of life can be devastating. After our lives are in pieces, we may realize that we have acted unwisely and want to change, but where do we start?

"How can men be wise?" the psalmist asks. "The only way to begin is by reverence for God. For growth in wisdom comes from obeying his laws" (Psalm 111:10). God has given clear instructions for life. When we have enough reverence for God that we are willing to accept his instructions as the basis for all of our decisions, we have a good starting point.

Jesus said, "All who listen to my instructions and follow them are wise, like a man who builds his house on solid rock. Though the rain comes in torrents, and the floods rise, and the storm winds beat against his house, it won't collapse for it is built on rock" (Matthew 7:24-25). Listening to what the Bible says is the next step toward walking in wisdom. Filling our minds with God's instructions will lead us to follow them. This will also help us turn away from those things God says are wrong. Job tells us, "Look, to fear the Lord is true wisdom, to forsake evil is real understanding" (Job 28:28).

Turning our lives over to God is a wise move! Like most aspects of recovery, walking in wisdom is a process that we grow into. These three elements are the groundwork: reverence for God, listening to his instructions, and following them.

True wisdom begins as we stand in awe of God's love and care for us.

STEP FOUR

We made a searching and fearless moral inventory of ourselves.

Jesus said, "Why worry about a speck in the eye of a brother when you have a board in your own? . . . First get rid of the board. Then you can see to help your brother" **(Matthew 7:3-5).**

DAY 1 Facing the Sadness

Bible Reading: Nehemiah 8:7-10

We made a searching and fearless moral inventory of ourselves.

Most of us falter at the prospect of making an honest personal inventory. The rationalizations and excuses abound for avoiding this step. The bottom line is, we know that there is an enormous amount of sadness awaiting us. And we fear the pain that facing the sadness will bring.

The Jewish exiles who returned to Jerusalem after captivity in Babylon had lost touch with God. During the exile, they hadn't been taught his laws; so naturally, they hadn't practiced them either. After rebuilding the city walls and the temple, the priests gathered the people together to read the book of the law. The people were overwhelmed with grief and began sobbing, because their lives in no way measured up. The priests said to them, "Don't cry on such a day as this! For today is a sacred day before the Lord your God—it is a time to celebrate with a hearty meal and to send presents to those in need, for the joy of the Lord is your strength" (Nehemiah 8:9-10).

That day marked the beginning of the Festival of Tabernacles, a required Jewish feast which celebrated their escape from bondage in Egypt and God's care for them while they wandered in the wilderness.

When we set out to face the pain and sadness of making a moral inventory, we will need the "joy of the Lord" to give us strength. This joy comes from recognizing, even celebrating, God's ability to bring us out of bondage and to care for us as we pass through the sadness toward a new way of life.

Our joy in the Lord helps us to face the sadness within ourselves.

DAY 2 God's Standard

Bible Reading: James 1:21-25

We made a searching and fearless moral inventory of ourselves.

When making an inventory, some kind of list is usually used to help take stock of what's on hand. If we've lived our lives with dysfunctional influences, our idea of what's "normal" probably won't be a very good measuring stick for evaluating our lives. We'll need another standard to help us take account of where we are.

The Jewish exiles who returned to Jerusalem had grown up in captivity. They started their inventory by finding a new standard. "The laws of God were read aloud to them for two or three hours, and for several more hours they took turns confessing their own sins" (Nehemiah 9:3).

The apostle Paul ridiculed the idea that we could measure our lives by the people around us. He said this of the Corinthian believers: "Their trouble is that they are only comparing themselves with each other, and measuring themselves against their own little ideas. What stupidity! . . . Our goal is to measure up to God's plan for us" (2 Corinthians 10:12-13).

James wrote, "Humbly be glad for the wonderful message we have received, for it is able to save our souls. . . . But if anyone keeps looking steadily into God's law for free men, he will not only remember it, but he will do what it says, and God will greatly bless him in everything he does" (James 1:21-25).

In doing our moral inventory, we will get better results if we use God's Word as a measuring stick. This should give us the perspective we need as we seek to sort out our lives.

Our recovery involves coming to terms with ourselves as we really are.

DAY 3 Confession

Bible Reading: Nehemiah 9:1-3

We made a searching and fearless moral inventory of ourselves.

The heart of our moral inventory will probably deal with our destructive habits, defects of character, the wrongs we've done, the consequences that we now live with, and the hurt we've caused others. It's like sifting through all the garbage. This part is painful, but a necessary part of throwing away those rotten habits and behaviors that are spoiling the rest of our lives.

The returned Jewish exiles are described as "confessing their own sins" (Nehemiah 9:3); this phrase speaks volumes. The word *confessing* means "to bemoan something by wringing of the hands" and also "to throw away." The word *sins* means "offenses and their occasions"; it can also refer to habitual sinfulness and the consequences of such behavior.

This can serve as a model for us to follow. We can list the occasions of our offenses, our destructive habits, and the consequences we've brought into our lives and the lives of others. Let's also look at what was done within the process of "confessing their own sins." They owned each part; they bemoaned each part; and then they threw it all away. Their inventory was a time of cleaning out the garbage. After this they were better able to make a new start.

In dealing with the garbage in our lives we can "own" it by taking personal responsibility for our choices and actions. We can "bemoan" it by allowing ourselves to grieve. We can "throw it away" by leaving it behind and turning toward the future.

Our time of confession should be a time of celebration.

DAY 4 Family Influence

Bible Reading: Nehemiah 9:34-38

We made a searching and fearless moral inventory of ourselves.

Our family of origin has had an influence on who we are today. Some of us want to pretend that our families were, or are, nearly perfect. Others of us may tend to avoid responsibility for our actions by blaming our families. Whatever the case, when we think about our own lives, we also need to deal with our families and the effects they have had on who we are today.

We're told that the returned Jewish exiles "took turns confessing their own sins and those of their ancestors" (Nehemiah 9:3). They blamed their ancestors for their captivity and the difficult situation they were facing. They said, "They [our ancestors] refused to turn from their wickedness. So, now we are slaves here in the land of plenty that you gave to our ancestors! . . . And we serve them [conquering kings] at their pleasure and are in great misery" (Nehemiah 9:35-37).

It's all right to admit the truth about what brought us into bondage. This might very well involve the wrongs committed by our parents and family. It's all right to express our anger and regret over what's been done to us. We have a right to hold others accountable and grieve over the negative effects they've had on our lives. That is part of the real picture. It's not all right to use this as an excuse for our wrong choices or for staying in bondage. They may be partly responsible for bringing us to this place. We're responsible for moving on to a better place for ourselves and our children.

Past generations helped create our present circumstances; our confessions can free us for a better future.

DAY 5 Constructive Sorrow

Bible Reading: 2 Corinthians 7:8-11

We made a searching and fearless moral inventory of ourselves.

We all have to deal with sorrow. We may try to stuff it down and ignore it. We may try to drown it or avoid feeling it by intellectualizing. But sorrow doesn't go away. We need to accept the sorrow that will be a part of the inventory process.

Not all sorrow is bad for us. The apostle Paul had written a letter to the church in Corinth. It made them very sad because Paul was confronting them about something that they were doing wrong. At first he was sorry that he had hurt them. But later he said, "Now I am glad I sent it, not because it hurt you, but because the pain turned you to God. It was a good kind of sorrow you felt, the kind of sorrow God wants his people to have. . . . For God sometimes uses sorrow in our lives to help us turn away from sin and seek eternal life. We should never regret his sending it. . . . Just see how much good this grief from the Lord did for you! You no longer shrugged your shoulders, but became earnest and sincere, and very anxious to get rid of the sin" (2 Corinthians 7:8-11).

Jeremiah said, "Although God gives . . . grief, yet he will show compassion too, according to the greatness of his loving-kindness. For he does not enjoy afflicting men and causing sorrow" (Lamentations 3:32-33).

This grief was good, for it came from honest self-evaluation, not morbid self-condemnation. We can learn to accept our sorrow as a positive part of our recovery, not just as punishment.

Honest self-examination can lead us to a sorrow that inspires our growth.

DAY 6 Coming out of Hiding

Bible Reading: Genesis 3:6-13

We made a searching and fearless moral inventory of ourselves.

Many of us have spent our lives in a state of hiding, ashamed of who we are inside. We may hide by living double lives, using our drug of choice to make us feel like someone else, or by self-righteously setting ourselves above others. Step Four involves uncovering the things we've been hiding, even from ourselves.

After Adam and Eve disobeyed God, "suddenly they became aware of their nakedness, and were embarrassed. So they strung fig leaves together to cover themselves around the hips. . . . The Lord God called to Adam, 'Why are you hiding?' And Adam replied, 'I heard you coming and didn't want you to see me naked. So I hid'" (Genesis 3:7-10). Human beings have been covering up and hiding ever since!

Jesus consistently confronted the religious leaders for their hypocrisy. The word *hypocrite* describes a person who pretends to have virtues or qualities that he really doesn't have. One time Jesus said to them, "Hypocrites! You are so careful to polish the outside of the cup, but the inside is foul with extortion and greed. . . . First cleanse the inside of the cup and then the whole cup will be clean" (Matthew 23:25-26).

When the real person inside comes out of hiding, we'll have to deal with some dirt! Making this inventory is a good way to "cleanse the inside"; and some of that cleansing may involve bathing our lives with tears. It is only by uncovering the hidden parts of ourselves that we'll be able to change the outer person, including our addictive/compulsive behaviors.

Confessing our hidden parts brings healing and restoration.

DAY 7 Finger Pointing

Bible Reading: Matthew 7:1-5

We made a searching and fearless moral inventory of ourselves.

There have probably been times when we've avoided our own wrongs and problems by pointing the finger at someone else. We may be out of touch with our internal affairs because we are still blaming others for our moral choices. Or perhaps we avoid examining ourselves by making moral inventory of the people all around us.

When God asked Adam and Eve about their sin, they both pointed the finger at someone else. "'Have you eaten fruit from the tree I warned you about?' 'Yes,' Adam admitted, 'but it was the woman you gave me who brought me some; and I ate it.' Then the Lord God asked the woman, 'How could you do such a thing?' 'The serpent tricked me,' she replied" (Genesis 3:11-13). It seems to be human nature to blame others as our first line of defense.

We also may avoid our own problems by evaluating and criticizing the lives of others. Jesus tells us, "And why worry about a speck in the eye of a brother when you have a board in your own? . . . Hypocrite! First get rid of the board. Then you can see to help your brother" (Matthew 7:3, 5).

While doing this step, we must constantly remind ourselves that this is a season of *self*-examination. We must guard against drifting off into blaming and examining the lives of others. There will be time in the future for helping others after we've taken responsibility for our own lives.

Our inventory should turn our focus from what others have done to what we can do.

DAY 8 Love Overcomes Fear

Bible Reading: 1 John 4:16-19	**We made a searching and fearless moral inventory of ourselves.**

The thought of making a fearless moral inventory may sound like an impossible task. Looking at our lives on a moral basis can be very frightening. How can we get to the place where the word *fearless* can actually describe the moral inventory we make?

The apostle John said, "As we live with Christ, our love grows more perfect and complete; so we will not be ashamed and embarrassed at the day of judgment, but can face him with confidence and joy, because he loves us and we love him too. We need have no fear of someone who loves us perfectly; his perfect love for us eliminates all dread of what he might do to us" (1 John 4:17-18).

Love is the key. God, who is the final judge of all morality, loves us perfectly. He doesn't just love us if we're perfect. Perhaps we've had people withhold love and shame us for our faults and failures. If we've only known love to be conditional, it only makes sense that admitting our faults causes us to be afraid of losing the love and acceptance we all need.

To eliminate the fear, we need to surround ourselves with unconditional love from God and other people. Only unconditional love will cover our shame and give us confidence that no matter what we find when we look at ourselves, we will always be loved. The apostle Peter affirmed this by saying, "Most important of all, continue to show deep love for each other, for love makes up for many of your faults" (1 Peter 4:8).

Our moral inventory needs a constant review from the perspective of God's love.

DAY 9 A Searching Examination

Bible Reading:
2 Timothy 1:9-11

We made a searching and fearless moral inventory of ourselves.

Searching is more than just casually looking around; it implies an intense desire to discover what we're looking for. What could motivate us to make a *searching* moral inventory, especially since we know we'll be uncovering our inadequacies?

God is not looking for people good enough to deserve his love. Instead, God wants to find people who will identify their inadequacies as a place for his love and kindness to fit into their lives. If this is true, why shouldn't we be enthusiastic about searching, even for our failures? Every deficiency, every need, every shortcoming can make room for the love of God to be displayed prominently in our lives. The apostle Paul wrote to Timothy, saying, "It is he [God] who saved us and chose us for his holy work, not because we deserved it but because that was his plan long before the world began—to show his love and kindness to us through Christ" (2 Timothy 1:9).

If we approach our inventory with the intention of looking for places in our lives where God's mercy and love have the chance to make up for our failings, we can be enthusiastic about both the good and bad that we find there. Jude tells us, "Keep yourselves in the love of God, *looking for* the mercy of our Lord Jesus Christ unto eternal life" (Jude 1:21, NKJV, emphasis added). Knowing that God is looking for places to display his love in our lives, we can make an intense, yet fearless, search.

Our fearless internal search brings to light areas of our lives desperate for God's love and mercy.

DAY 10 God's Mercy

Bible Reading: Revelation 20:11-15

We made a searching and fearless moral inventory of ourselves.

We may wish we could avoid making a moral inventory; it's normal to want to hide from examination. But in our hearts, we probably sense that a day will come when we'll have to look carefully at our lives.

The Bible tells us there's a day coming when an inventory will be made of every life. No one will be able to hide. In John's vision he saw "a great white throne and the one who sat upon it, from whose face the earth and sky fled away, but they found no place to hide. I saw the dead, great and small, standing before God; and The Books were opened, including the Book of Life. And the dead were judged according to the things written in The Books, each according to the deeds he had done. . . . And if anyone's name was not found recorded in the Book of Life, he was thrown into the Lake of Fire" (Revelation 20:11-12, 15).

It's best to do our own moral inventory now to make sure we're ready for the one to come. Anyone whose name is in the Book of Life is saved. This includes all whose sins have been atoned for by the death of Jesus. Those who refuse God's offer of mercy are left to be judged on the basis of their own deeds recorded in "The Books." No one will pass that test! Perhaps now is a good time to make sure our names are in the right book. And when we know our lives are covered with God's forgiveness, we will be able to examine them fearlessly.

We can be fearless in our inventory because we have been loved and accepted by God.

STEP FOUR

DAY 11 Understanding the Past

Bible Reading:
1 Corinthians
3:10-15

We made a searching and fearless moral inventory of ourselves.

Our addictions may already have destroyed everything we've worked for—our family, friendships, finances—everything may be lost. Beginning recovery is like starting back at the foundation and building a whole new life. Making an inventory should help us consider what caused our losses in the first place. That way, we'll be able to rebuild with materials that will hold up under fire.

The apostle Paul wrote, "But he who builds on the foundation must be very careful. And no one can ever lay any other real foundation than that one we already have—Jesus Christ. . . . Everyone's work will be put through the fire so that all can see whether or not it keeps its value, and what was really accomplished. Then every workman who has built on the foundation with the right materials, and whose work still stands, will get his pay. But if the house he has built burns up, he will have a great loss. He himself will be saved, but like a man escaping through a wall of flames (1 Corinthians 3:10, 12-15).

Even though Paul was referring to the final judgment, this also applies to recovery. We know that what we used in building our old way of life didn't hold up. By doing our inventory, we can make sure that we don't experience further loss by repeating our past patterns, which are vulnerable to destruction. When future tests come, the lasting effects of our recovery and the rewards of our new way of life will be evident to all.

Since we have turned our lives over to God, he is the foundation on whom we must build.

DAY 12 Wonderfully Made

Bible Reading: *Psalm 139:13-18*

We made a searching and fearless moral inventory of ourselves.

Growing up, we may have been led to believe that we just weren't "good enough." We probably tried to become "good enough" by *doing*, since we weren't acceptable just as we were. We need to be careful as we make a moral inventory not to replay in our own minds all the old lies about our lack of value as human beings. This is not the purpose of the inventory! Using it this way can be detrimental to our recovery.

We need to replace the misconceptions about our self-worth with the truth. David reflected on God's view of us when he wrote: "You made all the delicate, inner parts of my body, and knit them together in my mother's womb. Thank you for making me so wonderfully complex! It is amazing to think about. Your workmanship is marvelous—and how well I know it. You were there while I was being formed in utter seclusion! You saw me before I was born and scheduled each day of my life before I began to breathe. Every day was recorded in your Book! How precious it is, Lord, to realize that you are thinking about me constantly! I can't even count how many times a day your thoughts turn towards me" (Psalm 139:13-18).

David's glimpse of the high value God places on our lives, even before we are born, shows that our value precedes *doing*. By faith we need to accept this foundational truth about our basic value as human beings. We must accept that our lives are worth the pain of working through recovery.

Aspects of God's perfect character are reflected in the lives of each and every person.

STEP FOUR

DAY 13 God's Likeness

Bible Reading: Genesis 1:25-31

We made a searching and fearless moral inventory of ourselves.

For most of us who have lived in bondage to our addictions, it's probably very easy for us to see the bad lurking within. It's much harder to see the qualities we have that are good or excellent. We may tend to see life in terms of all or nothing, good or bad. But we need to recognize that along with our shortcomings, we have also been made with an incredible potential for good.

At the end of the fifth day of creation, God had made everything except man and woman. "And God was pleased with what he had done" (Genesis 1:25). Then God created man and woman. "Like God did God make man; man and maid did he make them. And God blessed them and told them, 'Multiply and fill the earth and subdue it; you are masters of the fish and birds and all the animals.' . . . Then God looked over all that he had made, and it was excellent in every way" (Genesis 1:27-28, 31).

God made a distinction between his estimation of mankind and the rest of creation. He saw us as *excellent!* We were made in the image of God, with capacities far beyond mere animals. God was, and is, excited about us! He gave us abilities and responsibilities to reflect his own nature in all of creation.

Although we have a sin nature that came after the Fall, we are still created in the likeness of God. In doing our inventory, we need to see the good as well as the bad. Let's remind ourselves of the excellence and dignity inherent in being human as we honestly look at those things which miss the mark.

We are made to be like God and therefore share many of his characteristics and feelings.

DAY 14 Discovering Wisdom

Bible Reading: We made a searching and fearless
Proverbs 2:6-22 moral inventory of ourselves.

In recovery we come to realize that we're influenced by the people we're around. We welcome the support of those who are farther along on the road to recovery. We may rely heavily on the encouragement of our sponsor or others who are supportive of our new way of life. We will also come to see the negative influence of associating with people who are still living the kind of life from which we're trying to escape. Part of our inventory may include considering whom we choose to spend our time with and whether these decisions contribute to our recovery.

In Proverbs we are told, "Wisdom and truth will enter the very center of your being, filling your life with joy. You will be given the sense to stay away from evil men who want you to be their partners in crime—men who turn from God's ways to walk down dark and evil paths and exult in doing wrong, for they thoroughly enjoy their sins" (Proverbs 2:10-14). We are encouraged to "follow the steps of the godly instead, and stay on the right path, for only good men enjoy life to the full; evil men lose the good things they might have had, and they themselves shall be destroyed" (Proverbs 2:20-22).

Are we exercising wisdom by following the steps of those who are living the kind of life we truly desire? If we do this, we will find our lives to be filled with joy. We will also be spared the loss and destruction that await those who do not enter into recovery and continue down darkened pathways.

Even if we've made bad choices in the past, we can reclaim the lost parts of our lives by turning to choose the good.

STEP FOUR

DAY 15 Recognizing Strengths

Bible Reading: Judges 6:1-16

We made a searching and fearless moral inventory of ourselves.

For those of us who have lived in bondage to addictive/compulsive behaviors, loss of self-respect is a familiar feeling. It is easy to begin to see ourselves as chronically weak, small, even hopeless. We often fall into the rut of believing we're destined to bondage, poverty, and failure. When this view of ourselves and our lives persists, we give up the possibility of change. We settle for just trying to survive. We live in fear and shame, filling up with resentment as our lives remain in the pit. As we make our inventory, we should take time to test these kinds of assumptions about ourselves.

When we first meet Gideon, he is discouraged; he's a young man with little self-respect. His family was the poorest in a small tribe, and he was the least in his family. We first see him threshing wheat in a winepress, to hide the wheat from the enemy who would steal what little food he had. An angel appeared and called to him, "Mighty soldier, the Lord is with you!" (Judges 6:12). Gideon didn't look or feel like a mighty soldier, but God could see his potential. By the end of the story, Gideon had become the deliverer of his people (Judges 6–8). His first step toward success was to see himself as God saw him—as a "mighty warrior." Then he was able to hope in the possibility of freedom.

We can use our inventory to help us see ourselves in a new light and summon up the hope for a better life. Then, as God gives us the strength, we can pursue freedom from the bondage that surrounds us and our families.

We need to discover our special gifts and learn to focus them on the problems we face.

STEP FOUR

DAY 16 Seeking Truth

Bible Reading: Philippians 3:12-14

We made a searching and fearless moral inventory of ourselves.

Those of us in recovery all struggle to move out of a difficult past and into a healthier future. We can't change our past, yet it's hard to accept the truth about it. It's hard to face the things that others have done to us and all the mistakes we have made. Our energy can easily be spent trying to rewrite the past, a task at which we can never succeed. In Step Four we are simply trying to honestly evaluate our lives, including everything in our past.

Jesus said, "You will know the truth and the truth will set you free" (John 8:32). The path to freedom always leads through the truth, even the truth about our past. The apostle Paul once wrote to young Timothy: "Alexander the coppersmith has done me much harm. The Lord will punish him" (2 Timothy 4:14). Paul states the truth about someone who had hurt him but leaves the matter in God's hands. We, too, should honestly accept what has been done to us and then let it go, leaving it in God's hands.

Elsewhere, Paul examined his past, making an honest review of his earthly accomplishments, his wrongs, his mistakes, his family, his gains, and his losses. It was from this broad perspective that he could write these words: "I haven't learned all I should even yet, but I keep working toward the day when I will finally be all that Christ saved me for and wants me to be" (Philippians 3:12). When we face the truth about our past, we can finally let go of it. Then we can journey on into a healthier future.

We can be fearless in our inventory, knowing that the truth can only set us free.

DAY 17 Buried Pain

Bible Reading: Philippians 4:10-14

We made a searching and fearless moral inventory of ourselves.

Some of us have never accepted the hurtful circumstances of our lives. We may be living in denial to avoid the pain. We continue to struggle against the painful realities, to rebel against who we are or what has happened to us. There are others of us who have accepted the bad, even to the point where it feels normal and comfortable. Therefore, we repeat cycles of behavior that are destructive; but we can't receive the good.

The apostle Paul wrote, "I have learned how to get along happily whether I have much or little. I know how to live on almost nothing or with everything. I have learned the secret of contentment in every situation, whether it be a full stomach or hunger, plenty or want" (Philippians 4:11-12). When Paul wrote these words he was in a Roman prison waiting to hear if he would be executed. And yet, we hear no whining or complaining. Instead, he learned to accept the circumstances he could not change.

Working Step Four should be a time of learning to find serenity while also accepting ourselves and our lives as they are. Life isn't fair. It isn't predictable or controllable. It can be wonderfully rich in some ways and terribly difficult in others. We must be willing to face the hurt in our lives and consider how we have reacted to it. Then our discomfort can lead us to break the destructive cycles. And then we can learn to be content with the things we cannot change.

Contentment lies in knowing and accepting ourselves, while also trusting in Christ and his power.

DAY 18 Filling the Gaps

Bible Reading: Judges 4:1-21

We made a searching and fearless moral inventory of ourselves.

There are times when chaos reigns in our lives because others are not willing or able to fulfill the role they should play. When this happens we may suffer from the lack of leadership and protection.

The time of the judges was a time of confusion for Israel. Each person did what was right in his own eyes instead of obeying the law. They were oppressed by tyrants, one of whom was General Sisera, who "made life unbearable for the Israelis for twenty years" (Judges 4:3). At this time God chose Deborah to be a judge. Her job was to decide the disputes of the people.

One day Deborah summoned a man named Barak and told him that God would use him to defeat the army of Sisera. "'I'll go, but only if you go with me!' Barak told her" (4:8). So, Deborah agreed to go along, but she said, "I'm warning you now that the honor of conquering Sisera will go to a woman instead of to you!" (4:9). Barak lacked the faith to take on the responsibilities God had chosen him for. In the end, General Sisera did die at the hands of a woman. In the victory song, Deborah was honored. They sang, "Israel's population dwindled, until Deborah became a mother to Israel" (Judges 5:7).

When others don't fulfill their rightful duty and role, we have the option of finding a way to cope, with God's help. Deborah compensated for Barak's lack of faith. We don't have to endure the ongoing effects of other people's limitations. And we don't have to accept the painful circumstances that their weaknesses create.

Staying in daily contact with God will help eliminate some of the painful circumstances we might otherwise create.

DAY 19 Healthy Acceptance

Bible Reading: **We made a searching and fearless**
1 Samuel 25:1-34 **moral inventory of ourselves.**

When other people put us at risk or cause us pain, we may feel like there's nothing we can do. We may feel very comfortable in the role of victim and give in to our feelings of helplessness.

Abigail is a good example of someone who didn't give in to helplessness but had the wisdom to know what she could and couldn't change. Her husband, Nabal (which means "fool"), was "uncouth, churlish, stubborn, and ill-mannered" (1 Samuel 25:3). Before David became king, Nabal insulted his troops to the point that David and his men were on their way to kill him and anyone who got in their way. Through some fast thinking and some even faster talking, Abigail protected her family. She convinced David not to take vengeance into his own hands. A few weeks later Nabal was dead of natural, or perhaps supernatural, causes and Abigail became David's wife.

As part of our inventory, we might examine how we deal with other people who endanger us. Do we fall into the victim role and do nothing to protect ourselves from the results of their actions? Do we accept that we can't change them, or just resolve to try harder in our crusade? Acceptance of another's addiction or personality doesn't mean that we have to accept being the victim of their wrongs. We can give up our crusade to change them, without giving up our right to be treated with dignity.

We can improve our circumstances in life without demanding radical changes in the people close to us.

DAY 20 All or Nothing

Bible Reading:
1 Kings 19:3-18

We made a searching and fearless moral inventory of ourselves.

Perfectionists see the world in black and white. We may feel like we're superhuman, able to take on anything, until we discover a flaw. Then we come crashing down and consider ourselves to be worthless failures.

The prophet Elijah is one of the great heroes of the Bible. If anyone had reason to feel superhuman, it was he. He could pray and stop the rain for years. He commanded fire to come down from heaven and destroy his enemies. But even he could have a bad day. Let's consider his reaction after being threatened by Queen Jezebel. "'I've had enough,' he told the Lord. 'Take away my life. . . . I have worked very hard for the Lord God of the heavens; but the people of Israel have broken their covenant with you and torn down your altars and killed your prophets, and only I am left; and now they are trying to kill me too'" (1 Kings 19:4, 10). The Lord replied, "Incidentally, there are 7,000 men in Israel who have never bowed to Baal" (19:18).

Like Elijah, if we're perfectionists, we may think of ourselves as being above everyone else. We work very hard to please God and other people. But we can grow dangerously discouraged if it doesn't seem to work. This "all or nothing" way of thinking is something to watch for while working Step Four. If we don't allow ourselves to be less than perfect, we may find ourselves at great risk during the times when life reminds us that we are only human after all.

Often periods of failure follow our successes; we need to humbly recognize our limitations.

STEP FOUR

DAY 21 No Other Gods

Bible Reading:
Exodus 20:1-17

We made a searching and fearless moral inventory of ourselves.

Even if we don't practice a particular religion, we do worship something. Our hearts, souls, and minds can't exist in a vacuum. We're all under allegiance to some set of beliefs. Our love and need to be loved drive us to the feet of some god. Part of our inventory needs to include looking to see who or what brings us to our knees.

The first commandment God gave says: "You may worship no other god than me" (Exodus 20:3). He repeated the same command after the children of Israel had wandered forty years in the wilderness adding some explanations: "I am Jehovah your God who rescued you from slavery in Egypt. Never worship any god but me" (Deuteronomy 5:6-7). Once when Jesus was talking with some people, "a lawyer spoke up: 'Sir, which is the most important command in the laws of Moses?' Jesus replied, 'Love the Lord your God with all your heart, soul, and mind. This is the first and greatest commandment'" (Matthew 22:35-38).

If we want to reorder our lives according to God's design, it is helpful to start with the standard he set up—the Ten Commandments. He begins by simply asking that we recognize him as God. Are we willing to admit that our Creator and Rescuer is fully deserving of our wholehearted love and commitment? Are we willing to turn away from our other gods to worship him alone?

If we give God the proper place in our lives, all of his commandments should follow naturally.

DAY 22 False Images

Bible Reading:
1 Corinthians 10:12-14

We made a searching and fearless moral inventory of ourselves.

We may find that our imaginations are held captive by an image or ideal that makes demands of us. We may be focused on the image of "the perfect body," and find ourselves swept into compulsive eating disorders, depression, or sexual addictions. We may be focused on the image of "the good life," and find ourselves swept into workaholism, stealing, or lying to try to appease the image we worship. We may have an image of ourselves as "the black sheep of the family," and slavishly live our lives playing out that role.

We don't talk much about idol worship in our culture, except perhaps when we talk of celebrities. Idolatry can be defined as image worship; it may involve becoming a slave to the ideas an image represents. This is the second commandment: "You shall not make yourselves any idols: no images of animals, birds, or fish. You must never bow or worship it in any way; for I, the Lord your God, am very possessive. I will not share your affection with any other god!" (Exodus 20:4-5). The apostle Paul warned, "So, dear friends, carefully avoid idol worship of every kind" (1 Corinthians 10:14).

In his protective love, God warns us not to let devotion to an image enslave our lives. The images we worship are more likely to come through television or other media than from an idol carved from stone. But we need to ask ourselves, What are the images and ideas that drive our compulsive behaviors?

Taking inventory of the things we consider important may alert us to the false gods in our lives.

DAY 23 Integrity

Bible Reading: Matthew 5:33-37

We made a searching and fearless moral inventory of ourselves.

When we live in a world where we need to pretend in order to cope, it's hard to maintain integrity. We learn to lie to cover up our shameful circumstances. We may lie to ourselves by escaping into another world through our addictions. When we don't feel sure of ourselves, some of us even hide behind religious words and experiences. We might say things like "The Lord told me this . . ." or "I swear to God . . ." in order to validate our actions.

The third commandment says: "You shall not use the name of Jehovah your God irreverently, nor use it to swear to a falsehood. You will not escape punishment if you do" (Exodus 20:7). "You must never use my name to make a vow you don't intend to keep. I will not overlook that" (Deuteronomy 5:11). Jesus went further, "The law of Moses says, 'You shall not break your vows to God, but must fulfill them all.' But I say: Don't make any vows! . . . Don't even swear 'By my head!' for you can't turn one hair white or black. Say just a simple 'Yes, I will' or 'No, I won't.' Your word is enough. To strengthen your promise with a vow shows that something is wrong" (Matthew 5:33-34, 36-37).

Integrity is a key issue to consider while making our inventory. We need to ask ourselves where we are still in hiding. If we are making renewed vows, saying God ordained a specific course, perhaps we would do well to ask ourselves why we need all the extra endorsements.

Integrity will be the natural result of making an honest inventory of ourselves.

DAY 24 Being, Not Doing

Bible Reading: Exodus 20:8-11

We made a searching and fearless moral inventory of ourselves.

Some of us become addicted to our work and our accomplishments. It's not that we're just hardworking people; we use our activities to help us feel worthwhile. It's as though we believe deep inside that we are worthless, so we work and take care of others to earn the right to be loved. When our work is at the heart of our self-esteem, we have a hard time stopping whatever it is that gives us a feeling of value. We become slaves to what we do and can never do enough.

The fourth commandment says: "Remember to observe the Sabbath as a holy day. Six days a week are for your daily duties and your regular work, but the seventh day is a day of Sabbath rest before the Lord your God. On that day you are to do no work of any kind, nor shall your son, daughter, or slaves—whether men or women—or your cattle or your house guests. For in six days the Lord made the heaven, earth, and sea, and everything in them, and rested the seventh day; so he blessed the Sabbath day and set it aside for rest" (Exodus 20:8-11).

God gave the Hebrews this command when he brought them out of Egypt after four hundred years of slavery. The only value they had known had been measured by constant work. God reminds us with this command that he cares about who we are as well as about what we do.

God's command that we spend a day resting is clear evidence that he loves us.

DAY 25 Honoring Our Parents

Bible Reading: Deuteronomy 5:16

We made a searching and fearless moral inventory of ourselves.

We may feel a confusion of emotions as we relate to our parents. This is true especially if we've been abused during our childhood and bear the scars of that abuse. We may have been taught that failing to honor our parents is a sin. This raises some disturbing questions. How can we honor someone whose actions have been anything but honorable? Does this mean that we stay under their control and yield to their manipulations in order to please God?

The Bible does say, "Honor your father and mother (remember, this is a commandment of the Lord your God); if you do so, you shall have a long, prosperous life in the land he is giving you" (Deuteronomy 5:16). The word *honor* comes from a root word meaning "heavy"; it implies fixing weighty value on the relationship. We are to place high value on our parents' role in our lives.

This does not mean, however, that they have the right to destroy our lives just because they brought us into the world. Even Jesus said, "I have come to set a man against his father, and a daughter against her mother, . . . a man's worst enemies will be right in his own home!" (Matthew 10:35-36).

As we evaluate our lives, we can honor our parents by realizing the heavy impact they have had on us. We don't have to let them manipulate and abuse us in order to please God. But we can still choose to love them, even though we may need to set up boundaries in the relationship.

We can best honor our parents by the way we live our lives.

DAY 26 A Debt of Love

Bible Reading: Romans 13:8-10

We made a searching and fearless moral inventory of ourselves.

While under the influence of an addiction, we end up hurting ourselves, others we don't know, and those we love the most. We may be horrified at how we could have done such things to the people we love. Does that mean we don't love them? Or how could the people we love have done such things to us? Does that mean that they don't love us? What conclusions are we to draw from the sin that stabs at our lives?

"Pay all your debts except the debt of love for others—never finish paying that! For if you love them, you will be obeying all of God's laws, fulfilling all his requirements. If you love your neighbor as much as you love yourself you will not want to harm or cheat him or kill him or steal from him. And you won't sin with his wife or want what is his, or do anything else the Ten Commandments say is wrong. All ten are wrapped up in this one, to love your neighbor as you love yourself. Love does no wrong to anyone. That's why it fully satisfies all of God's requirements. It is the only law you need" (Romans 13:8-10).

At first glance we may conclude from this passage that anyone who practices the evils warned against in the Ten Commandments couldn't have love for others. But it may actually show us that when we hurt the ones we love, maybe we are loving them the way we love ourselves—very poorly. May God help us to love ourselves, so that we may learn to love others also.

It is our calling in life to love others and ourselves as God has loved us.

DAY 27 Handling Anger

Bible Reading: Matthew 5:20-22

We made a searching and fearless moral inventory of ourselves.

Some of us realize that all that's kept us from committing murder was the lack of opportunity at the moment we were in touch with the depth of our rage. Maybe we can stuff our ugly emotions down deep most of the time, only venting them when we're caught off guard or under the influence.

The law of Moses clearly says: "You must not murder" (Exodus 20:13). Moses went on to explain, "If anyone kills another out of hatred by throwing something at him, or ambushing him, or angrily striking him with his fist so that he dies, he is a murderer. . . . But if it is an accident—a case in which something is thrown unintentionally, or in which a stone is thrown without anger, without realizing it will hit anyone, and without wanting to harm an enemy—yet the man dies, then the people shall judge whether or not it was an accident" (Numbers 35:20-24). Jesus taught, "Under the laws of Moses the rule was, 'If you murder, you must die.' But I have added to that rule and tell you that if you are only *angry*, even in your own home, you are in danger of judgment!" (Matthew 5:21-22).

If we took the time to think about it, we may realize that we're still in danger because of the rage burning beneath the surface. In order for our recovery to be complete, we must dig up the anger, vent it appropriately, and let it go. This is a vital part of our recovery process, which we dare not neglect.

Unresolved anger becomes a violation of God's command to love.

DAY 28 Sexual Inventory

Bible Reading: **We made a searching and fearless**
Matthew 5:27-30 **moral inventory of ourselves.**

We're all sexual beings. For some of us sex becomes an addiction, used to medicate our pain. Instead of staying within the committed safety of marriage, as God prescribes, we overdose on sex, emotionally or physically. Any time the marriage bond is violated, deep wounds are created which damage our sense of security. This is true whether the damaged marriage involves our parents, ourselves, or both. Dealing properly with our sexuality is a vital part of our recovery.

Jesus taught us, "The laws of Moses said, 'You shall not commit adultery.' But I say: Anyone who even looks at a woman with lust in his eye has already committed adultery with her in his heart" (Matthew 5:27-28). One day, a group of lawyers brought a woman who had been caught in the act of adultery to Jesus and asked him to pass judgment. Jesus told them that they could stone her to death in accordance with the law, but only if a person without sin threw the first stone. "The Jewish leaders slipped away one by one, beginning with the eldest, until only Jesus was left in front of the crowd with the woman. Then Jesus stood up again and said to her, 'Where are your accusers? Didn't even one of them condemn you?' 'No, sir,' she said. And Jesus said, 'Neither do I. Go and sin no more'" (John 8:9-11).

The point of making an inventory of our sexuality is not to bring condemnation upon ourselves or others. It is to see where the wounds are and to move toward healing the devastation.

Left unchecked, wrong desires lead to wrong actions, which will lead us away from God and from our recovery.

DAY 29 Facing Loss

Bible Reading: John 10:1-13

We made a searching and fearless moral inventory of ourselves.

Addiction and stealing usually go hand in hand. Stealing is one way to fill our desperate needs when we have no other ways of getting them met. We may have been robbed ourselves and we feel violated, left with a deficit of our own. Somehow, in either case, we have to get to the point of being filled up. Both stealing and feeling ripped off are signs of a need that should be addressed.

Jesus told a story describing himself as a shepherd who has great love for us, his sheep. He also said, "I am the Gate for the sheep. . . . All others who came before me were thieves and robbers. . . . The thief's purpose is to steal, kill and destroy. My purpose is to give life in all its fullness" (John 10:7-8, 10). The apostle Paul warned, "If anyone is stealing he must stop it and begin using those hands of his for honest work, so he can give to others in need" (Ephesians 4:28).

In our inventory we will easily spot the obvious things we've stolen or had stolen from us. But we also need to look further. We need to look deeply to find the areas where we feel deprived. We need to discover the places where we want more than what others might consider our fair share. We need to uncover the empty places carved out by our previous losses. As we inventory our deficits, we can bring all of the sins and the deprivations beneath them to Jesus so that he can fill them. It will be out of this sense of fullness that we can begin to give.

Our inventory will uncover the empty places in our lives so God can fill them with his love and care.

DAY 30 Overcoming Envy

Bible Reading: Hebrews 13:5-6

We made a searching and fearless moral inventory of ourselves.

A major part of recovery deals with our tendency to create and live in a fantasy world. We escape the painful realities of our lives momentarily and trade them in for experiences that feel good. The pathway that leads to our addiction is paved with desires for the things, relationships, and experiences that we see in the lives of others and don't have ourselves.

One of the lesser known of the Ten Commandments says, "You must not be envious of your neighbor's house, or want to sleep with his wife, or want to own his slaves, oxen, donkeys, or anything else he has" (Exodus 20:17). "You must not burn with desire for another man's wife, nor envy him for his home, land, servants . . . nor anything else he owns" (Deuteronomy 5:21). Jesus also warned, "Beware! Don't always be wishing for what you don't have. For real life and real living are not related to how rich we are" (Luke 12:15). The writer of Hebrews said, "Stay away from the love of money; be satisfied with what you have. For God has said, 'I will never, *never* fail you nor forsake you'" (Hebrews 13:5).

Modern society and commercial advertising are designed to breed discontent. This is a threat to our recovery because it leads us into an emotional fantasy world. We need to make an inventory of the envy and covetousness lodged in our hearts and minds. Then we must treat these problems like a poison that will hurt us if allowed to remain in our lives.

Since only God can meet all our needs, true contentment can only be found in him.

STEP FIVE

We admitted to God, to ourselves, and to another human being the exact nature of our wrongs.

"If we confess our sins to him [God], he can be depended on to forgive us and to cleanse us from every wrong" **(1 John 1:8-9).**

STEP FIVE

DAY 1 Freedom through Confession

Bible Reading:
Romans 2:14-15

We admitted to God, to ourselves, and to another human being the exact nature of our wrongs.

All of us struggle with our conscience, trying to make peace within ourselves. We may try to deny what we've done, find excuses, try to squirm out from beneath the full weight of our conduct. We may work hard to be "good," trying to counteract our wrongs. We do everything we can to even out the internal score. In order to put the past to rest, we must stop rationalizing and admit the truth.

We are all born with a built-in buzzer that alerts us to what is wrong. God holds everyone accountable, "for down in their hearts they know right from wrong. God's laws are written within them; their own conscience accuses them, or sometimes excuses them" (Romans 2:14-15).

Part of Step Five is to stop this internal struggle and admit that wrong is wrong. It's a time to agree with God and our own conscience about our cover-up and the exact nature of our wrongs. We're like people who have been accused of crimes which they actually committed. We may have spent years constructing alibis, coming up with excuses, and trying to plea bargain. It's time to come clean. It's time to admit what we know deep down inside to be true: "Yes, I'm guilty as charged."

There is no real freedom without confession. What a relief it is to finally give up the weight of our lies and excuses. When we do confess, we will find the internal peace that we lost so long ago. We will also be one step closer to full recovery.

Admitting our failures is an essential step to forgiveness and healing.

DAY 2 God, Our Friend

Bible Reading: Hebrews 4:14-16

We admitted to God, to ourselves, and to another human being the exact nature of our wrongs.

Going to God can be scary. We may associate God with a condemning judge, a brutal father, or some other frightful image. Before we will be able to admit our wrongs to God, we'll need to feel confident that he is on our side.

In ancient times, people could not approach God on their own. The High Priest would offer a sacrifice to cover their sin, and then bring them before God. The High Priest was on their side, even though he had to acknowledge and deal with their sins. We have someone on our side, too. "Jesus the Son of God is our great High Priest who has gone to heaven itself to help us; therefore let us never stop trusting him. This High Priest of ours understands our weaknesses, since he had the same temptations we do, though he never once gave way to them and sinned. So let us come boldly to the very throne of God and stay there to receive his mercy and to find grace to help us in our times of need" (Hebrews 4:14-16). "For since he himself has now been through suffering and temptation, he knows what it is like when we suffer and are tempted, and he is wonderfully able to help us" (Hebrews 2:18).

We don't have to fear admitting our wrongs to God. In him we have a friend who understands our struggles and our suffering. When we go to him we won't have to flee from his condemnation. We will be welcome to stay at the throne of God to receive mercy. He will give us the grace we need in our struggle to recover.

When we face our wrongs, God understands and is able to help us.

DAY 3 Overcoming Denial

Bible Reading: Genesis 38:1-30

We admitted to God, to ourselves, and to another human being the exact nature of our wrongs.

Admitting our wrongs to ourselves can be the most difficult part of Step Five. Denial can be blinding! How can we be expected to admit to ourselves those things we are blind to? Here's a clue that can help us. We will often condemn in others the wrongs most deeply hidden within ourselves.

According to ancient Jewish law, a widow was entitled to marry the surviving brother of her husband in order to produce children. Tamar had been married successively to two brothers who died without giving her children. Her father-in-law, Judah, promised to give her his younger son also, but he never did. This left her alone and destitute. In an effort to protect herself, she disguised herself as a prostitute and became pregnant by Judah himself. And she kept his identification seal (Genesis 38:1-23).

When Judah heard that Tamar was pregnant and unmarried, he demanded her execution. "But as they were taking her out to kill her she sent this message to her father-in-law: 'The man who owns this identification . . . is the father of my child. Do you recognize them?' Judah admitted that they were his and said, 'She is more in the right than I am'" (Genesis 38:25-26).

It won't be easy to be honest with ourselves. "The heart is the most deceitful thing there is, and desperately wicked" (Jeremiah 17:9). However, we can look at those things we condemn in others as a clue to what may be lurking within ourselves.

It takes great courage to be honest with ourselves about ourselves.

DAY 4 Healing through Confession

Bible Reading: James 5:16-18

We admitted to God, to ourselves, and to another human being the exact nature of our wrongs.

Most of us resist the thought of admitting our wrongs to another person. We may think, *Isn't it enough to admit my faults to myself and to God? Why should I humiliate myself before another person who is no better than I am?*

It seems that there is healing power in the act of telling another person. James wrote, "Admit your faults to one another and pray for each other so that you may be healed. The earnest prayer of a righteous man has great power and wonderful results" (James 5:16). The apostle Paul also commented on this: "Share each other's troubles and problems, and so obey our Lord's command [to love your neighbor as yourself]. If anyone thinks he is too great to stoop to this, he is fooling himself" (Galatians 6:2-3).

We may laugh at the thought of finding a "righteous" person to confide in. We needn't worry; the word James uses doesn't mean self-righteous. He is referring to someone who is right in fulfilling duties both with God and man. This kind of person will be just and without prejudice, already made right with God through personal confession. Someone with this kind of righteousness won't be prejudiced against us.

When we find someone who has already dealt honestly with his struggle, our burden can be made lighter by sharing our own. Our confessor will also be able to pray for us in an understanding way. Such prayer can really make a positive impact on our recovery.

Confessing our faults opens up our lives to God's healing power.

DAY 5 Escaping Self-Deception

Bible Reading: Galatians 6:7-10

We admitted to God, to ourselves, and to another human being the exact nature of our wrongs.

We may fool ourselves into believing that we can simply bury our wrongs and go on, without ever having to admit them. In time, we all discover that those deeds we thought were buried once and for all were actually seeds. They grow and bear fruit. Eventually we have to deal with a crop of consequences and face the fact that self-deception doesn't work to our advantage.

"A man will always reap just the kind of crop he sows! If he sows to please his own wrong desires, he will be planting seeds of evil and he will surely reap a harvest of spiritual decay and death; but if he plants the good things of the Spirit, he will reap the everlasting life which the Holy Spirit gives him" (Galatians 6:7-8). "If we say that we have no sin, we are only fooling ourselves and refusing to accept the truth. But if we confess our sins to him [God], he can be depended on to forgive us and to cleanse us from every wrong" (1 John 1:8-9).

Step Five says good-bye to self-deception and hello to forgiveness and cleansing. We should note that there is cleansing from every wrong, not from "wrongdoing" in a general sense. Admitting the exact nature of our wrongs includes giving an account in exact and specific terms. It is only when we get specific that we will no longer be able to fool ourselves about the nature of our wrongs. Since we can't ignore God and get away with it anyway, we might as well come clean and be forgiven.

In recovery, planting our confessions will yeild a harvest of forgiveness.

DAY 6 Fear of Rejection

Bible Reading: Hebrews 4:12-16

We admitted to God, to ourselves, and to another human being the exact nature of our wrongs.

The thought of being totally honest about the exact nature of our wrongs causes us to hesitate for fear of rejection. How many times have we thought to ourselves, *If anyone ever knew the real me they wouldn't love me; they would probably leave me?*

Whether we like it or not, the Bible tells us that everyone will have to give an account of his life before God. "Yes, each of us will give an account of himself to God" (Romans 14:12). But, we don't have to worry about surprising him with any of the hidden details. "He knows about everyone, everywhere. Everything about us is bare and wide open to the all-seeing eyes of our living God; nothing can be hidden from him to whom we must explain all that we have done" (Hebrews 4:13).

This can be encouraging if we think about it. The very fact that he already knows all about us and still requires us to give an account must mean that there is some value for us in the experience. Since he already knows every detail of our thoughts and actions and hasn't rejected us, we don't have to fear his rejection. "But if we confess our sins to him, he can be depended on to forgive us and to cleanse us" (1 John 1:9).

We don't go through the process of admitting our wrongs to God for his information, but for our transformation. Once we find the courage to work through this step with God, we will find more courage to help us risk telling another human being.

God knows all our secrets, but he lovingly waits for us to reveal them to him.

DAY 7 Feelings of Shame

Bible Reading: John 8:3-11

We admitted to God, to ourselves, and to another human being the exact nature of our wrongs.

Shame has kept many of us in hiding. The thought of revealing ourselves to another human being stirs up feelings of shame and the fear of being publicly exposed.

"The Jewish leaders . . . brought a woman caught in adultery and placed her out in front of the staring crowd. 'Teacher,' they said to Jesus, '. . . Moses' law says to kill her. What about it?' . . . Jesus stooped down and wrote in the dust with his finger. They kept demanding an answer so he stood up again and said, 'All right, hurl the stones at her until she dies. But only he who never sinned may throw the first!' Then he stooped down again and wrote some more in the dust. And the Jewish leaders slipped away one by one . . . until only Jesus was left in front of the crowd with the woman" (John 8:3-9).

Many believe that it was Jesus' writing in the dust that caused the accusers to leave. Perhaps he was listing the secret sins of the Jewish leaders. If this is true, it gives us a beautiful picture of the kind of person Jesus is—a person with whom we can safely expose our secrets. Our confessor needs to be someone who is not surprised by sin and will not be waiting to condemn us. Such a person needs to take private note of our wrongs, writing them in the soft dust, not etching them in stone and posting them in public. Since shame can be a trigger for addictive behavior, we need to be careful about whom we choose.

With God's help we can accept his forgiveness and be released from our shame.

DAY 8 Restoring Relationships

Bible Reading: Matthew 18:15-18

We admitted to God, to ourselves, and to another human being the exact nature of our wrongs.

When we're grappling with addictions in our family, we are likely to draw away from people and from honest communication about our problems. Step Five is the place where we can return to the relationships that will help us face the truth. Paul spoke of the value of honesty, saying, "Stop lying to each other; tell the truth, for we are parts of each other and when we lie to each other we are hurting ourselves" (Ephesians 4:25).

Jesus even laid out specific instructions for dealing with people who have done wrong but are persisting in denial. He said, "If a brother sins against you, go to him privately and confront him with his fault. If he listens and confesses it, you have won back a brother. But if not, then take one or two others with you and go back to him again proving everything you say by these witnesses. If he still refuses to listen, then take your case to the church, and if the church's verdict favors you, but he won't accept it, then the church should excommunicate him" (Matthew 18:15-17).

Accountability and honesty in our relationships are essential to successful recovery. When we make ourselves accountable to others, the caring influence of the group can help to keep us on the right track. They can provide us with an objective perspective, helping us to admit the truth. We often find ourselves isolated as a result of our shame or our fear that we will be rejected if we ever reveal who we really are. Admitting our wrongs to a trustworthy person always helps to break down the isolation.

Lies destroy our relationships; the truth restores them.

DAY 9 Relief from Dishonesty

Bible Reading: Psalm 32:1-6

We admitted to God, to ourselves, and to another human being the exact nature of our wrongs.

Living a lie is miserable. Perhaps we carry the heavy burden of hiding our secret lives. Maybe we're avoiding God and withdrawing from people because of our fear of being found out.

Moses understood the price to be paid for trying to live a lie. He prayed, "We die beneath your anger; we are overwhelmed by your wrath. You spread out our sins before you—our secret sins—and see them all. No wonder the years are long and heavy here beneath your wrath. All our days are filled with sighing" (Psalm 90:7-9). David showed us the other side. "What happiness for those whose guilt has been forgiven! . . . What relief for those who have confessed their sins and God has cleared their record. There was a time when I wouldn't admit what a sinner I was. But my dishonesty made me miserable and filled my days with frustration. All day and all night your hand was heavy on me. My strength evaporated like water on a sunny day until I finally admitted all my sins to you and stopped trying to hide them. I said to myself, 'I will confess them to the Lord.' And you forgave me! All my guilt is gone. Now I say that each believer should confess his sins to God when he is aware of them, while there is time to be forgiven. Judgment will not touch him if he does" (Psalm 32:1-6).

Why should we live with the weight of dishonesty when relief is available to us? God already knows our secret sins anyway. Why continue to suffer needless agony when we can be relieved?

God wants to forgive; it has always been a part of his loving nature.

DAY 10 Both Good and Bad

Bible Reading: Romans 3:10-12

We admitted to God, to ourselves, and to another human being the exact nature of our wrongs.

We may see ourselves as different from other people—either much worse or much better. We may look down on ourselves and continually compare ourselves with "good" people. Or perhaps our addiction is more socially acceptable. We may console ourselves by placing ourselves above others whose sins seem worse than ours.

"As the Scriptures say, 'No one is good—no one in all the world is innocent.' No one has ever really followed God's paths, or even truly wanted to. Every one has turned away; all have gone wrong" (Romans 3:10-12).

The first chapter of Romans is often used to condemn sexual sins, or sexual addictions. People often skip over the last few verses, which condemn the more acceptable sins such as backbiting, disobedience to parents, or being a proud braggart. Right after this chapter, the apostle Paul speaks to people who see themselves as better than others: "'Well,' you may be saying, 'what terrible people you have been talking about!' But wait a minute! You are just as bad. When you say they are wicked and should be punished, you are talking about yourselves, for you do these very same things" (Romans 2:1).

Every one of us is made of the same stuff, both good and bad. We may act out in different ways; but in God's eyes, we're the same. When we focus on admitting our wrongs, it helps us remember that we're not so different from others after all.

We are all sinful, but we are also loved by God and valuable in his eyes.

STEP FIVE

DAY 11 Good Counselors

Bible Reading: Proverbs 15:22-33

We admitted to God, to ourselves, and to another human being the exact nature of our wrongs.

In recovery, we learn new ways of seeing things, new ways of responding, and new guidelines for making decisions. Our old patterns of thinking and living didn't work very well. Now that we're establishing new patterns, we'll need counselors. They will supply the support we need and will listen as we share our story.

King Solomon gives this advice, "Plans go wrong with too few counselors; many counselors bring success" (Proverbs 15:22). "With good counselors there is safety" (Proverbs 11:14). King David looked to God's word for counsel saying, "Your laws are both my light and my counselors" (Psalm 119:24). Isaiah prophesied of the Messiah (Jesus), saying, "For unto us a Child is born; unto us a son is given; and the government shall be upon his shoulder. These will be his royal titles: 'Wonderful,' 'Counselor,' 'The Mighty God,' 'The Everlasting Father,' 'The Prince of Peace'" (Isaiah 9:6).

When we surround ourselves with dependable counselors, we are developing a safety net. Good counsel can come from the Bible and from people. When we admit our wrongs to other people they can also become a source of counsel for our lives. They may be professionals who understand addiction and recovery. They might be people who know us and measure their advice by godly wisdom. Or perhaps they are people who have experienced what we're now going through. Find someone!

We need the help of those who can enlarge our vision and broaden our perspective.

DAY 12 Unending Love

Bible Reading:
Hosea 11:8-11

We admitted to God, to ourselves, and to another human being the exact nature of our wrongs.

We may be sorely aware of the deep shame, trouble, and pain inflicted on our families because someone (ourselves or someone we love) is acting out his addictions. We may be afraid of admitting the exact nature of our wrongs, because we don't understand how God could love someone who is so bad.

Hosea was a prophet to the rebellious nation of Israel. God used his life to demonstrate God's unconditional love for us. The Lord told Hosea to marry a prostitute. He married her, loved her, and devoted himself to her. She relapsed into her old ways, broke Hosea's heart, and brought shame on their family. She ended up falling into slavery. God then baffled Hosea by telling him, "Go, and get your wife again and bring her back to you and love her, even though she loves adultery. For the Lord still loves Israel though she has turned to other gods" (Hosea 3:1).

We may be asking, *How could God (or anyone) still love me?* But God asks, "Oh, how can I give you up? . . . How can I let you go? How can I forsake you? . . . My heart cries out within me; how I long to help you! . . . For I am God and not man; I am the Holy One living among you, and I did not come to destroy" (Hosea 11:8-9). There is absolutely nothing we can do or admit that would cause God to stop loving us! (See Romans 8:38-39.)

God is committed to us and our recovery even when we want to quit and run away.

DAY 13 Facing Consequences

Bible Reading:
1 Samuel
15:10-23

We admitted to God, to ourselves, and to another human being the exact nature of our wrongs.

Part of admitting our wrongs involves having to consider and to accept the consequences of our actions. We may want to deny our wrongs and try to justify them. We may feel wrongly accused and defensive as we try to escape the accountability we must surely face some day.

Saul was the first king of Israel. At his coronation the people were told, "Now, if you will fear and worship the Lord and listen to his commandments and not rebel against the Lord, and if both you and your king follow the Lord your God, then all will be well" (1 Samuel 12:14). But Saul disobeyed the Lord. "Then the Lord said to Samuel, 'I am sorry that I ever made Saul king, for he has again refused to obey me'" (15:10-11). When Samuel confronted Saul, he denied doing any wrong and put up his defenses. So Samuel replied, "Rebellion is as bad as the sin of witchcraft, and stubbornness is as bad as worshiping idols. And now because you have rejected the word of Jehovah, he has rejected you from being king" (15:23). Saul then led his entire family and country into years of civil war, as he fought to remain king. He finally died at his own hand, surrounded by enemy troops. His three sons died with him.

There's no escaping the consequences of our actions. But, when we admit our wrongs and face the consequences, we may spare ourselves and our loved ones years of additional pain.

While we may not escape the consequences of our actions, we can experience God's forgiveness.

DAY 14 Denial Leads to Bondage

Bible Reading: John 8:30-36

We admitted to God, to ourselves, and to another human being the exact nature of our wrongs.

Living in denial is living dishonestly. How many times have we lied to ourselves and others, saying, "I can stop any time I want!" Or "I have the right to choose how I live my own life!" Or "My behavior doesn't affect anyone but me!" Ironically, as we asserted our freedom to live as we chose, we soon lost the freedom to choose anything other than our addiction; we became enslaved to it.

Jesus said to some would-be disciples, "'You are truly my disciples if you live as I tell you to, and you will know the truth, and the truth will set you free. . . . You are slaves of sin, every one of you. And slaves don't have rights, but the Son has every right there is! So if the Son sets you free, you will indeed be free. . . . Why can't you understand what I am saying? It is because you are prevented [by the devil] from doing so! . . . He was a murderer from the beginning and a hater of truth—there is not an iota of truth in him. When he lies, it is perfectly normal; for he is the father of liars'" (John 8:31-36, 43-44).

Spiritual forces swaying our lives have their roots in either truth or deceit. Truth leads to freedom; deceit to bondage and death. Denial is a lie that keeps us in slavery. When we're slaves to our addictions we lose the right to choose any other way of life. It's only when we break the denial, when we become brutally honest about our bondage, that there's any chance for real freedom.

Denial keeps us in bondage to our vices; confession leads us to recovery and freedom.

STEP FIVE

DAY 15 Aiming at Truth

Bible Reading: Ephesians 4:12-16

We admitted to God, to ourselves, and to another human being the exact nature of our wrongs.

We probably grew up believing lies about life, about ourselves, about our families. We may still experience confusion and uncertainty because we don't have a strong sense of what's true. The lies we believe about ourselves can play into our addictive ways. So we need to reexamine our lives in the light of what's true.

The apostle Paul talked about how the people who believed in Christ were to function like a single body. Each member is to be "filled full with Christ" (Ephesians 4:13), offering the gifts they have to help the whole body grow up into maturity. Since Jesus described himself as "the Truth" (John 14:6), and we are to be filled with him, our recovery process involves becoming "truth-full." Paul continued, "Then we will no longer be like children, forever changing our minds about what we believe because someone has told us something different, or has cleverly lied to us and made the lie sound like the truth. Instead, we will lovingly follow the truth at all times" (Ephesians 4:14-15).

Recovery can be like growing up all over again. As we grow, we need to continue to aim ourselves in the direction of what is true. In the past we measured truth against whatever sounded right to us at the time. Now we can have the sure measurement of God's Word and Jesus Christ himself. From this perspective we need to reevaluate our beliefs. What is true about God? What is true about me? What is right? What is wrong?

Commitment to the truth involves both our words and our actions.

DAY 16 Cleaning the Inside

Bible Reading:
Luke 11:39-44

We admitted to God, to ourselves, and to another human being the exact nature of our wrongs.

We often protect ourselves by focusing our attention on other people and their behaviors. That way we don't have to examine our own. We often stay in relationships where we seem powerless, for in doing so, we maintain built-in excuses for failure. We may also spend time looking down on others who are "worse" than we are, thus avoiding an examination of our own corruption. But in doing these things, we fail to take responsibility for our own recovery by honest self-examination.

Jesus confronted the Pharisees, saying, "You Pharisees wash the outside, but inside you are still dirty—full of greed and wickedness!" (Luke 11:39). Can you imagine polishing the outside of a cup, which is moldy on the inside, and then drinking from it? Of course not! But we do this in a spiritual sense because it's hard to deal with the "dirt" inside our hearts.

Step Five is all about cleaning the inside of our cup. We must begin by turning our eyes away from everyone else around us. This may include those we blame for our condition in life or those we condemn to make our wrongs seem less in comparison. Then we can get back to looking within ourselves. Every one of us has some residue of wrongdoing in our lives. When we admit this to God, to ourselves, and to another human being, we will experience the cleansing of humility and forgiveness. Then we'll have lives that can bring refreshment to others.

Our recovery not only requires that we look inward; it also demands that we confess what we find inside.

DAY 17 Receiving Forgiveness

Bible Reading:
Acts 26:12-18

We admitted to God, to ourselves, and to another human being the exact nature of our wrongs.

As we work our recovery program, we go through a process of accepting the truth about our lives and the consequences of our choices. We may feel like we have to earn forgiveness instead of just receiving it. We may find it easier to forgive others who have hurt us than to forgive ourselves for the hurt we have caused.

When Jesus confronted the apostle Paul, he gave him this mission: "Now stand up! For I have appeared to you to appoint you as my servant and my witness. . . . Yes, I am going to send you to the Gentiles, to open their eyes to their true condition so that they may repent and live in the light of God instead of in Satan's darkness, so that they may receive forgiveness for their sins and God's inheritance along with all people everywhere whose sins are cleansed away, who are set apart by faith in me" (Acts 26:16-18).

God's goal in sending his Word to us is that we may receive forgiveness and a full inheritance, like anyone else who turns to him. The process involves first opening our eyes to our true condition, which happens in Steps One, Two, and Four. This allows us the opportunity to repent, changing our minds so that we're in agreement with God and ready to admit our wrongs. God wants us to receive immediate forgiveness, based on the finished work of Christ. We're not second-class citizens in the kingdom of God. We don't have to work the rest of the Twelve Steps as a form of penance. Forgiveness awaits us right now, if we will only receive it.

We all share equally in God's promise of forgiveness as we confess our wrongs before him.

DAY 18 The Plumbline

Bible Reading: Amos 7:7-8

We admitted to God, to ourselves, and to another human being the exact nature of our wrongs.

The kind of instrument we use to measure our lives will often determine the kinds of problems we uncover. If we use a faulty guideline, we won't be able to make an accurate assessment. We may wonder why we aren't progressing in our recovery programs. It may be that we need to look closely at the measuring stick we are using to uncover our problem areas.

The prophet Amos recorded this vision: "The Lord was standing beside a wall built with a plumbline, checking it with a plumbline to see if it was straight. And the Lord said, . . . 'I will test my people with a plumbline'" (Amos 7:7-8).

A plumbline is a length of string that has a weight tied to one end. When you hold the string up, letting the weighted end hang down, gravity ensures that the string is perfectly vertical. When held next to a building structure, the plumbline provides something sure by which to check whether the building is "in line" with the physical universe or not. If a building is built in line with the plumbline, the structure will be sturdy and function well.

The same holds true in the spiritual realm. God's Word is our spiritual plumbline. Just as we can't argue with the law of gravity, we can't change the spiritual laws revealed in the Bible. It is to our advantage to measure our lives by that divine plumbline. And when things don't measure up, it is important that we admit there is a problem and start rebuilding accordingly.

God's Word is our plumbline, keeping us in line with his loving plans for us.

DAY 19 Admitting Hypocrisy

Bible Reading: Amos 5:21-24

We admitted to God, to ourselves, and to another human being the exact nature of our wrongs.

Many of us live two lives, one ruled by our addictions and passions, the other governed by the laws of religion or social respectability. We probably know the pain of living in both worlds and the fear of being found out.

During a period of peace and prosperity, Israel's upper class was living in luxury. Much of their wealth, however, was gained by exploiting the poor. They violated God's laws and worshiped idols, while still keeping up their "proper" religious duties. God said to them, "I hate your show and pretense—your hypocrisy of 'honoring' me with your religious feasts and solemn assemblies. I will not accept your burnt offerings and thank offerings. I will not look at your offerings of peace. . . . I want to see a mighty flood of justice—a torrent of doing good" (Amos 5:21-22, 24).

God sees through the external images we present and looks upon the heart. He understands the pain and bondage of living in hiding; he hates the pretending. Step Five is the time to face our hypocrisy. We need to stop trying to make up for the darkness inside by going overboard with religious displays. Let's stop singing louder to drown out the cry of our guilty conscience. We need to let God's justice convict us of every sin and let Jesus' blood cover it. Then we'll be able to honestly sing praises, move toward a whole, integrated life, and be free from pretending.

God wants us to have honest hearts, willing to show others who we really are.

DAY 20 Marking Off Boundaries

Bible Reading: Ephesians 4:17-19

We admitted to God, to ourselves, and to another human being the exact nature of our wrongs.

We may feel that we are somehow above the rules everyone else needs to live by. We may have grown so proud of ourselves and our power to "handle" our addiction that we've completely lost sight of right and wrong. At this point we have become slaves to our lusts. This is a time of great danger.

The apostle Paul warned, "Live no longer as the unsaved do, for they are blinded and confused. Their closed hearts are full of darkness; they are far away from the life of God because they have shut their minds against him, and they cannot understand his ways. They don't care anymore about right and wrong and have given themselves over to impure ways. They stop at nothing, being driven by their evil minds and reckless lusts" (Ephesians 4:17-19).

The Lord spoke through the prophet Amos: "Can horses run on rocks? Can oxen plow the sea? Stupid even to ask. . . . And just as stupid is your rejoicing in how great you are, when you are less than nothing—and priding yourselves on your own tiny power!" (Amos 6:12-13).

We may be deluded into believing that we can break all the rules and make a mockery out of what God says is right and good, but this isn't true. If this is what we believe, we may need the help of someone else to even determine what is wrong. Then we will be able to turn from it and be protected from the consequences.

We discover true freedom when we seek to become what God has designed us to be.

STEP FIVE

DAY 21 Filling the Empty Places

Bible Reading: 2 Timothy 3:14-17	**We admitted to God, to ourselves, and to another human being the exact nature of our wrongs.**

We may feel like we have to live with a deficiency. It seems that somehow something inside is missing, something we really needed in order to be complete. This feeling of being "less than" others can fuel our need for our addictions, to make us feel good or "normal."

The apostle Paul said, "The whole Bible was given to us by inspiration from God and is useful to teach us what is true and to make us realize what is wrong in our lives; it straightens us out and helps us do what is right. It's God's way of making us well prepared at every point, fully equipped to do good to everyone" (2 Timothy 3:16-17).

God has a plan to deal with that sense of lack in our lives. He wants to fill up that "something" that is missing that makes us feel like we need our addiction to be normal. He knows that we need help to be "complete" and "fully equipped." His Word is there to give us the tools we need to compensate for our lack. God's Word is also given for correction, to restore us to an upright state.

When we let addictions become the focal point of our lives, we're always off balance. We need to align our lives to the Word of God, admitting our wrongs and needs to God. This will allow us to be fully restored and to find what we need to balance our lives.

Confession opens us to God's equipping power, filling the empty places inside us.

DAY 22 Gods That Can't Satisfy

Bible Reading: Jeremiah 2:10-26

We admitted to God, to ourselves, and to another human being the exact nature of our wrongs.

We've all become slaves to gods that cannot satisfy. We run after that elusive "high" that only heightens our thirst for more. In the process, we lose our sense of appropriate guilt. We regret getting caught, but fail to mourn the deeper tragedy of repeatedly returning to the wrong well to satisfy our thirst.

God spoke through Jeremiah: "For my people have . . . forsaken me, the Fountain of Life-giving Water, and they have built for themselves broken cisterns that can't hold water! Why has Israel become a nation of slaves? . . . Why don't you turn from all this weary running after other gods? But you say, 'Don't waste your breath. I've fallen in love with these strangers and I can't stop loving them now!' Like a thief, the only shame that Israel knows is getting caught" (Jeremiah 2:13-14, 25-26).

God knows how thirsty we are. He's the fountain that gushes with the water that can truly satisfy. A cistern is a man-made holding tank. Our addictions are like "broken cisterns" that don't stay full. The fundamental mistake being pointed out here is that we're running repeatedly to the wrong source for our satisfaction. Instead of just being sorry for "getting caught," God wants us to realize the deeper wrong. He wants us to return to him, find true satisfaction, and eliminate our need to keep going back to our addictions. Admitting our wrongs should include the sources we've turned to that don't fully satisfy.

We can replace the cracked cisterns of our addictions with the life-giving fountain that God promises.

DAY 23 Joyful Confession

Bible Reading: Isaiah 43:25–44:5

We admitted to God, to ourselves, and to another human being the exact nature of our wrongs.

Our wrongs may have been left unattended for a long time. Our lives may seem like parched fields where good things just don't grow anymore. Years of denial have left the stubble of pain on the landscape of our lives. We look at the lives of our children and feel ashamed. We see the desolation they suffer because we didn't have the means to meet even our own needs, let alone theirs.

The Lord wants our wrongs brought before him so that he can flood them with forgiveness. He spoke through Isaiah: "I, yes, I alone am he who blots away your sins for my own sake and will never think of them again. Oh, remind me of this promise of forgiveness, for we must talk about your sins. Plead your case for my forgiving you. . . . I will give you abundant water for your thirst and for your parched fields. And I will pour out my Spirit and my blessings on your children. They shall thrive like watered grass, like willows on a river bank" (Isaiah 43:25-26; 44:3-4).

We don't have to leave our wrongs scattered over the landscape of our past. The Lord longs to overcome them with loving forgiveness, so that we can spring to life once again. The forgiveness is instantaneous, erasing all the wrongs in our past. God longs to replenish the landscapes of our lives and our children's lives so that we will be beautiful to behold. When we admit our wrongs to God we can do so joyfully, reminding him of his wonderful promises!

When God forgives us, we don't have to worry that he might remind us later of our past offenses.

DAY 24 Blinding Rationalization

Bible Reading:
Hosea 12:6-7

We admitted to God, to ourselves, and to another human being the exact nature of our wrongs.

When we constantly have to rationalize our behavior to get around a guilty conscience or to cover up for something, we begin to lose sight of how to accurately measure our lives. We may have cheated for so long that we now find it difficult to measure out the "exact nature of our wrongs." At this point, we may need an objective person to help us. We may have lost the ability to be impartial in our judgment.

God says, "You must be impartial in judgment. Use accurate measurements—lengths, weights, and volumes—and give full measure" (Leviticus 19:35). The Lord demands fairness in every business deal. The book of Proverbs says, "A just balance and scales are the Lord's; all the weights in the bag are his work" (Proverbs 16:11). "Oh, come back to God. Live by the principles of love and justice, and always be expecting much from him, your God. But no, my people are like crafty merchants selling from dishonest scales—they love to cheat" (Hosea 12:6-7).

We should never underestimate the power of rationalization to warp our perspective on our sins. God requires impartial judgment, a task we may not be able to manage on our own. It is helpful and crucial to admit the exact nature of our wrongs to another human being. He should be able to see the blind spots in our lives better than we can. His perspective will help us adjust our understanding so that it better matches reality.

God's measure of success is different than ours; he calls us to honest confession.

STEP FIVE

DAY 25 Confession Brings Mercy

Bible Reading: Psalm 51:1-6

We admitted to God, to ourselves, and to another human being the exact nature of our wrongs.

Many of the wrongs we need to confess are shameful. They are kept in the dark because we can't bear to look at what they reflect about our human condition. We somehow know deep in our being that we have violated the way things "should have been." It sometimes takes the reflection of another person to help us see the truth about our actions.

Before the prophet Nathan confronted King David about his sins, David had gone on with his life as if nothing were wrong. After Nathan informed David of God's judgment because of his adultery with Bathsheba and his murder of her husband, Uriah, David responded by writing this psalm. "O loving and kind God, have mercy. Have pity upon me and take away the awful stain of my transgressions. Oh, wash me, cleanse me from this guilt. Let me be pure again. For I admit my shameful deed—it haunts me day and night. It is against you and you alone I sinned, and did this terrible thing. You saw it all, and your sentence against me is just" (Psalm 51:1-4).

It is human nature to want to cover our shameful deeds and to hide from God. When we are forced to face the reality of the situation, we can follow David's example. We can recall God's nature, which is full of love, kindness, and mercy. Then we should realize that we have sinned against God, not just another person, and we should recognize that God saw it all. After this, we must confess accordingly, accepting his verdict and sentence.

No sin is too great to be forgiven!

DAY 26 Joy Restored

Bible Reading: Psalm 51:7-15

We admitted to God, to ourselves, and to another human being the exact nature of our wrongs.

When we admit that we're sinners, like everyone else, we may assume that we're disqualified from being used by God to lead others. We may look up to those who seem so proud that God has kept them from sin and feel worthless in comparison.

In his confession of adultery and murder, David prays, "Don't toss me aside, banished forever from your presence. Don't take your Holy Spirit from me. Restore to me again the joy of your salvation, and make me willing to obey you. Then I will teach your ways to other sinners, and they—guilty like me—will repent and return to you" (Psalm 51:11-13). David understood that admitting his wrongs would provide a bridge to other hurting souls.

This is quite different from the prayer he prayed as a young man, who had yet to realize that he was a sinner like the rest of us. Here's part of that prayer: "I hate the sinners' hangouts and refuse to enter them. . . . Don't treat me as a common sinner or murderer who plots against the innocent and demands bribes. No, I am not like that, O Lord; I try to walk a straight and narrow path of doing what is right; therefore in mercy save me" (Psalm 26:5, 9-11).

Admitting our sins doesn't disqualify us from being used of God. Recognizing the sin in our lives can only make us more useful to him. It allows us to glorify God for his grace and it removes any reasons we might have for exalting ourselves.

The more we've experienced God's forgiveness, the more we desire his presence and his joy.

DAY 27 Crying to God

Bible Reading: Psalm 38:9-16

We admitted to God, to ourselves, and to another human being the exact nature of our wrongs.

We may need to pay the price for our wrongs in order to wake up and admit them. And as we suffer those consequences, the pain may be increased by seeing our loved ones and friends draw back from us, while our enemies close in for the kill. Those we love may withdraw in order to deal with their own pain, leaving us feeling abandoned. Those we wish would leave us alone prepare to attack and destroy us.

David knew what this was like. He prayed this prayer when experiencing the consequences of his wrongs: "My loved ones and friends stay away, fearing my disease. Even my own family stands at a distance. Meanwhile my enemies are trying to kill me. They plot my ruin and spend all their waking hours planning treachery. But I am deaf to all their threats; I am silent before them as a man who cannot speak. I have nothing to say. For I am waiting for you, O Lord my God. Come and protect me. Put an end to their arrogance, these who gloat when I am cast down" (Psalm 38:11-16).

Sometimes there's nothing we can say that will make up for what we've done. Instead, it's a time to call out to God for his protection. God can help us to deal with our wrongs. He can draw our loved ones back to us and put an end to the arrogance of those who gloat over our downfall. God is not one of our enemies. He doesn't enjoy our pain. But, he will often use the natural consequences of our actions to get our attention.

As we confess to others, we need to be silent as they respond, and depend on God for protection.

DAY 28 Stop and Listen

Bible Reading: Isaiah 28:16-22

We admitted to God, to ourselves, and to another human being the exact nature of our wrongs.

We've tried time and again to take care of ourselves. Maybe we learned early on that no one else would; at least that's the belief we've built our lives on. Time and again we find that life tends to overwhelm us, especially when we turn to our addictions to try to meet our needs. It just doesn't work.

"But the Lord God says, 'See, I am placing a Foundation Stone in Zion—a firm, tested, precious Cornerstone that is safe to build on. He who believes need never run away again. I will take the line and plummet of justice to check the foundation wall you built; it looks so fine, but it is so weak a storm of hail will knock it down! The enemy will come like a flood and sweep it away, and you will be drowned. . . . Again and again that flood will come and carry you off, until at last the unmixed horror of the truth of my warnings will finally dawn on you' " (Isaiah 28:16-17, 19).

When life comes crashing in, and we realize that our attempts to take care of ourselves don't quite make it, we have a choice. We can run away again, or we can stop and get the message God is sending. The pain God allows in our lives and the dissatisfactions we feel are meant to wake us up to the dangers of our chosen lifestyles. This will help us transfer our dependence to God, who can provide us with a solid foundation for living.

In the midst of our confessions, we need to continue to listen to what God may be saying to us.

DAY 29 God Understands

Bible Reading:
Psalm 38:1-22

We admitted to God, to ourselves, and to another human being the exact nature of our wrongs.

We may know the anguish of feeling like we deserve the suffering in our life. Sins carry their own painful consequences, many of them in the form of physical disease and discomfort. It's a terrible thing to realize that our pain may be discounted by others because we brought it upon ourselves. We may have encountered self-righteous people who look down on us in our pain, as if to say, "Well, that should teach you! I bet you'll never do that again!" They don't seem to understand the power the addiction holds over us.

David prayed, "O, Lord, don't punish me while you are angry! Your arrows have struck deep; your blows are crushing me. Because of your anger my body is sick, my health is broken beneath my sins. They are like a flood, higher than my head; they are a burden too heavy to bear. My wounds are festering and full of pus. Because of my sins I am bent and racked with pain. My days are filled with anguish. . . . How constantly I find myself upon the verge of sin; this source of sorrow always stares me in the face. I confess my sins; I am sorry for what I have done" (Psalm 38:1-6, 17-18).

We can call out to God in the midst of our pain. He has compassion on us, even if we brought the pain upon ourselves. We can admit that we're still on the verge of sin in the same prayer that says how truly sorry we are. Such is the nature of addiction. People may never understand, but God does.

As we confess, we need to admit that we are always on the verge of falling.

DAY 30 Confession versus Guilt

Bible Reading: Genesis 42:1-26

We admitted to God, to ourselves, and to another human being the exact nature of our wrongs.

Sometimes we've lived a lie for so long, and built so much of our lives on a false foundation, that we're afraid to admit the truth. It would mean dismantling much of the good we've worked for in order to go back and explain. But we're plagued with guilt and fear of exposure, constantly looking over our shoulder. We may fear divine judgment and human vengeance, forfeiting years of peace. We may interpret everything that goes wrong in our lives as just punishment for the lie we're living.

This was the case for the brothers of Joseph, who sold him into slavery and told their father he was dead. Their story is told in Genesis 37–50. We see later that they interpreted their trouble with the Egyptian officials as God's punishment for their hidden sins. When they tried to explain why they couldn't leave their young brother Benjamin, they had to repeat the lie that Joseph was dead. They didn't realize that the man they were addressing was their brother Joseph. They were snared in their own lies and tormented by fears of retribution. When Joseph finally revealed himself and offered forgiveness, they found it hard to believe and receive.

When we refuse to take the risk of uncovering lies, we're condemning ourselves to a life of guilt. It may be hard to face the truth, but it isn't as bad as living with the heavy burden of the lies. With a clean conscience, there is freedom and hope for a good life.

It may be hard to admit the truth, but that's the path to our recovery.

STEP SIX

We were entirely ready to have God remove all these defects of character.

***"And so, dear brothers, I plead with you to give your bodies to God. Let them be a living sacrifice, holy—the kind he can accept"* (Romans 12:1).**

STEP SIX

DAY 1 Discovering Hope

Bible Reading:
John 5:1-9

We were entirely ready to have God remove all these defects of character.

How can we honestly say that we're *entirely* ready for God to remove our defects of character? If we think in terms of all or nothing, we may get stuck here because we will never feel entirely ready. It's important to keep in mind that the Twelve Steps are guiding ideals. No one can work them perfectly. Our part is to keep moving, to get as close as we can to being ready.

In Jesus' day there was a pool where people came in hope of finding miraculous healing. "One of the men lying there had been sick for thirty-eight years. When Jesus saw him and knew how long he had been ill, he asked him, 'Would you like to get well?' 'I can't,' the sick man said, 'for I have no one to help me into the pool at the movement of the water. While I am trying to get there, someone else always gets in ahead of me.' Jesus told him, 'Stand up, roll up your sleeping mat and go on home!' Instantly the man was healed! He rolled up the mat and began walking!" (John 5:5-9).

This man was so crippled that he couldn't go any farther on his own. He camped as near as he could to a place where there was the hope of recovery. God met him there and brought him the rest of the way. For us, "entirely ready" may mean getting as close to the hope of healing as we can in our crippled condition, using the support available to us. When we do, God will meet us there and take us the rest of the way.

Our confession readies us for God's work of cleansing and releasing.

DAY 2 God's Abundant Pardon

Bible Reading: Isaiah 55:1-9

We were entirely ready to have God remove all these defects of character.

People tell us to repent and stop thinking the way we do. Most of us would give anything to do this. If it were only that simple to put a stop to our obsessive thoughts! When we're starving emotionally, it's almost impossible to stop thinking about what has fed that hunger, even when we realize it doesn't satisfy.

People don't seem to understand. They may quote a verse like, "Let men cast off their wicked deeds; let them banish from their minds the very thought of doing wrong!" (Isaiah 55:7). But we think, *How? My thoughts seem to be out of my control.*

God does understand. He put that verse into the larger context of dealing with the hunger within our soul. He said, "Why spend your money on food that doesn't give you strength? Why pay for groceries that do you no good? Listen and I'll tell you where to get good food that fattens up the soul! Come to me with your eyes wide open. Listen, for the life of your soul is at stake. . . . Let them turn to the Lord that he may have mercy upon them, and to our God, for he will abundantly pardon!" (Isaiah 55:2-3, 7). The word translated *abundantly* can be understood to mean "in progressively increasing measure each time we come."

We need to fight our addictions on two fronts: dealing with the hunger deep inside us, and changing our thoughts of doing wrong. Neither battle is easily won; each requires our daily readiness for God to satisfy our hunger and remove our defects of character.

God not only forgives us, but also promises to satisfy the hunger we feel deep inside.

DAY 3 Healing the Brokenness

Bible Reading: Psalm 51:16-19

We were entirely ready to have God remove all these defects of character.

If we have sincerely practiced the previous steps, we have probably found enough pain inside to break our hearts. Facing the fact that brokenness is part of the human condition can be crushing. But if we've arrived at this point, it is probably a sign that we are ready for God to change us.

King David, as a young man, wasn't ready for God to change his defects of character because he didn't recognize that they were there. He prays, "Don't treat me as a common sinner. . . . No, I am not like that, O Lord; I try to walk a straight and narrow path of doing what is right; therefore in mercy save me" (Psalm 26:9-11). He approached God on the basis of his own merit.

It wasn't until later in his life when he was confronted with his sins of adultery and murder that he was able to say, "I was born a sinner, yes, from the moment my mother conceived me" (Psalm 51:5). He also said, "You don't want penance; if you did, how gladly I would do it! . . . It is a broken spirit you want—remorse and penitence. A broken and a contrite heart, O God, you will not ignore" (Psalm 51:16-17).

Jesus taught, "Those who mourn are fortunate! for they shall be comforted" (Matthew 5:4). God isn't looking for evidence of how good we are or how hard we try. He only wants us to mourn over our brokenness. Then he will not ignore our needs, but will forgive us, comfort us, and cleanse us.

We can't please God by what we do; he looks at the attitudes of our hearts.

DAY 4 Crossing the Barriers

Bible Reading:
Joshua 3:1-17

We were entirely ready to have God remove all these defects of character.

For those of us who've used dysfunctional patterns to govern our lives, crossing over into an entirely new way of living takes some preparation. We may see where we're supposed to end up, but we don't know how to get there.

Israel had wandered for forty years in the wilderness. Finally they arrived at the Jordan River and were able to see the Promised Land. But still, there was no way for them to cross the river. They were instructed, "When you see the priests carrying the Ark of God, follow them. You have never before been where we are going now, so they will guide you" (Joshua 3:3-4). God miraculously stopped the flow of the river and the people focused their attention on the Ark of God as they crossed on dry ground.

We, too, have never before been where we are now going. We can be guided by focusing on what the Ark represents. "Inside the ark were the tablets of stone with the Ten Commandments written on them, and a golden jar with some manna in it, and Aaron's wooden cane that budded" (Hebrews 9:4). These represented God's presence, his law, his promised provision, and a warning against rebellion to "ward off further catastrophe" (Numbers 17:10).

As God helps us cross the final barriers we need to remember that his law is there to guide us and he will provide our daily bread. We also need to bear in mind the dangers of rebellion. With this focus and preparation, we will be ready to move ahead.

We can move ahead with confidence when our eyes are on God.

DAY 5 Attitudes and Actions

Bible Reading: Philippians 3:12-14

We were entirely ready to have God remove all these defects of character.

Getting "entirely ready" to have God remove "all" our defects of character sounds impossible. In reality we know that such perfection is out of reach. This is another way of saying that we're going to do our best to approach a lifelong goal, which no one ever completes this side of eternity.

The apostle Paul expressed a similar thought. He said, "I don't mean to say I am perfect. I haven't learned all I should even yet, but I keep working toward that day when I will finally be all that Christ saved me for and wants me to be. . . . Forgetting the past and looking forward to what lies ahead, I strain to reach the end of the race and receive the prize for which God is calling us up to heaven" (Philippians 3:12-14).

This combination of a positive attitude and energetic effort is a part of the mystery of our cooperation with God. Paul said, "Be even more careful to do the good things that result from being saved, obeying God with deep reverence, shrinking back from all that might displease him. For God is at work within you, helping you want to obey him, and then helping you do what he wants" (Philippians 2:12-13).

We'll need to practice these steps the rest of our lives. We don't have to demand perfection of ourselves. It is enough to keep moving ahead as best we can. We should look forward to our rewards, with hopes of becoming all God intends us to be.

Hoping in Christ, we can let go of past guilt and look ahead to the good things God has planned for us.

DAY 6 Long-Lasting Change

Bible Reading: Matthew 15:16-20	**We were entirely ready to have God remove all these defects of character.**

When we were consumed with addictive/compulsive behaviors, we considered the behaviors to be "the problem." When we are sober and not acting out our compulsions, we realize that "the problem" goes much deeper. We used to think, *If I could only change my behavior, everything would be fine*. Now that we're in recovery, and the behavior may be under control, it's time to look to the state of our innermost being to get to the heart of the problem.

Early in his life King David prayed, "Dismiss all the charges against me" (Psalm 26:1), focusing on his deeds. Later in life, he was able to pray on a deeper level, "Create in me a new, clean heart, O God, filled with clean thoughts and right desires" (Psalm 51:10).

Jesus explained the true source of our problem: "Evil words come from an evil heart and defile the man who says them. For from the heart come evil thoughts, murder, adultery, fornication, theft, lying and slander" (Matthew 15:18-20). We needn't worry, though. God is in the business of heart transplants. He promised Israel, "I will take from you your hearts of stone and give you tender hearts of love for God, so that you can obey my laws and be my people, and I will be your God" (Ezekiel 11:20).

Being entirely ready means that we want God to go deeper than dealing with our destructive behaviors. We want him to change our motives and create a new, clean heart within us.

Who we are deep down matters more to God than who we may appear to be on the surface.

DAY 7 Removed, Not Improved

Bible Reading:
Romans 6:5-11

We were entirely ready to have God remove all these defects of character.

Most of us have made numerous attempts at self-improvement. Perhaps, we've consciously tried to improve our attitudes, our education, our appearance, or our habits. We probably have had some success in self-improvement on some level. However, when it comes to our struggles with defects of character, chances are we've only experienced deep frustration.

There is a reason for our frustration. These character defects can only be removed, never improved! The illustration given us in the Bible is that these defects of character must be put to death, as Jesus was, with the hope of new life to follow. The apostle Paul wrote, "Your old evil desires were nailed to the cross with him; that part of you that loves to sin was crushed and fatally wounded, so that your sin-loving body is no longer under sin's control, no longer needs to be a slave to sin" (Romans 6:6). "Those who belong to Christ have nailed their natural evil desires to his cross and crucified them there" (Galatians 5:24).

There is no Band-Aid cure for these defects of character. They have been fatally wounded and must die their death on the cross. This process is never easy. Who goes to a crucifixion without some measure of anxiety? But when we accept this and allow God to remove our defects, we will be surprised by the new life that greets us on the other side.

Before, we were slaves to our addictions; now, we can choose to have God remove all the old destructive patterns.

DAY 8 Telling the Truth

Bible Reading: Colossians 3:9-11

We were entirely ready to have God remove all these defects of character.

Lying can be habitual. We may even have lied to ourselves, pretending we don't have a problem with lying. We may have learned to cover up our problems by becoming excellent liars. We can see the unhappiness caused by our lies, how they've hurt us and our loved ones. And lying is one of the defects we can give up with many promised benefits.

Think about these promises: "Do you want a long, good life? Then watch your tongue! Keep your lips from lying" (Psalm 34:12-13). "Don't tell lies to each other; it was your old life with all its wickedness that did that sort of thing; now it is dead and gone. You are living a brand new kind of life that is continually learning more and more of what is right, and trying constantly to be more and more like Christ who created this new life within you" (Colossians 3:9-10). "Stop lying to each other; tell the truth, for we are parts of each other and when we lie to each other we are hurting ourselves" (Ephesians 4:25).

There are great benefits to truthfulness. What other virtue is accompanied by such promises? Honesty is vital to recovery. Since lying may be second nature to us, it may be difficult to change. Part of any successful recovery involves guarding our lips and our thoughts, to rid ourselves of the lies that hurt us and others. Since this may have been a lifelong way of coping, we must accept that learning to tell the truth is a gradual process.

Telling the truth is an excellent way to build bridges and break down barriers.

DAY 9 Results Reveal Value

Bible Reading: Hebrews 12:5-11

We were entirely ready to have God remove all these defects of character.

Some phases of our recovery may be very painful; it may feel to us like we're being punished. We may assume that the bad things happening are because we are bad. And we may begin to believe that God doesn't love us.

It may hurt when God removes these defects, but this in itself is a display of love. The Bible says, "My son, don't be angry when the Lord punishes you. . . . For when he punishes you, it proves that he loves you. When he whips you it proves you are really his child. Let God train you, for he is doing what any loving father does for his children. Whoever heard of a son who was never corrected? . . . God's correction is always right and for our best good, that we may share his holiness. Being punished isn't enjoyable while it is happening—it hurts! But afterwards we can see the result, a quiet growth in grace and character" (Hebrews 12:5-7, 10-11).

Our recovery is a time of correction; it's a time of facing problems and character flaws, and changing incorrect beliefs. There may be seasons when we do have to pay for our past. God will use this time to redirect our lives toward a better life. His correction isn't arbitrary or abusive, but it's still painful. Knowing that God's discipline demonstrates his love for us can be comforting in the midst of the pain. It helps to remember that his love will only allow that which is for our ultimate good.

When God corrects us, he proves his loving concern for us.

DAY 10 A New Identity

Bible Reading:
1 Corinthians
6:9-11

We were entirely ready to have God remove all these defects of character.

Our addictions may be so ingrained in us that we define our identity by them. It may feel like we are predisposed to behave as we do. And yet we're condemned for our behavior that feels out of our control! How can we let go of seeing ourselves primarily in terms of the kinds of addictions that dominate our lives?

One passage in Scripture seems to identify people by their behavior. It says, "Those who live immoral lives, who are idol worshipers, adulterers or homosexuals—will have no share in his Kingdom. Neither will thieves, or greedy people, drunkards, slanderers, or robbers." This doesn't seem fair. We feel like we'll never be able to escape our addictive nature. But the passage goes on, "There was a time when some of you were just like that, but now your sins are washed away, and you are set apart for God; and he has accepted you because of what the Lord Jesus Christ and the Spirit of our God have done for you" (1 Corinthians 6:10-11). "When someone becomes a Christian he becomes a brand new person inside. He is not the same anymore. A new life has begun!" (2 Corinthians 5:17).

God doesn't just erase the behavior. When we identify ourselves with Christ, he wants to give us a new identity. We'll always remember what we were and realize that our sin nature and our body may always be predisposed to a particular addiction. We'll still slip up, but we should no longer see our addiction as the definition of who we are.

God accepts us because our identity is found in Christ.

STEP SIX

DAY 11 Transformed from the Inside

Bible Reading: Romans 12:1-2

We were entirely ready to have God remove all these defects of character.

How many times have we wished that we could be someone else? Perhaps part of the reason we act out our addictions is because we can't stand ourselves. Self-hatred is often associated with addictive/compulsive personalities. If we don't like who we are, it's reassuring to know that we can change dramatically.

The apostle Paul wrote, "Present your bodies a living sacrifice, holy, acceptable to God, which is your reasonable service. And do not be conformed to this world, but be transformed by the renewing of your mind, that you may prove what is that good and acceptable and perfect will of God" (Romans 12:1-2, NKJV).

The words *conformed* and *transformed* describe processes that happen to things that are changeable or unstable. In this case, we are the changeable things in mind. *Conformed* refers to an outward change to make one thing appear like another. *Transformed* describes a change from the inside out. It comes from the same word that describes a caterpillar changing into a butterfly.

We all have great potential for change. We've tried to change our outward behavior and found that it doesn't last. As we yield ourselves to God in the cocoon of the recovery process, he will renew our minds. He will begin to remove our defects of character, transforming us inwardly so that it affects both our character and our behavior.

God has good, pleasing, and perfect plans for us, his children.

DAY 12 Seeking Wisdom

Bible Reading:
Proverbs 3:13-23

We were entirely ready to have God remove all these defects of character.

None of us set out with the goal of becoming addicted. We were seeking something else—escape from the pain, perhaps something to make up for our losses and brokenness or maybe an inner desire to self-destruct. Unfortunately, the things we seek are not able to satisfy our deepest needs and desires.

Our needs are legitimate. The defect that needs to be changed is our tendency to go the wrong way to try to meet them. The Bible says, "Have two goals: wisdom—that is, knowing and doing right—and common sense. Don't let them slip away, for they fill you with living energy, and bring you honor and respect. They keep you safe from defeat and disaster and from stumbling off the trail" (Proverbs 3:21-23).

Wisdom leads to the benefits most of us want out of life. When we seek wisdom, as if it were a hidden treasure, we'll find the other things we desire. "The man who knows right from wrong and has good judgment and common sense is happier than the man who is immensely rich! For such wisdom is far more valuable than precious jewels. Nothing else compares with it. Wisdom gives: a long, good life, riches, honor, pleasure, and peace" (Proverbs 3:13-17). As we change our focus and begin to seek after wisdom, we will find our lives more fulfilled and secure. This may also help us avoid the destructive paths we've previously taken as we have tried to fulfill our own unmet needs and desires.

Common sense is given to everyone; wisdom is given only to those who follow God.

DAY 13 Repairing Our Boundaries

Bible Reading: 2 Chronicles 32:5-9

We were entirely ready to have God remove all these defects of character.

Recovery involves repairing or building healthy boundaries in the places where our boundaries are weak or defective. Boundaries are the limits set in our lives for our protection. Perhaps boundaries have been violently trampled down through abuse or they may have grown weaker as we lost our ability to maintain limits. We let people walk all over us or let down our guard against our own destructive behavior.

In Bible times each city was fortified by boundary walls that served as protection from outside enemies. If these walls were weak or broken there was grave danger of an invasion and destruction. At one point in Israel's history an enemy was threatening to attack Jerusalem. The king "strengthened his defenses by repairing the wall wherever it was broken down and by adding to the fortifications, and constructing a second wall outside it. He . . . encouraged them with this address: 'Be strong, be brave. . . . We have the Lord our God to fight our battles for us!' This greatly encouraged them" (2 Chronicles 32:5-8).

Part of the recovery process involves repairing our boundaries. We can also construct a second wall of defense by developing a strong support network around us. We will still need to be brave and remember that whatever enemies we face in the form of destructive behaviors, there is someone with us who is far greater. We, too, can let this greatly encourage us!

Looking through the eyes of faith helps us to see the support that God provides around us.

DAY 14 Courage to Change

Bible Reading: 2 Chronicles 15:1-16

We were entirely ready to have God remove all these defects of character.

There comes a point in recovery when we need to face ourselves. We need to acknowledge the wrongs we've committed and the harm we've brought because of our slavery. It takes courage to make the preparations necessary to allow God to change our lives and relationships in ways supporting our recovery.

King Asa was a man who lived at a time when the people of Israel had given themselves over to the worship of idols. They had turned away from God and the way of life they knew to be right. A messenger of God told the king: "'The Lord will stay with you as long as you stay with him! Whenever you look for him, you will find him. But if you forsake him, he will forsake you.' . . . When King Asa heard this message . . . he took courage and destroyed all the idols in the land . . . and he rebuilt the altar of the Lord" (2 Chronicles 15:2, 8). Asa even removed his mother from her position of power because she had been influential in Israel's idolatry.

Allowing God to remove all our defects of character takes courage, because the changes he makes in us will affect every part of our lives. The time will come when we need to crush and burn the "idols" we've served, to go against the crowd, to make a commitment to God, and even to separate ourselves from those people who do not contribute to our recovery. When we do these things, we will find that the Lord will be there for us, encouraging us as we set things straight.

Stay in contact with people who love God and you will find the courage to change.

DAY 15 Leaving the Familiar

Bible Reading: Matthew 14:23-33

We were entirely ready to have God remove all these defects of character.

Having God remove our defects can be frightening. No matter how bad life gets we tend to feel at home with what's familiar. We may stay trapped in destructive life patterns because we fear change. But if we wait for all the fear to go away before we take courageous steps, we'll never make significant progress.

Courage isn't the absence of fear. Courage means to seize the strength you find within you, to encourage yourself, to be obstinate or steadfastly minded. It doesn't mean being free of fear. It means finding enough strength to take the next step.

In the account where Jesus walks on the water, the disciples are terrified when they see him. "Then Peter called to him, 'Sir, if it is really you, tell me to come over to you, walking on the water.' 'All right,' the Lord said, 'come along!' So Peter went over the side of the boat and walked on the water toward Jesus. But when he looked around at the high waves, he was terrified and began to sink. 'Save me, Lord!' he shouted. Instantly Jesus reached out his hand and rescued him" (Matthew 14:28-31).

Peter gathered up enough courage to take one step. He ventured out into a new experience. When he got in over his head, he called out and found the help he needed. We, too, only need to summon the courage to take the next step. This doesn't mean that we won't feel fear or need help. It does mean that with God's help, we'll make it. All we need is the courage to take just one more step.

We need to walk with our eyes on Jesus, not on the situations we face.

DAY 16 Removing Self-Hatred

Bible Reading: Psalm 139:13-18

We were entirely ready to have God remove all these defects of character.

Many of us have spent our lives trying to be someone we're not. Our addictive/compulsive behaviors may revolve around this desperate attempt to escape from ourselves. Maybe we have difficulty accepting our personality, our appearance, our handicaps, even our talents. Perhaps we spend our lives trying to be what someone else wants us to be because we feel that who we are is not enough. We may do all we can to distance ourselves from our inner being because we are so deeply ashamed of who we are.

Self-hatred is a defect of character that needs to be removed. It breeds the sin of covetousness, that is, longing to be in someone else's situation or have what they have. The psalmist wrote, "Thank you for making me so wonderfully complex! It is amazing to think about. Your workmanship is marvelous" (Psalm 139:14). Saying we are God's "workmanship" means that we're unique and beautiful masterpieces, works of poetry. Beauty and value are designed into our very fiber, by virtue of our Creator.

One important step in our recovery is to allow God to remove self-hatred, helping us to value ourselves for who we are. We have been miraculously created and we are treasured by God. And this has been true since the time in our mother's womb, long before we could *do* anything to earn it! As we begin to see how unique and special we are—embraced and accepted by God himself—our strides toward recovery should grow faster and longer.

We need to see ourselves as God does—a creature, wonderfully crafted, made by the very hands of God.

DAY 17 Removing Impatience

Bible Reading: James 1:1-4

We were entirely ready to have God remove all these defects of character.

We would all love to have an instant recovery. Many times our addictive behavior has its source in trying to fill an inner void with some form of immediate pleasure. When we enter into recovery, we have to admit that there is no immediate "fix" for the needs we have deep within. We need to prepare for God to remove our impatience. Recovery comes in seasons and takes time.

The Bible says, "Is your life full of difficulties and temptations? Then be happy, for when the way is rough, your patience has a chance to grow. So let it grow, and don't try to squirm out of your problems. For when your patience is finally in full bloom, then you will be ready for anything, strong in character, full and complete" (James 1:2-4).

It's nice to know that the trials of life have significant value. They are sent as our friends, to help us mature and develop the kind of character that isn't dependent on outside sources for fulfillment. The difficult seasons of life are like the fire that purifies precious metal. They are designed to burn away the impurities and leave us better than before. The process takes time, but it's worth it because of the strength, purity, and beauty that result.

When we finally accept that there's no shortcut on the way to wholeness, we will be able to find joy in each season of recovery. We will develop patience, true maturity, and lasting fulfillment as God replaces our defects with his character.

Our continued struggles are prime opportunities for growth and healing.

DAY 18 God's Will, God's Way

Bible Reading: Matthew 26:36-39

We were entirely ready to have God remove all these defects of character.

As we work through the steps of recovery, we look up a long, difficult road toward a better life. And though we know the goal is worthy of our commitment, we often find the challenge of the process overwhelming. As God goes about removing our defects, we may wish there were some other way. We may feel fear, a lack of confidence, deep anguish, and a host of other emotions which threaten to stop us in our tracks.

Jesus understands how we feel. He had a similar experience the night he was arrested. His friends were nearby, but when he needed them they were asleep. He told his friends, "My soul is crushed with horror and sadness to the point of death" (Matthew 26:38). As he realized the enormity of the pain he would face, he looked for some other way. He was not immediately able to accept the path set before him. Instead, he struggled and prayed the same thing three times, "My Father! If it is possible let this cup be taken away from me. But I want your will, not mine" (26:39). Finally he found the grace to accept God's plan.

We may be overwhelmed as we face our own crosses on the way to a new life. But during such times of stress, we can look to Jesus for encouragement. As we look to him, we can express our deepest emotions. We can be honest about our struggle and cry out for help. We also can be confident that we'll be given the strength we need for the next step.

Because of the anguish Jesus experienced, he can truly relate to our suffering.

DAY 19 Removing Hate

Bible Reading: Jonah 1–4

We were entirely ready to have God remove all these defects of character.

When people have hurt us deeply it is easy to hate and wish for vengeance. But holding tightly to these feelings can easily become a defect of character. The bitterness threatens our recovery because it causes us to blame others for our problems. It may scare us to think of forgiving those who have hurt us. We may be afraid that releasing our hatred will require us to condone the bad things people have done to us.

Jonah felt this way, too. He hated the people of Nineveh for their cruelty toward Israel. God told Jonah to go and warn them of the destruction planned for them. Instead, he tried to run away by boarding a ship going the opposite direction. The Lord caused a life-threatening storm, and Jonah ended up in the belly of a great fish. Suddenly, the Lord had Jonah's attention and Jonah reluctantly obeyed. Jonah preached to the people of Nineveh, they changed their ways, and God put off his planned destruction. Jonah complained, "This is exactly what I thought you'd do. . . . That's why I ran away. . . . I knew how easily you could cancel your plans for destroying these people" (Jonah 4:2).

We won't be able to remove our bitterness alone. And it will never be easy to accept that God wants to rescue even the people we hate. We'll need to allow God to change our hearts as we work toward forgiving those who have hurt us. This will take time. God only asks that we be willing to let him begin the work.

We can only become bitter after we've forgotten how much God has forgiven us.

DAY 20 Taking Time to Trust

Bible Reading:
1 Samuel 13:6-14

We were entirely ready to have God remove all these defects of character.

We're all susceptible to the negative influences of others. We may get pushed into rushed decisions by peer pressure and find ourselves in trouble as a result. This weakness should alert us to a defect in our lives and our need for help.

Saul had this defect but refused God's help. Israel was at war. In the midst of battle it was required that a priest offer sacrifices. Samuel told Saul that he would come at an appointed time to offer a sacrifice. Saul waited and began to feel pressured because his troops were leaving him. He knew it was against God's law for anyone other than a priest to offer sacrifices, but he let the pressure get to him. Saul did it himself. As soon as he had finished, Samuel arrived. "'You fool!' Samuel exclaimed. 'You have disobeyed the commandment of the Lord your God. He was planning to make you and your descendants kings of Israel forever, but now your dynasty must end; for the Lord wants a man who will obey him'" (1 Samuel 13:13-14).

If Saul had waited one more hour he would have kept his kingdom. Our tendency to be unduly influenced by others needs to be replaced with strength from God and faith in his plan.

When we take the time to wait for God, he will meet and bless us according to our needs.

DAY 21 Recovering Childhood

Bible Reading:
1 Corinthians
13:11-12

We were entirely ready to have God remove all these defects of character.

Many of us spend our lives trying to fill up the empty spaces. Perhaps, we missed out on a carefree childhood. We may have had to take care of our parents when they should have been taking care of us. Maybe our real needs were never met, leaving a deficit that prompts us to fulfill even our unhealthy desires. Our addictions are fed by the sense that we deserve some comfort in our pain-filled lives.

During childhood our needs should have been met—and immediately! But for many of us, they weren't. We may have learned to cope by giving ourselves what we wanted when we wanted it. Now we literally spoil ourselves to make up for the needs that weren't filled when they should have been.

The apostle Paul used this illustration: "When I was a child I spoke and thought and reasoned as a child does. But when I became a man my thoughts grew far beyond those of my childhood" (1 Corinthians 13:11). Children can only see the moment. As adults we can see a bigger picture and allow a long-range perspective to lend wisdom to our choices.

Some of us haven't yet put away childish things. We can't get back our lost childhood. Demanding immediate pleasure and relief from pain is a defect that ultimately brings unhappiness. We need to let it go and allow God to address the deep unmet needs from childhood as we work through recovery.

Our addictions have kept us from growing up; our recovery allows us to put away childish things.

DAY 22 Time to Change

Bible Reading: Deuteronomy 7:21-24

We were entirely ready to have God remove all these defects of character.

If our inner selves were transformed overnight, major changes would take place in our lives and relationships. We may fear some of these changes. We may be afraid that God will thrust us into a new way of life that we won't be able to handle. We do want new lives, but we know how fierce and tenacious our character defects can be, making us pause at the thought of dealing with them.

As the people of Israel were about to conquer the Promised Land, Moses said to them: "No, do not be afraid of those nations, for the Lord your God is among you, and he is a great and awesome God. He will cast them out a little at a time; he will not do it all at once, for if he did, the wild animals would multiply too quickly and become dangerous. He will do it gradually, and you will move in against those nations and destroy them" (Deuteronomy 7:21-23).

Israel's entrance into the Promised Land parallels our journey into a new life. Their conquest and removal of the enemy nations is similar to the conquests we have over our character defects. God understands that sudden, dramatic changes would endanger us. He will never expect us to maintain a life completely different from what we know. But he wants us to remember that he is with us. And he will cast out our defects a little at a time so we can handle the changes. We'll then be able to gradually move into a new life, experiencing victory one step at a time.

God could change us in an instant, but often he chooses to change us slowly, one step at a time.

DAY 23 God Wants Our Recovery

Bible Reading: Isaiah 59:15-21

We were entirely ready to have God remove all these defects of character.

Some of our families may attack us for trying to discover a better life. But despite their opposition, we know we can't go another step in the wrong direction. We're tired of being separated from God. We want more from life. Can God really step in and change the course of our lives?

"Listen now! The Lord isn't too weak to save you. And he isn't getting deaf! He can hear you when you call! But the trouble is that your sins have cut you off from God" (Isaiah 59:1-2). God understands the obstacles we face. He said through Isaiah, "Yes, truth is gone, and anyone who tries a better life is soon attacked. The Lord saw all the evil and was displeased to find no steps taken against sin. He saw no one was helping you, and wondered that no one intervened. Therefore he himself stepped in to save you through his mighty power and justice" (59:15-17).

Our relationships with God really can be transformed, our defects removed, the future of our families, bright. "'This is my promise to them,' says the Lord: 'My Holy Spirit shall not leave them, and they shall want the good and hate the wrong—they and their children and their children's children forever'" (59:21).

When we get tired of holding God off and allow him to come into our lives, he will fight for our recovery. He will send his Holy Spirit to stay with us and transform our affections. He will cause us to want the things that are good and to hate all the defects.

When our recovery becomes overwhelming, God personally steps in to help.

DAY 24 Avoiding Rationalization

Bible Reading:
1 Samuel 15:7-23

We were entirely ready to have God remove all these defects of character.

We may feel we are ready to have God remove *all* our defects of character. At the same time, however, we may have unwittingly organized our lives in a way that preserves some of the defects that should be removed. We call this rationalization, and sometimes we don't even know we're doing it!

King Saul claimed to be fully committed to obeying God's will. He would have sworn that he was ready to have God remove all his defects of character, but he had kept a few, rationalizing them. Samuel confronted Saul about this: "'And he [God] sent you on an errand and told you, "Go and completely destroy the sinners, the Amalekites, until they are all dead." Then why didn't you obey the Lord? Why did you rush for the loot and do exactly what God said not to?' 'But I *have* obeyed the Lord,' Saul insisted. 'I did what he told me to; and I brought King Agag but killed everyone else. And it was only when my troops demanded it that I let them keep the best of the sheep and oxen and loot to sacrifice to the Lord.' Samuel replied, 'Has the Lord as much pleasure in your burnt offerings and sacrifices as in your obedience? Obedience is far better than sacrifice'" (1 Samuel 15:18-22).

We need to ask God to show us the things we've rationalized into being acceptable. It is easy for us to overlook some of our defects. It may be helpful at this point in recovery to have someone else double-check our list.

Selective obedience is just another form of disobedience.

DAY 25 Removing Deeper Hurts

Bible Reading: Jonah 4:4-8

We were entirely ready to have God remove all these defects of character.

When we are upset, we often depend on our addictions to make us feel better. But as we get rid of our addictions, we then face the deeper character defects that God wants to heal. Our addictions function as places of "shelter" from our pain. But when those "shelters" are removed, deep anger may surface, exposing yet deeper character flaws that need healing.

Jonah had a glaring defect of character: he couldn't seem to forgive and have compassion on the people he hated. When God decided not to destroy them, Jonah threw a temper tantrum. "Then the Lord said, 'Is it right to be *angry* about *this?*' So Jonah went out and sat sulking on the east side of the city. . . . The Lord arranged for a vine to grow up quickly and to spread its broad leaves over Jonah's head to shade him. . . . The next morning . . . [the vine] withered away and died. Then when the sun was hot, God ordered a scorching east wind to blow on Jonah, and the sun beat down upon his head until he grew faint and wished to die" (Jonah 4:4-8).

God did this to show Jonah that the real problem wasn't the loss of his shelter. Hatred was the real problem. The removal of our sheltering addictions may expose deeper problems. This may spark defensive anger as God touches our deepest hurts. It's all right to let the anger out. But it's also important to let God take the real problem, too.

We can bring our anger to God; he's big enough to handle it lovingly.

DAY 26 Taking Time to Grieve

Bible Reading: Genesis 23:1-4; 35:19-21

We were entirely ready for God to remove all these defects of character.

The pathway to recovery and finding new life also involves the death process. The different means we used to cope were "defective," but still, they did give us comfort or companionship. Giving them up is often like suffering the death of a loved one.

Abraham and his grandson, Jacob, both lost loved ones as they traveled to the Promised Land. "Sarah . . . died in Hebron in the land of Canaan; there Abraham mourned and wept for her. Then, standing beside her body, he said . . . 'Here I am, a visitor in a foreign land, with no place to bury my wife. Please sell me a piece of ground for this purpose.' . . . So Abraham buried Sarah there" (Genesis 23:1-4, 19). A generation later, Jacob was given a new name, Israel, and the promise of a great heritage in the Promised Land. On his way there, he, too, lost his beloved wife. She died while giving birth to their son, Benjamin. "So Rachel died, and was buried near the road to Ephrath (also called Bethlehem). And Jacob set up a monument of stones upon her grave, and it is there to this day. Then Israel journeyed on" (Genesis 35:19-21).

As we journey toward our new lives, we will necessarily lose some of our defective ways of coping. When this happens, we need to stop and take time to give our losses a proper burial. We need to put them away, cover the shame, and allow ourselves to grieve the loss of something very familiar to us. When the time of grieving is over, we, too, can journey on.

We need to grieve our loss of the familiar so we can be ready for the new to come.

DAY 27 New for Old

Bible Reading: Matthew 26:17-28

We were entirely ready to have God remove all these defects of character.

There are many rituals involved in the addictive process. These bring comfort and a sense of security to our lives. When we give up the rituals associated with acting out our addictions, we have a real need to replace them with new ones.

The Jewish people celebrated Passover to commemorate how God had delivered them from the Angel of Death by commanding that they sprinkle a lamb's blood on their doorposts; this proved that the people inside the house belonged to God. Jesus became the Lamb of God to take away the sins of the world, thus abolishing the need to rely on the sacrificial lamb of Passover. But Jesus, in removing the need for this important ritual, replaced it with a new one. "On the first day of the Passover ceremonies . . . Jesus took a small loaf of bread and blessed it and broke it apart and gave it to the disciples and said, 'Take it and eat it, for this is my body.' And he took a cup of wine and gave thanks for it and gave it to them and said, 'Each one drink from it, for this is my blood, sealing the New Covenant. It is poured out to forgive the sins of multitudes'" (Matthew 26:17, 26-28).

When preparing to have our defects removed, we need to anticipate the loss of rituals that made us feel safe. We need to find new rituals and ceremonies to celebrate the truth of our new promises without acting out our addictions.

God wants to support us as we walk on the paths he's made for us.

DAY 28 Taking Our Time

Bible Reading: Esther 2:12-14

We were entirely ready to have God remove all these defects of character.

As we go about removing our defects, the pathway to recovery may seem very negative. It might be refreshing to discover that sometimes defects are removed as we lavish ourselves with good things.

The story of Esther is a kind of dream come true. The king needs a new queen. So he searches for the most beautiful girl in his kingdom. Esther is one of the girls selected as a candidate for this royal beauty contest. She was given a special menu of royal foods and was favored with beauty treatments. She was given a luxurious apartment with seven maids to take care of her. "The instructions concerning these girls were that before being taken to the king's bed, each would be given six months of beauty treatments with oil of myrrh, followed by six months with special perfumes and ointments. Then, as each girl's turn came for spending the night with King Ahasuerus, she was given her choice of clothing or jewelry she wished, to enhance her beauty" (Esther 2:12-13).

This sounds wonderful! Who wouldn't welcome getting the royal beauty treatment? Surely, all the girls were beautiful, but they all had defects. Notice that the beauty treatment took a whole year. They were also given choices of the items they wanted to enhance their natural beauty. When God sets out to remove our defects, he has plans to lavish us with good things. No matter how good we may look, all of us can use some help. And we need to realize that real transformations take time.

We gave time to our addictions; now we need to give time to our recovery.

DAY 29 Loving Support

Bible Reading: John 3:14-17

We were entirely ready to have God remove all these defects of character.

We may find it hard to believe that anyone would want us—really want us—just as we are. It may be especially hard to believe that a holy God would consider us worthy of his love, and so much so that he would sacrifice the life of his Son to make us his own. That's the stuff of fairy tales; and we probably aren't used to thinking of our lives in terms of "happily ever after."

And yet, "God loved the world so much that he gave his only Son so that anyone who believes in him shall not perish but have eternal life" (John 3:16). The apostle Paul went on to describe a love story that has the power to cleanse and transform the beloved. (In this case, that's us!) He wrote, "And you husbands, show the same kind of love to your wives as Christ showed to the Church when he died for her, to make her holy and clean, washed by baptism and God's Word; so that he could give her to himself as a glorious Church without a single spot or wrinkle or any other blemish, being holy and without a single fault" (Ephesians 5:25-27).

When we are ready to have God remove all of our defects, our decision is welcomed by a loving God. He accepts us as we are, with nothing hidden from his all-seeing eyes. Baptism symbolizes the burial of our old life and a resurrection to a new one. He will continue his transforming work until every defect is wiped away.

God's involvement with us is always based on his love for us.

DAY 30 Our Promised Future

Bible Reading: Revelation 21:3-6

We were entirely ready to have God remove all these defects of character.

As we think about God removing our defects of character, we probably find ourselves dwelling on the defects themselves. Removing them may seem to be an overwhelming task—even if God has promised to do the work! We may have a hard time visualizing the beautiful scene where all the defects are gone from our lives. Perhaps, if we could catch a glimpse of life beyond recovery, beyond the defects and the pain, we would shout for joy. What hope is inspired when, by faith, we take hold of our promised future!

The apostle Paul wrote, "And I am sure that God who began the good work within you will keep right on helping you grow in his grace until his task within you is finally finished" (Philippians 1:6). The apostle John wrote, "I heard a loud shout from the throne saying, 'Look, the home of God is now among men, and he will live with them and they will be his people, yes, God himself will be among them. He will wipe away all tears from their eyes, and there shall be no more death, nor sorrow, nor crying, nor pain. All of that has gone forever.' And the one sitting on the throne said, 'See, I am making all things new!' And then he said . . . 'Write this down, for what I tell you is trustworthy and true: It is finished! I am the A and the Z—the Beginning and the End. I will give to the thirsty the springs of the Water of Life—as a gift!'" (Revelation 21:3-6).

One day the defects will be gone and we will be satisfied!

No matter what we face today, God writes the last chapter—there is still hope!

STEP SEVEN

We humbly asked him to remove our shortcomings.

God said, "Come, let's talk this over! . . . No matter how deep the stain of your sins, I can take it out and make you as clean as freshly fallen snow" **(Isaiah 1:18).**

DAY 1 Declared "Not Guilty"

Bible Reading: Romans 3:23-28

We humbly asked him to remove our shortcomings.

What are our shortcomings? We all realize that we have them. Is this just another way of saying that we've fallen short of our personal ideals? At some time, all of us have held high ideals; we've used them to define what we think life should be like. But most of us learned early on that we couldn't measure up to them. And worse yet, we have often fallen short of the expectations of others, and we certainly haven't fulfilled all that God desires of us. Oh, the weight of guilt we carry! Oh, the pain to think of how we've disappointed those we love! Oh, the longing for some way to make up the difference between what we are and what we should be!

The apostle Paul once wrote, "Yes, all have sinned; all fall short of God's glorious ideal; yet now God declares us 'not guilty' of offending him if we trust in Jesus Christ, who in his kindness freely takes away our sins" (Romans 3:23-24). Paul goes on to ask, "Then what can we boast about doing to earn our salvation? Nothing at all. Why? Because our acquittal is not based on our good deeds; it is based on what Christ has done and our faith in him. So it is that we are saved by faith in Christ and not by the good things we do" (3:27-28).

When God removes our shortcomings, he does a great job! "He has removed our sins as far away from us as the east is from the west" (Psalm 103:12). We can trust God to remove our shortcomings, moment by moment, if we humble ourselves to accept his way. That means having faith in Jesus Christ to make up for our lack in both character and action.

No matter how great our sins, God's grace is greater.

DAY 2 Pride Born of Hurt

Bible Reading: Luke 11:5-13

We humbly asked him to remove our shortcomings.

Our pride can keep us from asking for what we need. We may have grown up in families or relationships where we were consistently refused, ignored, or disappointed. No one listened when we asked that our needs be met. Some of us may have reacted by determining to become self-sufficient. We were not going to ask for help. In fact, we were going to strive to never need anyone's help ever again!

It is this type of pride, born of hurt, that will hold us back from asking God to remove our shortcomings. Jesus said, "Keep on asking and you will keep on getting; keep on looking and you will keep on finding; knock and the door will be opened. Everyone who asks, receives; all who seek, find; and the door is opened to everyone who knocks" (Luke 11:9-10). "If a child asks his father for a loaf of bread, will he be given a stone instead? If he asks for fish, will he be given a poisonous snake? Of course not! And if you hard-hearted, sinful men know how to give good gifts to your children, won't your Father in heaven even more certainly give good gifts to those who ask him for them?" (Matthew 7:9-11).

We must come to the place of giving up our prideful self-sufficiency; we must be willing to ask for help. And we can't ask for help just once and be done with it. We must be persistent and ask repeatedly as the needs arise. When we practice Step Seven in this way, we can be assured that our loving heavenly Father will respond by giving us good gifts and by removing our shortcomings.

God promises to lovingly respond when we ask him for help.

DAY 3 Becoming Like Clay

Bible Reading: Jeremiah 18:1-6

We humbly asked him to remove our shortcomings.

Giving up control may be difficult for us. When we get ready for God to remove our shortcomings, we still may want to control how he does it. We're so used to calling the shots that we'll ask for God's help as long as he does it on our terms. We may demand that the changes happen on our timetable, or in the order we feel ready to give them up, or at a speed convenient to us.

God doesn't work that way. That is why humility is such an important part of this step. God told Jeremiah to go to the house of the potter to learn a lesson. Jeremiah said, "I did as he told me, and found the potter working at his wheel. But the jar that he was forming didn't turn out as he wished, so he kneaded it into a lump and started again. Then the Lord said: . . . Can't I do to you as this potter has done to his clay? As the clay is in the potter's hand, so are you in my hand" (Jeremiah 18:3-6). God told Isaiah, "Woe to the man who fights with his Creator. Does the pot argue with its maker? Does the clay dispute with him who forms it, saying, 'Stop, you're doing it wrong!' or the pot exclaim, 'How clumsy can you be!'?" (Isaiah 45:9).

When we put our lives in God's hands he will reshape them as he sees fit. It is our attitude of humility that allows us to accept the fact that he is the Creator. Our new life may be similar to the one we left behind, or entirely different. God is the master craftsman. Whatever he does, we can trust that he will recreate our life beautifully once we get out of his way!

When we ask him to, God reshapes our lives into something wonderful.

DAY 4 Humility Vs. Humiliation

Bible Reading: Luke 14:8-14

We humbly asked him to remove our shortcomings.

No one wants to be disgraced. Maybe one reason we hesitate to ask God to remove our shortcomings is for fear of being humiliated. Perhaps people have put us down or publicly embarrassed us in an attempt to turn us away from our addiction. We wonder if God will do the same if we ask him to change us.

God's goal is not to put us down, but rather to lift us up. He wants us to be spared embarrassment. Jesus showed this when he taught, "If you are invited to a wedding feast, don't always head for the best seat. For if someone more respected than you shows up, the host will bring him over to where you are sitting and say, 'Let this man sit here instead.' And you, embarrassed, will have to take whatever seat is left at the foot of the table! Do this instead—start at the foot; and when your host sees you he will come and say, 'Friend, we have a better place than this for you!' Thus you will be honored in front of all the other guests. For everyone who tries to honor himself shall be humbled; and he who humbles himself shall be honored" (Luke 14:8-11). We are promised, "If you will humble yourselves under the mighty hand of God, in his good time he will lift you up" (1 Peter 5:6).

God's goal is to spare us further humiliation and to lift us up once again to a position of respectability. This will happen at the time he knows is good for us, not necessarily when we feel ready. Our attitude of humility will help us wait for God to restore us in his good time.

Humility is not self-degradation; it is realistic affirmation.

DAY 5 Into the Open

Bible Reading: Philippians 2:5-9

We humbly asked him to remove our shortcomings.

Our pride often causes us to hide behind defenses during the recovery process. We may hide behind our good reputation, our position, or delusions of superiority. We may feel such inner shame that we go overboard to cover up with a self-righteous public identity. Those of us who have tried to protect ourselves in this way will need a dramatic change of attitude.

The apostle Paul wrote, "Your attitude should be the kind that was shown us by Jesus Christ, who, though he was God, did not demand and cling to his rights as God, but laid aside his mighty power and glory, taking the disguise of a slave and becoming like men. And he humbled himself even further, going so far as actually to die a criminal's death on a cross. Yet it was because of this that God raised him up to the heights of heaven and gave him a name which is above every other name" (Philippians 2:5-9). The author of Hebrews wrote, "Keep your eyes on Jesus, our leader and instructor. He was willing to die a shameful death on the cross because of the joy he knew would be his afterwards; and now he sits in the place of honor by the throne of God" (Hebrews 12:2).

We can ask God to change our attitudes. When he deals with our pride, we will be able to stop hiding behind our reputation. We will allow ourselves to become "anonymous," known as just another person struggling with addiction. When we humbly yield to God in recovery, he promises us future honor and the restoration of a good name.

The deeper our relationship with God, the deeper our humility.

DAY 6 Made of Gold

Bible Reading:
2 Timothy
2:20-22

We humbly asked him to remove our shortcomings.

Our shortcomings and character defects can interfere with our ability to make positive contributions. We probably wish God would make our problems disappear in an instant. Then, we think, we could find our purpose in life or be useful once again.

God wants our lives to be worthwhile, but we must remember that truly valuable things take time to purify. Peter reminds us that our faith (reliance upon God for complete recovery) "is being tested as fire tests gold and purifies it" (1 Peter 1:7). When gold is purified it is melted by severe heat. In the molten state, the impurities rise to the surface where they can be skimmed off. The gold is then allowed to cool again and the process is repeated, over and over, until the gold is pure enough for its intended purpose. God will deal with us likewise, continually revealing and removing our shortcomings in an ongoing process.

God is moving us toward a goal. The apostle Paul told Timothy, "In a wealthy home there are dishes made of gold and silver as well as some made from wood and clay. The expensive dishes are used for guests, and the cheap ones are used in the kitchen or to put garbage in. If you stay away from sin you will be like one of these dishes made of purest gold—the very best in the house—so that Christ can use you for his highest purposes" (2 Timothy 2:20-21).

His goal is to help us stay away from sin, one day at a time, as he continues to remove our shortcomings. This lifelong process will purify us and make us useful for God's highest purposes.

Our recovery is a refining process that burns away impurities.

DAY 7 A Humble Heart

Bible Reading: Luke 18:10-14

We humbly asked him to remove our shortcomings.

After examining ourselves closely (as we did in Steps Four, Five, and Six), we may feel cut off from God. Considering the scope of what we have done, we may feel unworthy to ask God for anything. Maybe our problem behaviors are despised as the lowest kind of evil by those whom we consider respectable. We may struggle with self-hatred. Our genuine remorse may cause us to wonder if we even dare approach God to ask for his help.

We are welcome to come to God, even when we feel this way. Jesus told this story: "Two men went to the Temple to pray. One was a proud, self-righteous Pharisee, and the other a cheating tax collector. The proud Pharisee 'prayed' this prayer: 'Thank God, I am not a sinner like everyone else, especially like that tax collector over there! For I never cheat, I don't commit adultery, I go without food twice a week, and I give to God a tenth of everything I earn.' But the corrupt tax collector stood at a distance and dared not even lift his eyes to heaven as he prayed, but beat upon his chest in sorrow, exclaiming, 'God, be merciful to me, a sinner.' I tell you, this sinner, not the Pharisee, returned home forgiven!" (Luke 18:10-14).

Tax collectors were among the most despised members of Jewish society. Pharisees, on the other hand, commanded the highest respect. Jesus purposely chose this illustration to show that it doesn't matter where we fit in society's hierarchy. It is the humble heart that opens the door to God's forgiveness.

As we humbly seek God each day, we will discover his mercy.

DAY 8 A Forgiven Past

Bible Reading: Psalm 103:1-16

We humbly asked him to remove our shortcomings.

We may have a hard time believing in God's forgiveness. We may think, *After all I've done, I don't feel like I should expect anyone to completely forgive me*. Maybe we feel that we've done such horrible things, or hurt people so badly, that there's no way our sins could ever be erased entirely. Even if we could be forgiven, who could ever forget the things we've done?

When we think of people we know—the people we've hurt—perhaps these fears are well founded. But when it comes to forgiveness from God, we need to remember that his ways are higher than man's ways. The psalmist wrote, "He [God] has not punished us as we deserve for all our sins, for his mercy toward those who fear and honor him is as great as the height of the heavens above the earth. He has removed our sins as far away from us as the east is from the west" (Psalm 103:10-12). God has said, "Come, let's talk this over! . . . No matter how deep the stain of your sins, I can take it out and make you as clean as freshly fallen snow. Even if you are stained as red as crimson, I can make you white as wool!" (Isaiah 1:18). "I, yes, I alone am he who blots away your sins for my own sake and will never think of them again" (Isaiah 43:25).

Part of our recovery is to accept complete forgiveness from God. When we come to God through the atoning blood of Jesus Christ, his forgiveness is complete. We may keep track of our failures, adding every fall to the long list we carry against ourselves. But God doesn't keep lists of our past sins; in his eyes we are clean.

Because God forgives and forgets, we need never wallow in the forgiven past.

DAY 9 God's Sensitivity

Bible Reading: Isaiah 42:1-7

We humbly asked him to remove our shortcomings.

Dealing with our own failings and weaknesses can be discouraging. Sometimes it doesn't seem fair that we have to face life with the burdens and emptiness we feel. Some of the things we've experienced have left us bruised and broken. The flame of hope seems to be wavering. In times when we feel weak like this, we need someone else to encourage us that God can make up for the injustices we've endured and the shortcomings we have.

God sent Jesus to meet our needs: "See my servant, whom I uphold; my Chosen One, in whom I delight. I have put my Spirit upon him; he will reveal justice to the nations of the world. He will be gentle—he will not shout nor quarrel in the streets. He will not break the bruised reed, nor quench the dimly burning flame. He will encourage the fainthearted, those tempted to despair. He will see full justice given to all who have been wronged" (Isaiah 42:1-3).

When we humbly ask God to remove our shortcomings we can point out the areas where we are hurting: "Here's where I'm bruised. This is where the light is dim and I can't see the way. Here's where I'm fainthearted and tempted to despair. This is where there has been a shortage of justice during the times I've been wronged and no one protected me." God gave this mission to Jesus: "You will open the eyes of the blind, and release those who sit in prison darkness and despair" (42:7). This is what God longs to do for us.

When you feel broken, bruised, or worthless, God gently picks you up and surrounds you with his care.

DAY 10 A New Freedom

Bible Reading: Isaiah 49:8-12

We humbly asked him to remove our shortcomings.

Many of us have lived life with a recurrent sense of dissatisfaction. There's a hunger and thirst inside that just can't be filled. Our problems seem like mountains, far too big for us to scale. Our own shortcomings seem like deep, dark valleys; they lead us away from all the positive goals we've set. We set out to deal with the mountains in life and find ourselves going down into the deep valleys of old patterns and addictions. Will we ever break free and find a better way?

God has said, "I am saying to the prisoners of darkness, 'Come out! I am giving you your freedom!' They will be my sheep, grazing in green pastures and on the grassy hills. They shall neither hunger nor thirst; the searing sun and scorching desert winds will not reach them any more. For the Lord in his mercy will lead them beside the cool waters. And I will make my mountains into level paths for them; the highways shall be raised above the valleys" (Isaiah 49:9-11).

God can free us from the constant hunger and thirst by providing new sources of nourishment for our souls. In his mercy, he will provide refreshing streams to satisfy us deeply. With God's help, some of the problems that now seem insurmountable will become approachable. He will help us find alternate routes to our goals without having to go back down the paths of addiction. We still have to face life's ups and downs. We still have to take the steps forward. But he can show us a new highway, above the valleys, which will lead us to where we want to go.

True freedom is discovered as God nourishes the hunger in our souls.

DAY 11 Irresistable Love

Bible Reading: Isaiah 53:1-6

We humbly asked him to remove our shortcomings.

Maybe we haven't given much thought to what it would take to remove our sins. It seems like once we've failed, or once our shortcomings have become evident, there is nothing that can really compensate for them. And yet we know the guilt and pain that come from continuing as we have in the past.

In God's eyes, our sins and shortcomings are very important. He can't just pretend that sin is all right. He knows the human suffering that results and longs to free us by removing the guilt and sin. Let's take a moment to consider what he went through in order to remove our shortcomings. "We despised him and rejected him—a man of sorrows, acquainted with bitterest grief. We turned our backs on him and looked the other way when he went by. He was despised, and we didn't care. Yet it was *our* grief he bore, *our* sorrows that weighed him down. And we thought his troubles were a punishment from God, for his *own* sins! But he was wounded and bruised for *our* sins. He was beaten that we might have peace; he was lashed—and we were healed! *We*—every one of us—have strayed away like sheep! *We*, who left God's paths to follow our own. Yet God laid on *him* the guilt and sins of every one of us!" (Isaiah 53:3-6).

Removing our sins was, and still is, very important to God. It cost him a great deal to purchase the gift of forgiveness, which he offers freely to us. It is a humbling experience to ponder what it took for God to be able to remove our shortcomings. How can we resist such love?

Since God has already overcome our shortcomings, we can approach him with both himility and confidence.

DAY 12 The Power of Asking

Bible Reading:
Isaiah 53:10-12

We humbly asked him to remove our shortcomings.

Most of us probably feel that since we don't really have a great relationship with God, we don't really have the grounds to expect him to remove our shortcomings. We may still see ourselves in a negative light. We may wonder why in the world God would do this for us.

Here's why: "It was the Lord's good plan to bruise him [Jesus] and fill him with grief. However when his soul has been made an offering for sin, then he shall have a multitude of children, many heirs. He shall live again and God's program shall prosper in his hands. And when he sees all that is accomplished by the anguish of his soul, he shall be satisfied; and because of what he has experienced, my righteous Servant shall make many to be counted righteous before God, for he shall bear all their sins" (Isaiah 53:10-11). The apostle Paul said, "For his Holy Spirit speaks to us deep in our hearts, and tells us that we really are God's children" (Romans 8:16).

We can expect God to remove our shortcomings because of all Jesus went through to make us righteous. Upon receiving Christ, we become children of God and heirs to many privileges. If we don't have this sense "deep in our hearts," perhaps we should consider whether we've accepted God's gift of forgiveness (see John 1:12). We may not feel like children of God, especially after a fall, but we can be sure that his promises are true. He offers new life and the removal of shortcomings to everyone willing to accept his offer.

The removal of our shortcomings is God's work alone—we only need to ask.

DAY 13 Clearing the Mess

Bible Reading: Isaiah 57:12-19

We humbly asked him to remove our shortcomings.

In many ways Step Seven represents a turning point in our recovery. It forms a bridge between the inner work of the first six steps and the final steps, which emphasize outer work—changes in behavior. Our shortcomings may seem to clutter the road out of our past. Just because we're working the steps doesn't mean that our lives are as they should be. Will God really come into the mess and lead us out?

"I will say, Rebuild the road! Clear away the rocks and stones. Prepare a glorious highway for my people's return from captivity. The high and lofty One who inhabits eternity, the Holy One, says this: I live in that high and holy place where those with contrite, humble spirits dwell; and I refresh the humble and give new courage to those with repentant hearts. . . . I have seen what they do, but I will heal them anyway! I will lead them and comfort them, helping them to mourn and to confess their sins" (Isaiah 57:14-15, 18).

God is a great help when it comes to clearing the way to a better future. He looks forward to removing our shortcomings so that we can better avoid being tripped up. When we come to him with humility, admitting that we still struggle with many of our shortcomings, he refreshes us and gives us the courage we need to go on. He isn't put off by the things we do. He sees what we do, but chooses to heal us anyway! He'll keep leading us toward recovery, one step at a time. He'll comfort us when we face sorrow and walk with us all the way.

God has seen the things we do, and he promises to heal us anyway!

DAY 14 God's Mercy

Bible Reading: Isaiah 64:5-9

We humbly asked him to remove our shortcomings.

When it comes to asking God to remove our shortcomings, we probably either feel like a professional sinner who is the scum of the earth and has no right to ask anything from him, or we feel like we're one of the godly ones, who sins occasionally (everybody does) but always tries to live a good life.

The prophet Isaiah said, "You [God] welcome those who cheerfully do good, who follow godly ways. But we are not godly; we are constant sinners and have been all our lives. Therefore your wrath is heavy on us. How can such as we be saved? We are all infected and impure with sin. When we put on our prized robes of righteousness we find they are but filthy rags. Like autumn leaves we fade, wither, and fall. And our sins, like the wind, sweep us away. Yet no one calls upon your name or pleads with you for mercy. Therefore you have . . . turned us over to our sins. And yet, O Lord, you are our Father. We are the clay and you are the Potter. We are all formed by your hand" (Isaiah 64:5-8).

Those of us who feel like the "bad guys" may not call on God because we still feel disqualified. If we do call on God, we have the advantage of recognizing our need for God's mercy. Those of us who feel like a "good guy" probably call on God often, and pride ourselves for doing so. The obstacle for us is that we may not plead for God's mercy, because we're not convinced we really need it. We all need to humbly plead for God's mercy. When we do, he can reshape us, leaving our shortcomings out of the formula.

God rejects us when we come brandishing our "good works"; he accepts us when we come seeking his mercy.

DAY 15 Knowing God

Bible Reading:
2 Peter 1:2-4

We humbly asked him to remove our shortcomings.

As we work through recovery, humility develops naturally as we realize our powerlessness over life, even over ourselves. We want a good life and we want our character to change in ways that will make this possible. In asking God to remove our shortcomings, we dare to reach out to the One who has the power we need.

The apostle Peter was a man with many admitted character flaws. His relationship with Jesus brought him face to face with his own weaknesses. He found that he wasn't able to live up to his own values, let alone the values of Jesus. But God dramatically changed his character to the point that he began to reflect the very character of Jesus. He left us with this advice: "Do you want more and more of God's kindness and peace? Then learn to know him better and better. For as you know him better, he will give you, through his great power, everything you need for living a truly good life: he even shares his own glory and his own goodness with us! And by that same mighty power he has given us all the other rich and wonderful blessings he promised; for instance, the promise to save us from the lust and rottenness all around us, and to give us his own character" (2 Peter 1:2-4).

This is Peter's secret for discovering the good life: Get to know God better and better. It is a growing love relationship with God that will open the door to a life untainted by our present character flaws. God has the mighty power to give us everything we need; and everything we need is found in him as he instills his character in us.

The power of recovery doesn't come from within; it comes from knowing God better and better.

DAY 16 Eyes of Love

Bible Reading: Hebrews 12:10-13

We humbly asked him to remove our shortcomings.

Most of us probably aren't used to getting the things we ask for. How can we have confidence that God will hear our prayers? How do we know he will answer when we ask him to remove our shortcomings?

The apostle Paul wrote, "Long ago, even before he made the world, God chose us to be his very own, through what Christ would do for us; he decided then to make us holy in his eyes, without a single fault—we who stand before him covered with his love" (Ephesians 1:4). God's primary goal is to make us holy, that is, to paint his character into our lives. Looking through the eyes of love, he already sees us as we will look when his work is done. Then he works out his goals for us in the arena of everyday life. The Bible tells us: God's correction is always right and for our best good, that we may share his holiness" (Hebrews 12:10). We can be sure that our holiness—the removal of our shortcomings—is God's will.

The apostle John wrote, "And we are sure of this, that he will listen to us whenever we ask him for anything in line with his will. And if we really know he is listening when we talk to him and make our requests, then we can be sure that he will answer" (1 John 5:14-15).

It is clearly God's will to have our shortcomings removed. And he has promised to give us anything we ask for within his will. Therefore, we can have full confidence that God will remove our shortcomings in his time.

We can ask with confidence because God looks at us with eyes of love.

DAY 17 In God's Time

Bible Reading: 2 Peter 3:8-9

We humbly asked him to remove our shortcomings.

We may be impatient to have our weaknesses and shortcomings removed immediately. It's hard to struggle along, feeling we don't have what it takes to live the life God wants for us. We may wish that he would just wave his magic wand, and *poof!* . . . a perfect person!

The Bible makes it clear that it is God's plan to perfect us. But it is also clear that God doesn't always work according to our timetable. Even the birth of the Messiah had to wait until "the right time." The apostle Paul wrote, "But when the right time came, the time God decided on, he sent his Son, born of a woman, born as a Jew, to buy freedom for us who were slaves to the law so that he could adopt us as his very own sons" (Galatians 4:4-5).

The apostle Peter left us another reminder: "But don't forget this, dear friends, that a day or a thousand years from now is like tomorrow to the Lord. He isn't really being slow about his promised return, even though it sometimes seems that way. But he is waiting, for the good reason that he is not willing that any should perish, and he is giving more time for sinners to repent" (2 Peter 3:8-9).

God has "the right time" planned for us, too. He takes everything into account when he decides how and when our prayers will be answered. It may seem like he's too slow in fulfilling his promises. But we can be sure that if he is slow in acting, it's for a good reason. In the meantime, he supplies the strength we need to continue in recovery, even with our shortcomings.

However long our road to recovery, with God we're always "right on time."

DAY 18 A Thorough Washing

Bible Reading:
1 Peter 3:18-21

We humbly asked him to remove our shortcomings.

When we ask God to remove our shortcomings, we show that we want our sins to be washed away. We may be burdened by what we've learned about ourselves while working the previous steps. We may feel dirty, and trapped; unable to make a break from our old life.

God realizes our need to feel clean and new. He has given us the command to accomplish this through baptism. The ceremonial dipping in water symbolically demonstrates our desire to have our sins or shortcomings washed away. The apostle Peter explained it this way: "In baptism we show that we have been saved from death and doom by the resurrection of Christ; not because our bodies are washed clean by the water, but because in being baptized we are turning to God and asking him to cleanse our *hearts* from sin" (1 Peter 3:21).

In describing his own conversion, the apostle Paul said, "A man named Ananias . . . came to me, and standing beside me said, . . . 'The God of our fathers has chosen you to know his will and to see the Messiah and hear him speak. You are to take his message everywhere, telling what you have seen and heard. And now, why delay? Go and be baptized, and be cleansed from your sins, calling on the name of the Lord'" (Acts 22:12-16).

Some of us may never have been baptized, but the Bible urges us to do so. God has prescribed this special act for our healing. Baptism demonstrates our exit from an old life and our entrance into a new one. Why delay?

As we humbly ask God to remove our sins, he promises to wash and cleanse our hearts.

DAY 19 Breaking the Pattern

Bible Reading: Romans 6:1-4

We humbly asked him to remove our shortcomings.

We want to believe that there's another kind of life available to us. We don't want to continue sinning, watching our lives being ruined. We vividly recall the baffling power sin has held over us in the past. Why should we believe that this power can be broken? How can we hope for freedom in the future?

As the apostle Paul taught about God's grace, some of his listeners asked this question: "Well then, shall we keep on sinning so that God can keep on showing us more and more kindness and forgiveness?" Paul replied like this: "Of course not! Should we keep on sinning when we don't have to? For sin's power over us was broken when we became Christians and were baptized to become a part of Jesus Christ; through his death the power of your sinful nature was shattered. Your old sin-loving nature was buried with him by baptism when he died; and when God the Father, with glorious power, brought him back to life again, you were given his wonderful new life to enjoy" (Romans 6:1-4).

When we choose to obey God by being baptized, we're symbolizing a spiritual truth. The nature inside us, which was bound to sin, has been united with Jesus at the crucifixion. When he died, it died. When we're covered by water in baptism, that symbolizes the burial of our old sin nature. When we come up from the water, that symbolizes our resurrection to a new way of life. Being united with Christ in his death and resurrection gives us the opportunity to live free from bondage to sin.

When we become one with Jesus Christ, the power of our past is broken.

DAY 20 A Major Miracle

Bible Reading: Joshua 10:5-15

We humbly asked him to remove our shortcomings.

At this point in recovery, we may feel that nothing short of a major miracle will win the battles we face. We may have been badly beaten as we tried to fight our addictions in the past. We probably concluded that we were too weak to win. What could be different now that will bring victory over our shortcomings?

When we fight alone, we are too weak to win. But if we call on the Lord to fight with us, it's a different story. Joshua was called upon to help an ally fight against several attacking enemies. "'Don't be afraid of them,' the Lord said to Joshua, 'for they are already defeated! I have given them to you to destroy'" (Joshua 10:8). Just as God promised, Israel won a decisive victory. "As the men of Israel were pursuing and harassing the foe, Joshua prayed aloud, 'Let the sun stand still over Gibeon, and let the moon stand in its place over the valley of Aijalon!' And the sun and the moon didn't move until the Israeli army had finished the destruction of its enemies! . . . The Lord stopped the sun and moon—all because of the prayer of one man. But the Lord was fighting for Israel" (Joshua 10:12-14).

It may take a major miracle to overcome the foes we face; but God is in the miracle business! He declares that every shortcoming is already defeated and given to us to destroy. When we call out to God for help in the heat of battle, we can have confidence in receiving his help. When the Lord is fighting for us, he won't stop until all our shortcomings are wiped out!

When we feel discouraged we must remember that God has already won the battle.

STEP SEVEN

DAY 21 Supportive Friends

Bible Reading: Mark 2:1-12

We humbly asked him to remove our shortcomings.

Our personal weaknesses can cripple our lives, leaving us handicapped. Some of us have lived a long time in this condition. We've come to the point of not being able to go to God for help on our own. We may need to rely on the help and the faith of others who don't have the same handicaps we do. They may be able to take us to where we can receive God's healing touch.

Here's a relevant story: While Jesus was preaching at a crowded house, "four men arrived carrying a paralyzed man on a stretcher. They couldn't get to Jesus through the crowd, so they dug through the clay roof above his head and lowered the sick man on his stretcher, right down in front of Jesus. When Jesus saw how strongly they believed that he would help, Jesus said to the sick man, 'Son, your sins are forgiven!' . . . Then, turning to the paralyzed man, he commanded, 'Pick up your stretcher and go on home, for you are healed!'" (Mark 2:3-5, 11).

This man faced what seemed like insurmountable obstacles in his hope for recovery. His friends risked embarrassment to carry him to the place where he could receive forgiveness and wholeness. If we are crippled by our addictions and personal "handicaps," the road to healing may be more difficult for us than for others who don't have the same shortcomings. We may have to rely on friends to carry us until we receive the healing that will make us able to move out on our own two feet.

While in recovery we often need the support and help from friends to bring about our healing.

DAY 22 A Singular Focus

Bible Reading: Mark 10:46-52

We humbly asked him to remove our shortcomings.

We may face a special challenge as we seek recovery: there may be people watching us who don't believe we'll ever make it. If this is so, we'll need the humility to aggressively seek help despite the added distraction of people looking on. They may treat us with disrespect and tell us to give up our hopes of healing. But we don't have to listen!

Think about this story: "Later, as they [Jesus and his disciples] left town, a great crowd was following. Now it happened that a blind beggar named Bartimaeus . . . was sitting beside the road as Jesus was going by. When Bartimaeus heard that Jesus from Nazareth was near, he began to shout out, 'Jesus, Son of David, have mercy on me!' 'Shut up!' some of the people yelled at him. But he only shouted the louder, again and again, 'O Son of David, have mercy on me!' When Jesus heard him he stopped there in the road and said, 'Tell him to come here.' So they called the blind man. 'You lucky fellow,' they said, 'come on, he's calling you!' Bartimaeus yanked off his old coat and flung it aside, jumped up and came to Jesus. 'What do you want me to do for you?' Jesus asked. 'O Teacher,' the blind man said, 'I want to see!' And Jesus said to him, 'All right, it's done. Your faith has healed you.' And instantly the blind man could see, and followed Jesus down the road!" (Mark 10:46-52).

We, too, need to keep calling out for God's help regardless of the negative responses of those around us. He'll hear our earnest cry and heal us, to the astonishment of those who say it'll never happen!

Recovery and healing is our primary task; let no one distract us from it!

STEP SEVEN

DAY 23 New Hearts

Bible Reading: Ezekiel 36:22-27	We humbly asked him to remove our shortcomings.

We may feel like we don't deserve God's help because of the way our behavior has tarnished his reputation. These feelings may be especially strong if we were Christians while we were acting out our addictions. Can we really expect God's help again after we've let him down?

The people of Israel were created to represent the Lord to the rest of the world. But instead of obeying him and making him proud of them, they embarrassed him by worshiping idols and behaving in sinful ways. But the Lord didn't give up on them. He spoke through the prophet Ezekiel: "Therefore say to the people of Israel, 'The Lord God says: I am bringing you back again but not because you deserve it; I am doing it to protect my holy name which you tarnished among the nations. . . . Your filthiness will be washed away, your idol worship gone. And I will give you a new heart—I will give you new and right desires—and put a new spirit within you. I will take out your stony hearts of sin and give you new hearts of love. And I will put my Spirit within you so that you will obey my laws and do whatever I command'" (Ezekiel 36:22, 25-27).

God will deliver us from our shortcomings to bring glory to his name, not because we deserve it. When people see how much God does for us, they may believe that he can help them, too. If we've tarnished his reputation, he has the power to restore us in a way that will make up for the damage and bring glory to himself.

Our continued recovery, even when we've suffered a relapse, brings great honor to God.

DAY 24 A Good Future

Bible Reading: Titus 2:11-14

We humbly asked him to remove our shortcomings.

We can hope for recovery in spirit, mind, and body. In the past we may have concluded that we just couldn't change. But by now, our attitude may be changing; we may have come to believe there is a way out. This hopeful disposition will help us to turn to God and begin again. Perhaps for the first time, we can now look forward to a future filled with promised blessings.

"May the God of peace himself make you entirely pure and devoted to God; and may your spirit and soul and body be kept strong and blameless until that day when our Lord Jesus Christ comes back again. God, who called you to become his child, will do all this for you, just as he promised" (1 Thessalonians 5:23-24).

"For the free gift of eternal salvation is now being offered to everyone; and along with this gift comes the realization that God wants us to turn from godless living and sinful pleasures and to live good, God-fearing lives day after day, looking forward to that wonderful time we've been expecting, when his glory shall be seen. . . . He died under God's judgment against our sins, so that he could rescue us from constant falling into sin and make us his very own people, with cleansed hearts and real enthusiasm for doing kind things for others" (Titus 2:11-14).

God has promised us a wonderful future. In the present, he's in the process of rescuing us from constantly falling into sin. Our willingness to let go of the past and our expectations for good things in the future will help in our recovery.

We have great hope, because the power we need to recover comes from Jesus Christ, the greatest of healers.

DAY 25 Filling Our Needs

Bible Reading: Ephesians 3:14-19

We humbly asked him to remove our shortcomings.

Identifying our shortcomings should help to clarify our needs. We need resources, inner strength, love, direction, and power. And we don't just need these things once, we need them to be replenished constantly because it seems that we keep running out.

The apostle Paul prayed, "Out of his [God's] glorious, unlimited resources he will give you the mighty inner strengthening of his Holy Spirit. And I pray that Christ will be more and more at home in your hearts, living within you as you trust in him. May your roots go down deep into the soil of God's marvelous love; and may you be able to . . . experience this love for yourselves, though it is so great that you will never see the end of it or fully know or understand it. And so at last you will be filled up with God himself" (Ephesians 3:16-19).

"Don't act thoughtlessly, but try to find out and do whatever the Lord wants you to. Don't drink too much wine, for many evils lie along that path; be filled instead with the Holy Spirit, and controlled by him" (5:17-18).

The word *filled* in these passages means "to fill up completely" or "to make full." The verb tense used indicates that this is an ongoing process—we are to be filled up continually. True recovery only comes as we find a way to fill up the needs in our lives. Wherever we are short, God has the resources, love, direction, strength, and power to meet our needs. We can invite the Holy Spirit to fill us up every day.

God's love reaches into every corner of our experience.

DAY 26 Continuing Forward

Bible Reading: Colossians 1:9-14

We humbly asked him to remove our shortcomings.

Even when our recovery is progressing and we're doing well, we will face difficulties that may upset us. If we come from a dysfunctional family, our loved ones who are not in recovery will continue to experience problems and crises that will touch our lives. We need to have a source of constant contact with God so that we can keep on going no matter what happens.

The apostle Paul wrote, "So ever since we first heard about you we have kept on praying and asking God to help you understand what he wants you to do; asking him to make you wise about spiritual things; and asking that the way you live will always please the Lord and honor him, so that you will always be doing good, kind things for others, while all the time you are learning to know God better and better. We are praying, too, that you will be filled with his mighty, glorious strength so that you can keep going no matter what happens—always full of the joy of the Lord, and always thankful to the Father who has made us fit to share all the wonderful things that belong to those who live in the Kingdom of light. For he has rescued us out of the darkness and gloom of Satan's kingdom and brought us into the Kingdom of his dear Son, who bought our freedom with his blood and forgave us all our sins" (Colossians 1:9-14).

We need to be continually asking God to remove our shortcomings and fill us up. He can give us the joy, strength, thankfulness, wisdom, and spiritual understanding to handle whatever happens.

Filled with his glorious strength, we can keep going no matter what happens.

DAY 27 A Healing Fire

Bible Reading:
1 Peter 4:12-13

We humbly asked him to remove our shortcomings.

We all know how deeply imbedded some of our shortcomings are. When we're ready to let God remove them, we must be willing to let him do whatever it takes to get the job done.

When we ask God to remove our shortcomings and purify us, we should be prepared to take some heat. The best way to purify something precious is to melt it down with fire. Even in the Old Testament God commanded that precious metals be passed through fire for ceremonial purification. "Anything that will stand heat—such as gold, silver, bronze . . . shall be passed through fire in order to be made ceremonially pure" (Numbers 31:22-23).

Throughout the Bible there are allusions to God using fire to purify us. The apostle Peter wrote, "Dear friends, don't be bewildered or surprised when you go through fiery trials ahead, for this is no strange, unusual thing that is going to happen to you. Instead, be really glad—because these trials will make you partners with Christ in his suffering, and afterwards you will have the wonderful joy of sharing in his glory in that coming day when it will be displayed" (1 Peter 4:12-13). The author of Hebrews wrote, "Being punished isn't enjoyable while it is happening—it hurts! But afterwards we can see the result, a quiet growth in grace and character" (Hebrews 12:11).

God only uses fire on things that can take the heat and come out better in the end. He doesn't send trials to destroy us, but rather to purify us and develop our character. The fire hurts, but in the end it leaves something beautiful in our lives.

God can create something beautiful out of the ruined past.

DAY 28 God Our Helper

Bible Reading:
Exodus 3:1-12

We humbly asked him to remove our shortcomings.

The thought of facing life without an addictive "crutch" may be frightening. Most of us have suffered from feelings of inadequacy for most of our lives. Our addictions have helped us to deal with our inadequacies.

Even Moses felt inadequate at times. When God called him to free the Israelites from slavery in Egypt, he felt incompetent for the task. "'But I'm not the person for a job like that!' Moses exclaimed. . . . 'O Lord, I'm just not a good speaker. . . . I have a speech impediment.' 'Who makes mouths?' Jehovah asked him. 'Isn't it I, the Lord? Who makes a man so that he can speak or not speak, see or not see, hear or not hear? Now go ahead and do as I tell you, for I will help you to speak well, and I will tell you what to say.' But Moses said, 'Lord, please! Send someone else.' Then the Lord became angry. 'All right,' he said, 'your brother Aaron is a good speaker. . . . So I will tell you what to tell him, and I will help both of you to speak well, and I will tell you what to do'" (Exodus 3:11; 4:10-15).

God has the power to make up for any inadequacies we might have. He has the power to heal and transform our abilities. He can give us confidence in situations that are intimidating. If we still feel inadequate, even with God's promised presence and help, he is willing to give us someone to go with us and help us. That companion may be the Holy Spirit or a person who has what it takes to compensate for our shortcomings.

When God is with us, no situation is too difficult or too frightening.

STEP SEVEN

DAY 29 Strength from Humility

Bible Reading: Isaiah 6:1-7

We humbly asked him to remove our shortcomings.

If we want to experience humility and have a sincere desire to have our shortcomings removed, we need to seek after God. When we catch a glimpse of his holiness, we will be humbled and transformed.

The prophet Isaiah shares this experience: "The year King Uzziah died I saw the Lord! He was sitting on a lofty throne, and the Temple was filled with his glory. Hovering about him were mighty, six-winged angels of fire. . . . They sang, 'Holy, holy, holy is the Lord Almighty; the whole earth is filled with his glory.' Such singing it was! It shook the Temple to its foundations, and suddenly the entire sanctuary was filled with smoke. Then I said, 'My doom is sealed, for I am a foul-mouthed sinner, a member of a sinful, foul-mouthed race; and I have looked upon the King, the Lord of heaven's armies.' Then one of the mighty angels flew over to the altar and with a pair of tongs picked out a burning coal. He touched my lips with it and said, 'Now you are pronounced "not guilty" because this coal has touched your lips. Your sins are all forgiven'" (Isaiah 6:1-7).

Isaiah's experience took the form of a supernatural vision. At just a glimpse of God's holiness, he became acutely aware of his own deep need for cleansing. We may never see God as Isaiah did, but we can experience God's presence in a place of worship. As we develop the habit of worshiping God, we will find growing humility in our lives and a growing desire to have him purify us fully.

How amazing that we can see God's greatness and our contrasting sinfulness, yet still experience his forgiveness!

DAY 30 Weakness Transformed

Bible Reading:
1 Samuel
17:17-51

We humbly asked him to remove our shortcomings.

As we look at ourselves, we may see more shortcomings than we really have. And we may be underestimating the unique gifts God has given us. Some of the things we beg God to remove may have a good side to them that we just haven't grown to appreciate yet.

Young David went to visit his older brothers at the battlefield. When he heard the taunts of the giant, Goliath, he was ready for a fight. When David asked to be sent out to fight the giant, King Saul said, "Don't be ridiculous! . . . You are only a boy" (1 Samuel 17:33). Saul finally gave in to David's requests. "Then Saul gave David his own armor. . . . David put it on, strapped the sword over it, and took a step or two to see what it was like. . . . 'I can hardly move!' he exclaimed, and took them off again. Then he picked up five smooth stones from a stream and put them in his shepherd's bag and, armed only with his shepherd's staff and sling, started across to Goliath" (17:38-40). David used the stones and sling to kill the giant.

The things that appeared to be David's shortcomings were actually strengths. While growing up, David learned to compensate for his small stature by learning to use the slingshot to protect the flocks. Some of our apparent shortcomings may have taught us to compensate in positive ways. They may work for us and don't need to be removed. They just need to be reframed in our thinking and handed over to God for his purposes.

When seen from God's perspective, even some of our shortcomings can become strengths.

STEP EIGHT

We made a list of all persons we had harmed and became willing to make amends to them all.

***Jesus taught, "If you are . . . offering a sacrifice to God, and suddenly remember that a friend has something against you, . . . go and apologize and be reconciled to him"* (Matthew 5:23-24).**

DAY 1 Forgiven to Forgive

Bible Reading: Matthew 18:23-35

We made a list of all persons we had harmed and became willing to make amends to them all.

Listing all the people we've harmed will probably trigger a natural defensiveness. With each name we put on our list, another mental list may begin to form—a list of the wrongs that have been done against us. How can we deal with the resentment we hold toward others, so we can move toward making amends?

Jesus told a story: "A king . . . decided to bring his accounts up to date. In the process, one of his debtors was brought in who owed him $10 million!" (Matthew 18:23-24). The man begged for forgiveness. "Then the king was filled with pity for him and released him and forgave his debt. But when the man left the king, he went to a man who owed him $2,000 and grabbed him by the throat and demanded instant payment" (18:27-28). This was reported to the king. "And the king called before him the man he had forgiven and said, 'You evil-hearted wretch! Here I forgave you all that tremendous debt, just because you asked me to—shouldn't you have mercy on others? . . .' Then the angry king sent the man to the torture chamber until he had paid every last penny due. So shall my heavenly Father do to you," Jesus said, "if you refuse to truly forgive your brothers" (18:32-35).

When we look at all that God has forgiven us, it makes sense to choose to forgive others. This also frees us from the torture of festering resentment. We can't change what they did to us, but we can write off their debt and become willing to make amends.

The value we place on God's forgiveness is best measured by our willingness to forgive others.

DAY 2 Grace-Filled Living

Bible Reading: Romans 12:17-21

We made a list of all persons we had harmed and became willing to make amends to them all.

Most of us probably have relationships in which we are holding grudges. Sure, we've hurt them, but they've hurt us, too. We become like children quarreling back and forth: "You hit me first!" "I did not!" Somehow, it just doesn't seem fair to let them off the hook! Now, we're supposed to become willing to make amends to everyone? Even those who have wronged us? How?

The apostle Paul left us this advice: "Never pay back evil for evil. Do things in such a way that everyone can see you are honest clear through. Don't quarrel with anyone. Be at peace with everyone, just as much as possible. Dear friends, never avenge yourselves. Leave that to God, for he has said that he will repay those who deserve it. . . . Instead, feed your enemy if he is hungry. If he is thirsty give him something to drink. . . . Don't let evil get the upper hand, but conquer evil by doing good" (Romans 12:17-21).

This is not impossible. We are not called to create peace, only to be at peace "as much as possible." We are not required to say that others don't deserve punishment, only to turn the job over to God. We don't give up a quarrel because someone else is necessarily right, but for the sake of our recovery. We can't change other people, but we can ask God for the courage to change ourselves.

This may seem all backwards, but God's ways are not our ways. As we turn our will and our lives over to God, we will learn that his ways do work.

If we've really experienced God's grace, we'll want to pass it on to others.

DAY 3 Overcoming Loneliness

Bible Reading: Ecclesiastes 4:9-12

We made a list of all persons we had harmed and became willing to make amends to them all.

Feelings of loneliness and isolation go along with the guilt and shame we feel about who we are or what we've done. We may feel so cut off from others that we feel lonely even when we're around other people. Our fear of being hurt, our guilt and self-hatred, can make us unable to believe in the love others have for us. We can feel all alone in the struggle even when there are people beside us who love us and want to help. Being willing to let their love in is part of our preparation for making amends.

Wise King Solomon observed: "Two can accomplish more than twice as much as one, for the results can be much better. If one falls, the other pulls him up; but if a man falls when he is alone, he's in trouble. Also, on a cold night, two under the same blanket gain warmth from each other, but how can one be warm alone? And one standing alone can be attacked and defeated, but two can stand back-to-back and conquer; three is even better, for a triple-braided cord is not easily broken" (Ecclesiastes 4:9-12).

Loneliness can break us and defeat our recovery process. When we prepare to make amends, we also need to prepare our hearts to accept whatever love, support, or friendship is offered in return. These supportive relationships, along with the third "strand" of God's supporting hand, will strengthen our lives considerably.

Making amends builds relationships, releasing the healing power of human companionship.

DAY 4 Scapegoats

Bible Reading: Leviticus 16:20-22

We made a list of all persons we had harmed and became willing to make amends to them all.

It's natural to hope that the people we've hurt will think better of us once we've sought to make amends. We may fear that there are some who will never upgrade their opinions about us, no matter what we do. In reality they may not, especially if they have chosen to use us as a scapegoat.

Before the coming of Jesus, the Jews were instructed to select a live goat which would carry away their sins. (When Jesus came, he became our scapegoat and took our sins upon himself.) The priest was to place his hands on this goat and confess over it all the sins of the people. "He [the priest] shall lay all their sins upon the head of the goat and send it into the desert, led by a man appointed for the task. So the goat shall carry all the sins of the people into a land where no one lives" (Leviticus 16:21-22).

Some of the people we've hurt will use us as their scapegoat. Since we have hurt them, they feel justified in sending us away with more than our share of the burden. They unconsciously place the blame for their pain on us, so we can carry it away. As their scapegoat, we play the role of removing something they were unable to deal with in any other way. Because of this, they may never welcome us back. We should prepare for this kind of response and realize that it says more about them than it says about us.

At times we will be forced to carry the pain of another; be thankful that God has agreed to do the same for us.

DAY 5 A Forgiving God

Bible Reading: Matthew 6:9-15

We made a list of all persons we had harmed and became willing to make amends to them all.

One motivation for preparing our list and making amends with the people we've hurt is the hope of having a clear conscience. We have lived with self-condemnation and probably hope that making amends will help us find forgiveness. Looking for forgiveness in the wrong places, however, may bring disappointment and give others unwarranted power over us.

The Bible doesn't teach us to go to people to find forgiveness. God is the one who grants forgiveness: "If we confess our sins to him [God], he can be depended on to forgive us and to cleanse us from every wrong" (1 John 1:9). Jesus taught us to pray: "Forgive us our sins, just as we have forgiven those who have sinned against us" (Matthew 6:12). He went on to explain, "Your heavenly Father will forgive you if you forgive those who sin against you; but if *you* refuse to forgive *them, he* will not forgive *you*" (6:14-15).

The purpose for making amends is to take personal responsibility for our behavior and the effect it has had on others. If those people respond by offering forgiveness, that is a nice bonus. Our forgiveness, however, is not in their hands. Forgiveness is with God in Jesus Christ. "For he [God] forgave all your sins, and blotted out the charges proved against you. . . . He took this list of sins and destroyed it by nailing it to Christ's cross. In this way God took away Satan's power to accuse you of sin" (Colossians 2:13-15).

By refusing to make amends, we deny our own sinfulness and our need of God's forgiveness.

DAY 6 The Fruit of Forgiveness

Bible Reading: 2 Corinthians 2:5-8

We made a list of all persons we had harmed and became willing to make amends to them all.

Some of the things we've done have earned us disapproval and possibly a loss of love. We have found that some people in our lives only love us if they can approve of our behavior. We may have struggled with bitterness toward them because we feel like they have been trying to punish us. If our "sins" have been made public, we may assume that we've lost the love of everyone who disapproves of our actions. This fear of rejection might deter us from reaching out to make amends.

In the young Corinthian church, a man was cut off from church fellowship when his sins were made public. After he turned around and tried to make amends, some people refused to welcome him back into the church. The apostle Paul told them: "Remember that . . . man I wrote about, who caused all the trouble. . . . I don't want to be harder on him than I should. He has been punished enough by your united disapproval. Now it is time to forgive him and comfort him. Otherwise he may become so bitter and discouraged that he won't be able to recover. Please show him now that you still do love him very much" (2 Corinthians 2:5-8). Some people will follow this advice and reaffirm their love for you when you go to them.

There will be some people who will respond with forgiveness, comfort, acceptance, and love. This will help us overcome the grief, the bitterness, and the discouragement we may feel. Their forgiveness will help us to move on with our recovery.

When we seek to make amends, we risk rejection; when we fail to do so, we risk losing the joy of forgiveness.

DAY 7 Unintentional Sins

Bible Reading: Leviticus 4:1-28

We made a list of all persons we had harmed and became willing to make amends to them all.

As we allowed our lives to get out of control, we probably hurt people without even realizing it. Many of the people on our list were hurt by our mistakes, not by something we did intentionally. We may not remember hurting some of them, and only realize it when someone points it out. Nevertheless, we still need to take responsibility for our actions by making amends.

When God gave the commandments, he included instructions for handling mistakes as well as intentional sins. He said, "These are the laws concerning anyone who unintentionally breaks any of my commandments. . . . If any one of the common people sins and doesn't realize it, he is guilty. But as soon as he does realize it, he is to bring as his sacrifice a female goat without defect to atone for his sin" (Leviticus 4:2, 27-28). "If by mistake you or future generations fail to carry out all of these regulations that the Lord has given you . . . then when the people realize their error, they must offer one young bull for a burnt offering. . . . And they shall be forgiven; for it was an error, and they have corrected it with their sacrifice" (Numbers 15:22-25).

We are responsible for the way our behavior has affected others. This is true even when we didn't realize we were hurting them. These unintentional sins need to be acknowledged and corrected as soon as we discover them. God forgives all our sins. In the recovery process, however, the unintentional sins need to be accounted for along with the more glaring ones.

Forgiveness from unintentional sins can be a source of unintentional joy.

DAY 8 Reaping Goodness

Bible Reading: Galatians 6:7-10

We made a list of all persons we had harmed and became willing to make amends to them all.

While in recovery, we learn to accept responsibility for our actions, even when we're powerless over our addictions. We come to realize that all our actions yield consequences. Some of us may have deceived ourselves into thinking we could escape the consequences of the things we did. But with time, it becomes clear that God has made accountability a necessary element of healthy human living.

"A man will always reap just the kind of crop he sows! If he sows to please his own wrong desires he will be planting seeds of evil and he will surely reap a harvest of spiritual decay and death; but if he plants the good things of the Spirit, he will reap the everlasting life that the Holy Spirit gives him" (Galatians 6:7-8).

The law of sowing and reaping can also work for us. God spoke through the prophet Hosea: "Plant the good seeds of righteousness and you will reap a crop of my love; plow the hard ground of your hearts, for now is the time to seek the Lord, that he may come and shower salvation upon you" (Hosea 10:12).

God says we *always* reap what we've sown. Even after we've been forgiven, we must deal with the consequences of our actions. It may take a season of time to finish harvesting the negative consequences from our past, but we shouldn't let this discourage us. Making our list of those we've harmed is a step toward planting good seeds. In time we'll see a good crop begin to grow.

Our small, everyday actions can produce long-term consequences for good.

DAY 9 Becoming Responsible

Bible Reading: 1 Thessalonians 4:9-12	**We made a list of all persons we had harmed and became willing to make amends to them all.**

Many of us know what it is like to be a burden on others. It is a common side effect of being controlled by an addictive/compulsive behavior. Sometimes our behaviors have caused us to lose our jobs or have made us unable to hold one down. As a result, we've found ourselves in financial need. This humiliation can affect our families in many ways. We may have caused loved ones great stress and shame because we haven't provided for their needs.

The apostle Paul taught us to follow this standard: "For you well know that you ought to follow our example: you never saw us loafing; we never accepted food from anyone without buying it; we worked hard day and night" (2 Thessalonians 3:7-8). "This should be your ambition: to live a quiet life, minding your own business and doing your own work. . . . [People] will trust and respect you, and you will not need to depend on others for enough money to pay your bills" (1 Thessalonians 4:11-12).

It is important for us to think about how our irresponsibility has affected others. Much pain may have been caused by our failure to provide for our families' needs. We need to reflect on how this failure has caused us to lose their respect and trust. The shame of not facing this aspect of our lives can be terribly discouraging. Once we face this and become willing to make amends, our self-respect will get quite a boost. This step will help us get rid of some of our daily stress, freeing us up to proceed with recovery.

Making amends is a sure way to rediscover our ability to be responsible.

DAY 10 A New Outlook

Bible Reading: Acts 10:10-17

We made a list of all persons we had harmed and became willing to make amends to them all.

Some of the hurt we've caused has resulted from wrong behaviors that can be changed. Some of it, however, has been caused by attitudes and characteristics that are deeply ingrained. They are so much a part of us that we're not sure where they end and where we begin. Can we change these deeply ingrained characteristics?

The apostle Peter was a devout Jew, even after he became a follower of Jesus. One day, as he was praying, "he fell into a trance. He saw the sky open and a great canvas sheet. . . . In the sheet were all sorts of animals, snakes, and birds [forbidden to the Jews for food]. Then a voice said to him, 'Go kill and eat any of them you wish.' 'Never, Lord,' Peter declared, 'I have never in all my life eaten such creatures, for they are forbidden by our Jewish laws.' The voice spoke again, 'Don't contradict God! If he says something is kosher, then it is.' . . . Peter was very perplexed" (Acts 10:10-17). Immediately after this vision passed, a group of non-Jews came and asked him to come and tell them about God. Peter agreed to go to the home of a Gentile, something that just wasn't done by a devout Jew. But the vision had shown him that his old way of life needed to change.

We're free to change by the power of God. We may look at some area of our life and say, "There's no way! I've never been able to do that, and I can't imagine that I ever will." Get ready! If God says we can, there's a whole new world out there.

As we continue in recovery, God is allowed to create something new out of our past.

DAY 11 Our Comforter

Bible Reading: John 16:8-15

We made a list of all persons we had harmed and became willing to make amends to them all.

We may wonder whether a particular name belongs on the list of those we've hurt. We may worry that we won't be able to determine who we've hurt. Or we may hesitate, fearing that our introspection will cause us to condemn ourselves too strongly. But we need not worry; we have a helper to help us handle these problems.

Jesus said, "If you love me, obey me; and I will ask the Father and he will give you another Comforter, and he will never leave you. He is the Holy Spirit, the Spirit who leads into all truth" (John 14:15-17). "And when he has come he will convince the world of its sin, and of the availability of God's goodness and of deliverance from judgment. . . . When the Holy Spirit, who is truth, comes, he shall guide you into all truth, for he will not be presenting his own ideas, but will be passing on to you what he has heard. He will tell you about the future" (John 16:8, 13).

The Holy Spirit is "God with us." We can ask the Holy Spirit to reveal to us all the names of those we have hurt. He will reveal them to us. The Holy Spirit comes to convict us of sin and remind us of God's goodness and deliverance from judgment. He is not there just to condemn us. Each pang of guilt can be given over to God for forgiveness the moment it arises. We don't need to worry about leaving someone off the list. The Holy Spirit can remind us about them later. Just write down everyone who comes to mind, asking God to give you the willingness to make amends.

As we face each new step, God will help us do and understand everything necessary to continue.

DAY 12 Our Debt of Love

Bible Reading: Luke 10:30-37

We made a list of all persons we had harmed and became willing to make amends to them all.

When we're self-consumed or consumed by someone else's addiction, we may hurt others by ignoring their needs.

Jesus told this story: "A Jew going on a trip from Jerusalem to Jericho was attacked by bandits. They stripped him of his clothes and money and beat him up and left him lying half dead beside the road. By chance a Jewish priest came along; and when he saw the man lying there, he crossed to the other side of the road and passed him by. A Jewish Temple-assistant walked over and looked at him lying there, but then went on. But a despised Samaritan came along, and when he saw him, he felt deep pity. Kneeling beside him the Samaritan soothed his wounds with medicine and bandaged them. Then he . . . nursed him through the night" (Luke 10:30-34). Jesus was making the point that it can be hurtful to ignore the needs we see around us. One of the laws of Moses said, "If you see your enemy trying to get his donkey onto its feet beneath a heavy load, you must not go on by, but must help him" (Exodus 23:5).

We owe love to one another. Those who depend on us for the love they need can be deeply hurt by our neglect. There are people who need us to "walk along beside" them when they're hurting. Whom have we ignored when we were so focused on ourselves, or on the addict in the family? Whose cries and needs have gone untended? Who has been harmed by our neglect?

Love demands that we act to meet the needs around us; that's how God loves us.

DAY 13 Giving Our Best

Bible Reading: Colossians 3:22-25

We made a list of all persons we had harmed and became willing to make amends to them all.

Though we've sometimes felt at our best while "under the influence," we can see in retrospect that this wasn't true. We're great at rationalizing. When our lives are consumed by addictions, we're just not at our best. Many of us may even have believed that our work was enhanced by our addictions. Being sober, we can look back at our work with new perspective. We probably realize that our job performance deteriorated and our attitudes suffered. The fact is: we weren't giving our best.

The apostle Paul wrote, "You slaves must always obey your earthly masters, not only trying to please them when they are watching you but all the time; obey them willingly because of your love for the Lord and because you want to please him. Work hard and cheerfully at all you do, just as though you were working for the Lord and not merely for your masters, remembering that it is the Lord Christ who is going to pay you, giving you your full portion of all he owns. . . . And if you don't do your best for him, he will pay you in a way that you won't like—for he has no special favorites who can get away with shirking" (Colossians 3:22-25).

We fill a needed role in society, however lowly we may estimate that role to be. God knows that our contribution matters. When we don't do our best, others are affected. When have people been harmed because we didn't do our best at work? Who has been hurt by the negative attitudes we may have displayed?

Regardless of our role in life, when we are in recovery we can be our best.

DAY 14 Internal Changes

Bible Reading: Luke 19:1-10

We made a list of all persons we had harmed and became willing to make amends to them all.

There are many kinds of thieves. Some of us stole to support our habits, when our addictions demanded it. Others of us have never stolen anyone's property, but are thieves in another sense. We may have robbed ourselves of opportunities or dignity. Perhaps, we've stolen the heart of someone's spouse or robbed our children of their childhood. All these robberies have victims.

The apostle Paul said, "If anyone is stealing, he must stop it and begin using those hands of his for honest work so he can give to others in need" (Ephesians 4:28). When Zacchaeus turned his life over to Christ he had to look at how many people he had cheated and stolen from in his unethical business deals. "Zacchaeus stood before the Lord and said, 'Sir, from now on I will give half my wealth to the poor, and if I find I have overcharged anyone on his taxes, I will penalize myself by giving back four times as much!'" (Luke 19:8).

Any time we take something that's not rightfully ours, or use something that doesn't belong to us without the permission of the rightful owner, that is stealing. People need to maintain clear boundaries of what belongs to them, whether in their material goods or in their committed relationships. If we have violated the boundaries and taken something belonging to others, we have spoiled their sense of security and brought them harm. We need to broaden our definition of stealing and ask God to show us everyone we've harmed in this way.

Changes we see on the outside usually reflect changes that have already happened on the inside.

DAY 15 Amends with Children

Bible Reading: Ephesians 6:1-4

We made a list of all persons we had harmed and became willing to make amends to them all.

All parents probably feel guilty at one time or another about how we have raised our kids. When there is addiction in the family, we are likely to be even harder on ourselves. We may just throw up our hands, giving up completely on parenting our children. If our needs weren't met during childhood, we may be totally at a loss; we may not know how to meet the needs of our little ones. We may be so overwhelmed by the responsibility of parenting that we stay in denial about how our life-styles affect them.

The apostle Paul wrote, "And now a word to you parents. Don't keep on scolding and nagging your children, making them angry and resentful. Rather, bring them up with the loving discipline the Lord himself approves, with suggestions and godly advice" (Ephesians 6:4). "Fathers, don't scold your children so much that they become discouraged and quit trying" (Colossians 3:21). Children also rely on their parents for their physical needs. Paul said, "Little children don't pay for their father's and mother's food—it's the other way around; parents supply food for their children" (2 Corinthians 12:14).

When we fail to provide for our children's needs, they are hurt. It may be hard to face because we feel so overwhelmed ourselves. We can make amends by letting them know that it's not their fault. We can reaffirm our love for them, and let them know that we're taking steps to change.

The fact of our recovery is best proven in our homes, with those we love.

DAY 16 Loving Submission

Bible Reading: Ephesians 5:21-33

We made a list of all the persons we had harmed and became willing to make amends to them all.

Those closest to us cannot escape being harmed by the consequences of our actions. If we are married, our addictions are harmful to our marriage partners, even if we hate to admit it.

The Bible tells us that marriage should be a relationship that satisfies the needs of both partners. The apostle Paul wrote, "Honor Christ by submitting to each other. . . . For since a man and his wife are now one, a man is really doing himself a favor and loving himself when he loves his wife! No one hates his own body but lovingly cares for it, just as Christ cares for his body the Church, of which we are parts. (That the husband and wife are one body is proved by the Scripture which says, 'A man must leave his father and mother when he marries, so that he can be perfectly joined to his wife, and the two shall be one.') . . . So again I say, a man must love his wife as a part of himself; and the wife must see to it that she deeply respects her husband—obeying, praising, and honoring him" (Ephesians 5:21, 28-31, 33).

God says that our lives are literally intertwined with the lives of our mates. It may be a healthy union or a dysfunctional one. In either case, we're united. The behavior of one always affects the other. Any time we fail to break the bonds with our parents, fail to love sacrificially, or fail to show respect for our spouse, we are hurting them and ourselves. Surely, they have hurt us, too; but for now, we're dealing with our own issues.

The most important amends we face are with those to whom we are closest.

DAY 17 Harming Ourselves

Bible Reading:
Luke 6:36-38

We made a list of all persons we had harmed and became willing to make amends to them all.

We all know that we've been hurt. But some of us are so focused on how we've been victimized and how others have hurt us that we fail to see how we've been hurting ourselves. We may spend a lot of time and energy on trying to change how others treat us, but to no avail. Perhaps we need to begin by looking at ways we've been hurting ourselves. Then we can work on changing them.

The Bible points out many danger areas where we are likely to hurt ourselves. Here are some of them: "Stop lying to each other; tell the truth, for we are parts of each other and when we lie to each other we are hurting ourselves" (Ephesians 4:25). "I say to run from sex sin. No other sin affects the body as this one does. When you sin this sin it is against your own body" (1 Corinthians 6:18). Jesus said, "Never criticize or condemn—or it will all come back on you. Go easy on others; then they will do the same for you. For if you give, you will get!" (Luke 6:37-38).

God loves us every bit as much as he loves the people we've harmed. He understands the actions that cause us pain and wants to help us avoid them. We may be guaranteeing our continued pain by continuing to do things that are guaranteed to hurt us. Being willing to make amends to ourselves includes being willing to renounce and give up the behaviors that destroy our lives. As we are willing to give these things up, we'll begin to find good things coming back our way.

When we've made bad choices, we first need to make amends to ourselves.

DAY 18 Making Amends with God

Bible Reading:
1 Corinthians 6:15-17

We made a list of all persons we had harmed and became willing to make amends to them all.

We're on intimate terms with God, whether we realize it or not. We've probably thought a lot about how our sins have hurt the people in our lives. But we may be surprised to find out how intimately acquainted God is with our sin, and the emotional impact it has on him.

The apostle Paul warned, "Don't cause the Holy Spirit sorrow by the way you live" (Ephesians 4:30). We can actually cause God grief by our actions, because the Holy Spirit of God is always with us. When we enter into sin, we take him with us. Paul explained, "Don't you realize that your bodies are actually parts and members of Christ? So should I take part of Christ and join him to a prostitute? Never! And don't you know that if a man joins himself to a prostitute she becomes a part of him and he becomes a part of her? For God tells us in the Scripture that in his sight the two become one person. But if you give yourself to the Lord, you and Christ are joined together as one person" (1 Corinthians 6:15-17). When Potiphar's wife attempted to seduce Joseph, the reason he gave for resisting was, "It would be a great sin against God" (Genesis 39:9).

God is our loving Father! We may not realize it, but God is intimately involved with our lives. He sees everything! He knows the pain in store for us when we make bad decisions. And he grieves deeply when we're doing things that will hurt us and his other loved ones. We need to ask ourselves when we may have caused God sorrow and grief.

Because God loves us so much, we hurt him deeply when we sin.

DAY 19 The Power of Words

Bible Reading: James 3:5-10

We made a list of all persons we had harmed and became willing to make amends to them all.

Words can hurt terribly! We've all said things that we regret. Stinging words leave their mark, and we can't take away the sting or erase the emotional impact they have. We may have made our tongues a tool of deception. Learning to tell lies expertly, we may have shattered someone's trust. We may have used our words to attack and wound our children and our spouses.

James recognized the terrible power of our words: "The tongue is a small thing, but what enormous damage it can do. A great forest can be set on fire by one tiny spark. And the tongue is a flame of fire. It is full of wickedness, and poisons every part of the body. And the tongue is set on fire by hell itself, and can turn our whole lives into a blazing flame of destruction and disaster. Men have trained, or can train, every kind of animal or bird that lives and every kind of reptile and fish, but no human being can tame the tongue. It is always ready to pour out its deadly poison. Sometimes it praises our heavenly Father, and sometimes it breaks out into curses against men who are made like God. And so blessing and cursing come pouring out of the same mouth" (James 3:5-10).

There seems to be no final cure for this unruly member of our body. We need to respect what great damage it can do. Kids may chant, "Sticks and stones can break my bones, but words will never hurt me." But this is a weak defense against a verbal weapon that can shatter our spirit. Whom have we hurt with our words?

Our words are like fire: we cannot control them or reverse the damage they cause.

DAY 20 Shared Addictions

Bible Reading: Proverbs 4:14-17

We made a list of all persons we had harmed and became willing to make amends to them all.

Most of us didn't fall into sin alone. We may have softened our guilt about falling into addiction by bringing other people along with us. Whatever the addiction, it seems there's a tendency to lure others into the same pit. Whom have we harmed by bringing them down with us?

Solomon warned, "Don't do as the wicked do. Avoid their haunts—turn away, go somewhere else, for evil men can't sleep until they've done their evil deed for the day. They can't rest unless they cause someone to stumble and fall. They eat and drink wickedness and violence!" (Proverbs 4:14-17). Peter warned of false teachers who used their position to take advantage of those who were emotionally needy. He said of them, "No woman can escape their sinful stare, and of adultery they never have enough. They make a game of luring unstable women" (2 Peter 2:14).

Solomon noted the power of seduction when he warned young men about the lure of a prostitute, "Don't go near her; stay away from where she walks, lest she tempt you and seduce you. For she has been the ruin of multitudes—a vast host of men have been her victims. If you want to find the road to hell, look for her house" (Proverbs 7:25-27).

We see the devastating effect we can have when we lure and seduce others to join us in sin. Whom have we harmed by breaking down their will to do good, and luring them back into trouble?

No one stands alone; our addictions are usually tied to the addictions of others.

DAY 21 Undoing the Damage

Bible Reading: Romans 8:28-30

We made a list of all persons we had harmed and became willing to make amends to them all.

We may feel a bit discouraged after thinking of all the people we've hurt. We see that even though we are willing to make amends, we won't be able to undo all the damage we've done. But there's still good reason to be encouraged.

The Bible has promised: "All that happens to us is working for our good if we love God and are fitting into his plans. For from the very beginning God decided that those who came to him—and all along he knew who would—should become like his Son, so that his Son would be the First, with many brothers. And having chosen us, he called us to come to him; and when we came, he declared us 'not guilty'" (Romans 8:28-30).

Here's how one sin was turned around to be used by God for good. Judah had sex with a woman he assumed to be a prostitute. She was really his widowed daughter-in-law, who was upset that he hadn't given her his other son for a husband. She had twin boys, Perez and Zerah, who had their grandpa for a father! (Genesis 38). Many were hurt by this unsavory situation.

Our hope lies in seeing how God can bring about good, even through our worst sins. In Matthew 1:3 we see that Perez and Zerah, the sons of Judah and Tamar, are in the direct lineage that brought Jesus Christ into the world! We can be encouraged that God has forgiven our sins and he has the power to bring good things out of horrible circumstances.

God can turn our greatest tragedies into events that bring honor to him.

DAY 22 No Small Sins

Bible Reading:
1 Samuel
21:1-10;
22:21-23

We made a list of all persons we had harmed and became willing to make amends to them all.

Sometimes we end up hurting innocent victims. When we started down the road seeking pleasure, or a path of safety or escape from our problems, we never imagined that our actions would lead to the destruction of innocent lives.

When young David was escaping from the wrath of King Saul, he ran to the priest, Ahimelech. "'The king has sent me on a private matter,' David lied. 'He told me not to tell anybody why I am here. . . . The king's business required such haste, and I left in such a rush that I came away without a weapon!' David explained" (1 Samuel 21:1-2, 8). The priest believed David's story and assisted him. But King Saul saw Ahimelech as a coconspirator, and had all eighty-five priests killed along with their entire families. Only one of Ahimelech's sons escaped to tell David what had happened. David responded, "Now I have caused the death of all of your father's family. Stay here with me, and I'll protect you. . . . Any harm to you will be over my dead body" (22:22-23).

David never intended to hurt anyone. He was just trying to cover his own tracks and get what he needed in his desperation. He recognized his responsibility and tried to do what he could after the tragedy. When people suffer innocently because of things we do, it will help them and their families if we acknowledge our responsibility and do whatever we can to help.

In recovery we must take responsibility for the consequences of our actions.

DAY 23 Healing with Parents

Bible Reading: Proverbs 17:25; 19:13, 26

We made a list of all persons we had harmed and became willing to make amends to them all.

Our parents are deeply connected to our lives on some level. And whether our families are intact or not, whether our parents acknowledge their love for us or not, whether they've made a mess of their lives or are a picture of perfection, they are still our parents. They once held us in their arms and had hopes and dreams that our lives could be better than their own. Parents are deeply vulnerable to hurt from their children. When our lives are damaged by the effects of addiction, our parents will be vulnerable to the pain.

Solomon had plenty to say about how wayward children can hurt their parents. Here are some of those comments from the book of Proverbs: "A rebellious son is a grief to his father and a bitter blow to his mother" (Proverbs 17:25). "A rebellious son is a calamity to his father" (19:13). "A son who is a member of a lawless gang is a shame to his father" (28:7). "A man who robs his parents and says, 'What's wrong with that?' is no better than a murderer" (28:24). "A son who mistreats his father or mother is a public disgrace" (19:26).

We have the capacity to cause grief, bitter sorrow, calamity, shame, and disgrace to our parents. These are many of the things we reap in our own lives when we are dominated by an addiction. Even if our parents have contributed to our problems, we can still take responsibility for our side of the relationship by doing what we can to make things right with them.

Coming to terms with our parents is an essential part of our recovery.

DAY 24 Missing the Party

Bible Reading:
Luke 15:28-32

We made a list of all persons we had harmed and became willing to make amends to them all.

When we think about making amends and reconciling relationships we may find that some places in our hearts are unwilling to take a step toward the other person. There may be unresolved anger, jealousy, and resentment; we may feel unable to forgive.

Jesus told a story about a man whose younger son took an early inheritance and left home. He wasted his money on riotous living and returned in desperate need. The older brother was angry and complained to his father. "'All these years I've worked hard for you and never once refused to do a single thing you told me to; and in all that time you never gave me even one young goat for a feast with my friends. Yet when this son of yours comes back after spending your money on prostitutes, you celebrate by killing the finest calf we have on the place.' 'Look, dear son,' his father said to him, 'you and I are very close, and everything I have is yours. But it is right to celebrate. For he is your brother; and he was dead and has come back to life! He was lost and is found!'" (Luke 15:28-32).

Unresolved anger, resentment, and jealousy are very harmful, even if we've done all the "good deeds" expected of us. We harm ourselves and others by our self-pity and emotional manipulation. If we face this kind of roadblock, we need to stop rehearsing everyone else's wrongs. We need to deal with the things that are keeping us from attending the "party" of life.

When we resist making amends we cut ourselves off from the joys of life.

DAY 25 Loving Hearts

Bible Reading: James 4:11-12

We made a list of all persons we had harmed and became willing to make amends to them all.

We can harm others by our attitudes as well as our actions. We may see ourselves as "righteous," assuming a superior attitude, ready to criticize at any moment. We may feel we have the right to criticize because others aren't measuring up to what we think should be expected. But our judgmental nagging doesn't seem to help others improve their performance.

James wrote, "Don't criticize and speak evil about each other, dear brothers. . . . Only he who made the law can rightly judge among us" (James 4:11-12). Here's an example of someone who was critical when he didn't understand the whole situation. When Eli the priest saw Hannah in the temple, he "noticed her mouth moving as she was praying silently and, hearing no sound, thought she had been drinking" (1 Samuel 1:12-13). Hannah was actually begging God to give her a child; her silent prayer was driven by a sad heart, not a drunken mind.

We are not God! We haven't been designated as the judge of the people around us. So we really don't have the right to criticize and speak evil of others. Besides, we may not fully understand the problems involved and may end up adding to them instead of helping. We need to consider how our negative, critical, and self-righteous attitudes have harmed others and become willing to make amends. Perhaps our focus on the wrongs of others is a way to avoid our own problems.

As God loves us, he wants to create loving hearts within us.

DAY 26 Full of Mercy

Bible Reading:
Matthew 9:10-13

We made a list of all persons we had harmed and became willing to make amends to them all.

In families where addictions are forceful, there's usually someone who falls into the role of being superhuman and self-righteous. In the family system, this person balances out the identified "addict," who feels subhuman. If we are one of the self-righteous ones, it is harder for us to identify ourselves because we don't look sick. We seem to be stable and have it all together. However, it can become very lonely as we separate ourselves from everyone whom we perceive to be below us.

The Pharisees once asked why Jesus associated with sinners. "Because people who are well don't need a doctor! It's the sick people who do! For I have come to urge sinners, not the self-righteous, back to God" (Matthew 9:10-13). Here's God's view of the self-righteous: "They say to one another, 'Don't come too close, you'll defile me! For I am holier than you!' They stifle me. Day in and day out they infuriate me" (Isaiah 65:5).

We may not realize how harmful self-righteousness can be. We can be hurting others by our lack of mercy, even though we're doing all the "right" things. Self-righteousness is hard to see in ourselves. We may need to ask our loved ones if this type of attitude has harmed them. Then we need to be willing to really listen to the answer they give.

As we become willing to make amends, mercy begins to grow in our hearts.

DAY 27 The Gift of Gratitude

Bible Reading: Luke 17:11-19

We made a list of all persons we had harmed and became willing to make amends to them all.

We can become so focused on our own struggles and pain that we forget to show gratitude to God or to the people who are instrumental in our healing. We may come to expect special treatment and forget that those who are showing care for our lives really deserve our thanks.

Jesus healed ten lepers and told them to go to the priests and show them that they were healed. "And as they were going, their leprosy disappeared. One of them came back to Jesus, shouting, 'Glory to God, I'm healed!' He fell flat on the ground in front of Jesus, face downward in the dust, thanking him for what he had done. This man was a despised Samaritan. Jesus asked, 'Didn't I heal ten men? Where are the nine? Does only this foreigner return to give glory to God?'" (Luke 17:14-18). The apostle Paul said, "No matter what happens, always be thankful, for this is God's will for you who belong to Christ Jesus" (1 Thessalonians 5:18).

Jesus was both God and man. As God he deserved the glory and the gratitude for the miracle of curing this incurable disease. Perhaps, in his humanity, his feelings were hurt by being so taken for granted. He didn't have to heal them. He extended himself out of love and compassion. Are there people in our lives who have reached out in loving compassion to help us, only to be taken for granted? Have we become so self-centered because of our own pain that we've failed to express gratitude to those who have helped us?

We receive the gift of great joy when we are able to receive God's other gifts with gratitude.

DAY 28 Sensitive Hearts

Bible Reading: Luke 16:19-31

We made a list of all persons we had harmed and became willing to make amends to them all.

One of the pitfalls of recovery is that we tend to become extremely self-focused and fail to see the needs of others. If we've been a rescuer, we can go overboard in our recovery and ignore valid needs. If we're medicating our pain through work, or some other drug or distraction, we can numb ourselves to the needs of others while we're numbing our own pain. Perhaps, we need to consider those around us who were needy while we were consumed with our own lives.

"'There was a certain rich man,' Jesus said, 'who was splendidly clothed and lived each day in mirth and luxury. One day Lazarus, a diseased beggar, was laid at his door. As he lay there longing for scraps from the rich man's table, the dogs would come and lick his open sores. Finally the beggar died and was carried by the angels to be with Abraham in the place of the righteous dead. The rich man also died and was buried, and his soul went into hell'" (Luke 16:19-23).

The point for us to consider is not that we may go to hell for neglecting the needs of others. Our salvation is insured by the blood of Jesus, which covers all of our sins. But we need to consider whether we have neglected the needs of those around us while we were consumed with addictions or with our recovery. Our children, spouse, or others may feel like they were bleeding on our doorstep and we didn't even notice because we were so self-consumed. Whom have we hurt by neglecting their valid needs?

Our recovery is only successful to the extent that we grow more sensitive to those around us.

DAY 29 Making Restitution

Bible Reading: Exodus 22:10-15

We made a list of all persons we had harmed and became willing to make amends to them all.

Irresponsibility is often associated with those who are caught up in addictive family systems. We may see ourselves as irresponsible and condemn ourselves. Or we may notice our irresponsible behavior, but excuse ourselves because of all that we've been dealing with. Or we may not even notice our irresponsible behavior, but have recurrent problems with others because we fail to respect their property.

The Bible clearly states, "If a man borrows an animal (or anything else) from a neighbor, and it is injured or killed, and the owner is not there at the time, then the man who borrowed it must pay for it" (Exodus 22:14). David once wrote, "Evil men borrow and 'cannot pay it back'! But the good man returns what he owes with some extra besides" (Psalm 37:21).

The Bible does tell us that it's important to take responsibility for the things we borrow. We may feel like we're being condemned as chronically evil if we've had a problem with irresponsibility. The word translated "evil men" really means one who is morally wrong or a person who acts badly. God sees irresponsible behavior as a bad action which can be corrected. He doesn't see us as hopelessly bad. Regardless of what we've been through, we are still held responsible to respect the property of others. We need to consider who we've harmed by being negligent or irresponsible with the use of their property.

Paying restitution builds bridges with others and establishes peace within ourselves.

DAY 30 Too Busy!

Bible Reading: Luke 10:38-42

We made a list of all persons we had harmed and became willing to make amends to them all.

We may be the one who tries to hold it all together in the family. We figure that if we don't take care of things, they just won't be taken care of. So we rush around trying to make sure that everything is as it should be. We may fume that others don't pitch in and help. We may simmer in our own self-pity, as we silently hope that someone will notice that we need help. We may hurt others by lashing out unexpectedly or by blaming them.

Jesus dealt compassionately with a woman who behaved in a similar way. Jesus and the disciples "came to a village where a woman named Martha welcomed them into her home. Her sister Mary sat on the floor, listening to Jesus as he talked. But Martha was the jittery type, and was worrying over the big dinner she was preparing. She came to Jesus and said, 'Sir, doesn't it seem unfair to you that my sister just sits here while I do all the work? Tell her to come and help me.' But the Lord said to her, 'Martha, dear friend, you are so upset over all these details! There is really only one thing worth being concerned about. Mary has discovered it—and I won't take it away from her!'" (Luke 10:38-42).

Martha deprived herself by trying to be available to everyone. She deprived herself of what she really needed, while playing the martyr. The result was resentment, self-pity, and indignation that no one came to her rescue. Whom have we hurt, ourselves included, by behaving as Martha did?

Keeping busy with the wrong things robs us of the even better things God has for us.

STEP NINE

We made direct amends to such people wherever possible, except when to do so would injure them or others.

"If anyone says 'I love God,' but keeps on hating his brother, he is a liar. . . . God himself has said that one must love not only God, but his brother too" (1 John 4:20-21).

STEP NINE

DAY 1 Keeping Promises

Bible Reading:
2 Samuel 9:1-9

We made direct amends to such people wherever possible, except when to do so would injure them or others.

How many people are still living in the shadow of our unkept promises? Is it too late to go back now and try to make it up to them?

King David had made some promises to his friend Jonathan. "One day David began wondering if any of Saul's family was still living, for he wanted to be kind to them, as he had promised Prince Jonathan" (2 Samuel 9:1).

Jonathan's only living son, Mephibosheth, had lived a long time with the pain of David's unkept promise. It had shaped his life-style, his emotional condition, the way he thought about himself. His grandfather, King Saul, had mistreated David before David became king. Perhaps Mephibosheth was afraid that David would mistreat him on account of his grandfather. Perhaps he had begun to take the guilt of his grandfather's sins upon himself. Generations of fear and guilt had been laid upon him—until David remembered and fulfilled his promise.

There are probably people in our lives who have been affected by promises we've failed to keep. It is important that we try to fulfill whatever promises we are able to. When we can't, the least we can do is to ask what our neglect meant to those we disappointed.

As we make amends we restore to others what rightfully belongs to them.

DAY 2 From Takers to Givers

Bible Reading: Luke 19:1-10

We made direct amends to such people wherever possible, except when to do so would injure them or others.

When we are feeding our addictions, it is easy to become consumed by our own needs. Nothing matters except getting what we crave so desperately. We may have to lie, cheat, kill, or steal; but that doesn't stop us. Within our families and community we become known as "takers," trampling over the unseen needs of others.

Zacchaeus had the same problem. His hunger for riches drove him to betray his own people by collecting taxes for the oppressive Roman government. He was hated by his own people as a thief, an extortioner, and a traitor. But when Jesus reached out to him, he changed dramatically. "Zacchaeus stood before the Lord and said, 'Sir, from now on I will give half of my wealth to the poor, and if I find I have overcharged anyone on his taxes, I will penalize myself by giving him back four times as much!' Jesus told him, 'This shows that salvation has come to this home today'" (Luke 19:8-9).

Zacchaeus went beyond just paying back what he had taken. For the first time in a long time, he saw the needs of others and wanted to be a "giver."

Making amends includes paying back what we've taken, whenever possible. Some of us may even seize the opportunity to go even further, giving even more. As we begin to see the needs of others and respond by choice, our self-esteem will rise. We will begin to realize that we can give to others, instead of just being a burden.

Making amends is the first step to becoming a giver.

DAY 3 Rebuilding Relationships

Bible Reading: Acts 15:36-41

We made direct amends to such people wherever possible, except when to do so would injure them or others.

How many times have we written people off because of some dispute in the distant past? Years pass and people change; yet we cling to our old ways of seeing them. Perhaps we never saw them very clearly in the first place! For some of us, making amends will include reviewing our relationships. We may need to change our estimation of some of those we've already judged.

Paul and Barnabas traveled together on a missionary journey, taking John Mark along as their assistant. When things got tough, the young man deserted them and went home. Later, Barnabas wanted to give John Mark another chance, but Paul refused. "Their disagreement over this was so sharp that they separated" (Acts 15:39). Much later in his life, Paul was put in prison. During that time, he wrote to Timothy and asked for John Mark. He said, "He is useful to me for ministry" (2 Timothy 4:11, NKJV).

The Bible doesn't tell us how Paul came to change his opinion of John Mark. Perhaps he realized that he hadn't been completely fair. Maybe John Mark had changed over the years. At some point, though, they had reestablished their relationship and repaired the emotional damage done.

Making amends includes going back and settling emotional accounts. When we've judged someone harshly, we need to reexamine our relationship with that person. If we expect others to change how they look at us, we will need to do the same for others.

By making amends, we become open to God's life-changing power.

DAY 4 Good Things from God

Bible Reading: Genesis 32:1-12

We made direct amends to such people wherever possible, except when to do so would injure them or others.

There may be people whom we've hurt so badly that they hate us. There may be considerable risks involved in going back to face them. The pain may not be erased, even after many years. But as difficult as such a meeting might be, it may help in our healing process—if God is leading us to do it.

Jacob had so injured his brother Esau through his crafty schemes that Esau had vowed to kill him. Jacob ran away, fearing for his life. Twenty years later God told him to return home. So Jacob sent messengers ahead of him to see what kind of reception he could expect. "The messengers returned with the news that Esau was on the way to meet Jacob—with an army of 400 men! Jacob was frantic with fear. . . . Then Jacob prayed, . . . 'O Lord, please deliver me from destruction at the hand of my brother Esau, for I am frightened—terribly afraid that he is coming to kill me. . . . But you promised to do me good'" (Genesis 32:6-7, 9-12).

We can learn from Jacob's example in this situation. First, we must be certain that God is leading us. We can pray earnestly, remembering his previous provisions and trusting in his promises. Then, asking for protection, we must take steps toward reconciliation.

God's call to make amends will lead us down a path toward good things.

DAY 5 Unfinished Business

Bible Reading: Philemon 1:13-16

We made direct amends to such people wherever possible, except when to do so would injure them or others.

Sometimes we need to complete unfinished business before we can move forward toward new opportunities in life. Some of us may have left a trail of broken laws and relationships behind us—things we need to address before moving on.

A new life doesn't excuse us from past obligations. While the apostle Paul was in prison, he led a runaway slave named Onesimus into a new life. Paul sent him back to his master, even though Onesimus risked the death penalty for his offense. Since his previous master was a friend of Paul's, and a Christian brother, they hoped that Onesimus would be forgiven.

Onesimus carried a letter to his master from Paul, which read "I really wanted to keep him [Onesimus] here with me . . . but I didn't want to do it without your consent. . . . He ran away from you for a little while so that now he can be yours forever, no longer only a slave, but something much better—a beloved brother. . . . If he has harmed you in any way or stolen anything from you, charge me for it" (Philemon 1:13-16, 18).

Before we can move ahead we must face the unfinished business of the past. This includes offering to pay back what we owe, coming clean with the law, and going back to the people from whom we ran away. We can't assume forgiveness from people, although we can hope for it. In some cases we may be surprised to find pardon and release from the bondage of our past.

Making direct amends will release us from our bondage to the past.

DAY 6 Something from Nothing

Bible Reading: Luke 15:11-24

We made direct amends to such people wherever possible, except when to do so would injure them or others.

Some of us may have stolen things from others, but now have no means of paying them back. How can we face the people we've wronged when we have nothing to offer? Since working through Step Eight, we should be willing to humbly approach the people we've wronged. But if we can't repay our debts, what's the point?

Jesus told a story about a young son who demanded an early inheritance and left home. He wasted his fortune on riotous living. He hit bottom, so to speak, and decided to go back to his father. He had nothing left of what he had taken and no means with which to ever repay his father. We can imagine his feelings as he rehearsed what he would say.

"So he returned home to his father. And while he was still a long distance away, his father saw him coming, and was filled with loving pity and ran and embraced him and kissed him. . . . His father said to the slaves, 'Quick! . . . We must celebrate with a feast, for this son of mine was dead and has returned to life. He was lost and is found.' So the party began" (Luke 15:20-24).

We may feel like we have nothing to offer. But to the people who love us, we are more important than anything else we could give them. The apostle Paul said, "Pay all your debts except the debt of love for others—never finish paying that!" (Romans 13:8). Though we may not be able to pay our debts right away, we can still offer our love.

Making amends can be the richest of gifts.

DAY 7 A Servant's Heart

Bible Reading: Philippians 2:1-8

We made direct amends to such people wherever possible, except when to do so would injure them or others.

At this point in recovery, most of us have experienced some major changes in our attitudes. At one time, we were so consumed by our addictions that we thought only of ourselves, failing to show any consideration for others. In this step, the focus is on the interests and needs of others.

The apostle Paul taught, "Don't be selfish; don't live to make a good impression on others. Be humble, thinking of others as better than yourself. Don't just think about your own affairs, but be interested in others, too" (Philippians 2:3-4). Whether we make direct amends to others, or choose not to because of the injury it would cause, we are concerned with protecting others from pain and suffering.

There may be situations where we will suffer if we go back to make amends. This is part of the work of recovery, and the potential pain should not deter us. The apostle Peter wrote, "If you do right and suffer for it, and are patient beneath the blows, God is well pleased. . . . Christ, who suffered for you, is your example. Follow in his steps: He never sinned, never told a lie, never answered back when insulted; when he suffered he did not threaten to get even; he left his case in the hands of God who always judges fairly" (1 Peter 2:20-23).

This step can be very difficult as we face the painful consequences of past actions. During this time, we need to turn our lives over to the care of God. He will fairly and wisely decide what will happen to us.

The best cure for selfishness is God's call to serve others.

DAY 8 Making Peace

Bible Reading: Matthew 5:23-25

We made direct amends to such people wherever possible, except when to do so would injure them or others.

We all suffer brokenness within ourselves, in our relationship with God, and in our relationships with others. Brokenness tends to weigh us down and can easily lead us back into our addictions. Recovery isn't complete until all areas of brokenness are mended.

Jesus taught, "So if you are standing before the altar in the Temple, offering a sacrifice to God, and suddenly remember that a friend has something against you, leave your sacrifice there beside the altar and go and apologize and be reconciled to him, and then come and offer your sacrifice to God" (Matthew 5:23-24). The apostle John wrote, "If anyone says 'I love God,' but keeps on hating his brother, he is a liar; for if he doesn't love his brother who is right there in front of him, how can he love God whom he has never seen?" (1 John 4:20).

Much of recovery involves repairing the brokenness in our lives. This requires that we make peace with God, within ourselves, and with others whom we've alienated. Unresolved issues in relationships can disable us from being at peace with God and ourselves. Once we go through the process of making amends, we must keep our minds and hearts open to anyone we may have overlooked. God will often remind us of relationships that need attention. When these come to mind, we should stop everything and go to those we've offended, seeking to repair the damage.

Making direct amends brings peace—with ourselves, others, and God.

DAY 9 Choosing to Love

Bible Reading:
Luke 6:27-36

We made direct amends to such people wherever possible, except when to do so would injure them or others.

As we set out to mend relationships, there are some things that are beyond our control. Some people may refuse to be reconciled, even when we do our best to make amends. This may leave us feeling like a victim. Once again we're stuck with the pain of unresolved issues. We may be left with negative feelings that continue to surface. What can we do to gain power in these situations?

Jesus said, "Listen, all of you. Love your *enemies.* Do *good* to those who *hate* you. Pray for the happiness of those who *curse* you; implore God's blessing on those who *hurt* you. . . . Love your *enemies!* Do good to *them!* Lend to *them!* And don't be concerned about the fact that they won't repay. Then your reward from heaven will be very great, and you will truly be acting as sons of God: for he is kind to the *unthankful* and to those who are *very wicked*" (Luke 6:27-28, 35).

We no longer need to be controlled by other people's dispositions. Even when we've done our best to make amends for the wrongs we've done, the situations may not change. And even when we've come to terms with the wrongs that have been done against us, our feelings may not change. But we don't have to be held captive by our feelings or the feelings of others. We can choose to act in a loving way. This will free us from being controlled by anyone other than God. As we choose to do good, our feelings will follow with time.

Our recovery is not decided by the responses of others; it is in God's hands alone.

DAY 10 Imperfect Love

Bible Reading:
John 21:14-19

We made direct amends to such people wherever possible, except when to do so would injure them or others.

We may wonder how we can love others but still hurt them. This paradox causes shame, sometimes erecting a barrier between us and the ones we love. We may be afraid to say that we love them, thinking, *If I really loved them, I wouldn't let them down the way I have.*

Peter had once sworn his love for Jesus. But then, after Jesus was arrested, Peter protected himself by denying that he even knew him. Jesus wasn't surprised. But Peter had a hard time forgiving himself. After Jesus rose from the dead, he had this conversation with Peter. "Jesus said to Simon Peter, 'Simon, son of John, do you love me more than these others?' 'Yes,' Peter replied, 'you know I am your friend.' . . . [A third time] he asked him, 'Simon, son of John, are you even my friend?' Peter was grieved at the way Jesus asked the question this third time. 'Lord, you know my heart; you know I am,' he said" (John 21:15-17).

Jesus allowed Peter to affirm his love the best he could and accepted him as he was. In this way, Jesus reduced the shame and restored the relationship. Shame and isolation can lead us back to our addictions. For the sake of our recovery, we must not let our shame cause us to avoid the people we love. It's all right if we love others imperfectly—no one is perfect. But we must keep our love relationships together until they've had time to heal.

Making amends for our imperfections will help us understand the true nature of love.

DAY 11 Covering the Past

Bible Reading: Ezekiel 33:10-16

We made direct amends to such people wherever possible, except when to do so would injure them or others.

When we walk down the wrong paths in life, we end up in bad places and experience devastating losses. If we go far enough down those paths, we endanger our very lives. We may wonder if we've already gone too far. Is a new way of life still possible, even if we turn from our old ways and make amends?

Even under the Old Testament laws, there was hope for those who chose to turn around and make amends. The Lord spoke through Ezekiel, saying, "O people of Israel, you are saying: 'Our sins are heavy upon us; we pine away with guilt. How can we live?' Tell them: 'As I live, says the Lord God, I have no pleasure in the death of the wicked; *I desire that the wicked turn from his evil ways and live.* Turn, turn from your wickedness, for why will you die, O Israel? For the good works of a righteous man will not save him if he turns to sin; and the sins of an evil man will not destroy him if he repents and turns from his sins.' . . . When I tell the wicked he will die, and then he turns from his sins and does what is fair and right—if he gives back the borrower's pledge, returns what he has stolen, and walks along the paths of right, not doing evil—he shall surely live. He shall not die. None of his past sins shall be brought up against him, for he has turned to the good and shall surely live" (Ezekiel 33:10-12, 14-16).

There's hope for everyone who turns around and makes amends. Our past sins can be overshadowed by the new life ahead of us.

Recovery leads to right actions, and then, to restitution.

DAY 12 Desperate Hunger

Bible Reading: Proverbs 6:30-31

We made direct amends to such people wherever possible, except when to do so would injure them or others.

There are conditions that drive us to our addictions. There's some need inside that makes it worth the risk involved. It deadens us to our own sense of what is right and wrong. We'll do anything to satisfy the hunger our addiction feeds. We wish people could understand that we don't risk everything good in our lives on a whim. We feel like we're starving. By now, we're coming to realize that although there are conditions that drive us to our addictions, we still must take responsibility for the wrong that we do.

King Solomon once wrote, "Excuses might even be found for a thief, if he steals when he is starving! But even so, he is fined seven times as much as he stole, though it may mean selling everything in his house to pay it back" (Proverbs 6:30-31).

God understands that there can be areas of starvation within us that drive us to do wrong. Certainly, once we identify those areas we will have more compassion for ourselves and from others who understand. But we're still responsible to make amends, even though this may be costly. The cost of making amends will help us face the immediacy of our need to deal with the starvation. Perhaps when we understand the hungers involved, we will be able to find the help we need to satisfy them. Only when the starvation is satisfied will we be able to remain free from our addictions.

In recovery we learn not to destroy ourselves through unwise actions.

DAY 13 Regaining Control

Bible Reading: Exodus 22:5-6

We made direct amends to such people wherever possible, except when to do so would injure them or others.

When we give in to our addictions, we feel isolated. We feel alone in our pain and need something to overcome it. We never expected our behaviors to affect the lives of others. We weren't thinking about the people around us; we were focused on our own pain. We just wanted to feel better. Our addictions seemed to promise us a way to destroy the pain without hurting anyone else.

The Old Testament says, "If the field is being burned off and the fire gets out of control and goes into another field so that the shocks of grain, or the standing grain, are destroyed, the one who started the fire shall make full restitution" (Exodus 22:6).

This law was especially important in the farming community of early Israel. It stated a person's responsibility for damages caused when his attempt to burn up thorns in his own field got out of control, and burned the valuable grain in adjoining fields. Here's an analogy: The thorns represent the pain we're trying to consume with the fire of our addictions. At first we don't realize how our lives are connected to others, or the damage that can result when our addictions get out of control. In retrospect, however, we can see how the fire of our addictions has destroyed much more than the thorns of our pain. Making amends means we need to account for all the losses that have resulted from the fire we started.

Making amends helps us take responsibility for the pain we've caused.

DAY 14 Civic Duty

Bible Reading: Matthew 17:24-27

We made direct amends to such people wherever possible, except when to do so would injure them or others.

We sometimes neglect our obligations because we disagree with the systems of which we are a part. This is a natural tendency. But it can become a greater problem when we're burdened with the pressures of addiction. Part of our recovery may involve realigning ourselves with some of society's expectations and demands, even when we may not be in full agreement with them.

Even Jesus had problems with the IRS of his day. Jesus asked Peter, "'Do kings levy assessments against their own people, or against conquered foreigners?' 'Against the foreigners,' Peter replied. 'Well, then,' Jesus said, 'the citizens are free! However, we don't want to offend them, so go down to the shore and throw in a line, and open the mouth of the first fish you catch. You will find a coin to cover the taxes for both of us; take it and pay them'" (Matthew 17:24-27).

The kings of Jesus' day drew their tax revenues from the nations they had conquered. Since Jesus was the Son of God, he should have been exempt from taxation by the Temple leaders—the representatives of God. Jesus still submitted himself to the demands of the society he lived in. We, too, need to be in good standing with our government. We need to pay our taxes and fulfill any other civic obligations demanded by the law.

We need to make things right even if we don't agree with all the stipulations.

DAY 15 Authorities

Bible Reading:
1 Peter 2:13-17

We made direct amends to such people wherever possible, except when to do so would injure them or others.

By turning our lives over to the care of God, we'll experience God's power for good. This will naturally lead us to make amends. We may be known for being at odds with society and the laws of the land. So when we begin to change, we may cause some heads to turn. People who have never experienced God's power will see the effect it's had on us. They will probably wonder what could have changed us so drastically.

The apostle Peter wrote, "For the Lord's sake, obey every law of your government: those of the king as head of the state, and those of the king's officers, for he has sent them to punish all who do wrong, and to honor those who do right. It is God's will that your good lives should silence those who foolishly condemn the Gospel without knowing what it can do for them, having never experienced its power. You are free from the law, but that doesn't mean you are free to do wrong. Live as those who are free to do only God's will at all times. Show respect for everyone. Love Christians everywhere. Fear God and honor the government" (1 Peter 2:13-17).

Obeying the law and meeting our obligations to society are important parts of making amends. We need to deal with our attitudes toward the laws of our land and the people in law enforcement. We may feel like we haven't hurt anyone, but if we've violated the law, we're responsible to face the consequences.

As we make amends we must face how we feel about authority figures.

DAY 16 Free from Fear

Bible Reading: Genesis 26:1-11

We made direct amends to such people wherever possible, except when to do so would injure them or others.

Making amends is one of the most difficult steps in recovery. So for encouragement, perhaps we should consider some of the benefits we can gain. Before coming clean, we live with the gnawing fear of being found out. Most addictions require us to live a lie; we are haunted by the hidden fear that everything is about to unravel. Our families also are burdened by hidden fears and shame. Setting out to make amends can change all this.

Here's a story of how one family was affected by having to live a lie. "Isaac stayed in Gerar. And when the men there asked him about Rebekah, he said, 'She is my sister!' For . . .he was afraid they would kill him to get her, for she was very attractive. But sometime later, King Abimelech, king of the Philistines, looked out of a window and saw Isaac and Rebekah making love. Abimelech called for Isaac and exclaimed, 'She is your wife! Why did you say she is your sister?' 'Because I was afraid I would be murdered,' Isaac replied" (Genesis 26:6-9).

Imagine the negative effect this lie had on Isaac and Rebekah's relationship. When they weren't pretending, they lived with constant fear. When we make amends and learn to live with the truth there is a great relief from fear. We are freed up from the pressures of always having to pretend to be something we're not. This relief can bring new life to all our intimate relationships.

In making amends we discover the freedom that comes by way of the truth.

DAY 17 Free from Shame

Bible Reading: Genesis 3:6-10

We made direct amends to such people wherever possible, except when to do so would injure them or others.

Before we make amends, constant guilt plagues our relationships with the people we've hurt. We actually give them power over us. We avoid them, feeling uncomfortable in social situations where they're present. We exclude them from our circle of friends. We become evasive and always hope that we won't have to deal with the shame of facing them. Living in hiding is not a good feeling.

Look at these two examples of people in hiding: "And as they [Adam and Eve] ate it, suddenly they became aware of their nakedness, and were embarrassed. So they strung fig leaves together to cover themselves around the hips. That evening they heard the sound of the Lord God walking in the garden; and they hid themselves among the trees. The Lord God called to Adam, 'Why are you hiding?' And Adam replied, 'I heard you coming and didn't want you to see me naked. So I hid'" (Genesis 3:7-10). "One day Cain suggested to his brother, 'Let's go out into the fields.' And while they were together there, Cain attacked and killed his brother. But afterwards the Lord asked Cain, 'Where is your brother? Where is Abel?' 'How should I know?' Cain retorted. 'Am I supposed to keep track of him wherever he goes?'" (4:8-9).

These are not stories of happy people! Living a lie necessarily forces us to live in shame and isolation. We begin to live constantly on the defensive. When we make amends, we're free to resume our relationships with God and others, and without the fear or shame.

Making things right with others will bring freedom from shame.

DAY 18 Surprised by Love

Bible Reading: Luke 15:18-21

We made direct amends to such people wherever possible, except when to do so would injure them or others.

Often our behaviors result not only in harming others, but also in alienating us from the people who love us. We begin to feel embarrassed around others. We wonder how we'll be received when we meet the people we've hurt. Step Nine says that we are to make *direct* amends wherever possible. This can be an intimidating task.

When the Prodigal Son was preparing to make direct amends to his father, he felt the need to rehearse a little speech. "'I will go home to my father and say, "Father, I have sinned against both heaven and you, and am no longer worthy of being called your son. Please take me on as a hired man."' So he returned home to his father. And while he was still a long distance away, his father saw him coming, and was filled with loving pity and ran and embraced him and kissed him. His son said to him, 'Father, I have sinned against heaven and you, and am not worthy of being called your son'" (Luke 15:18-21).

He didn't even get to finish his speech! His father embraced him, welcomed him home with loving pity, and threw the biggest party they'd ever had! One of the surprise benefits we may experience from making amends is that it may not be as hard as we expect. In some cases, those we love will have pity on us and be thrilled to see us at their door. They will embrace us, forgiving all the harm we've done in the past. These positive experiences should then help us face the more painful and difficult ones.

The hardest part of making amends is in making the decision to do so.

DAY 19 In the Light

Bible Reading: Psalm 19:7-11

We made direct amends to such people wherever possible, except when to do so would injure them or others.

When we're living under the influence of an addiction, we're likely to see the world in a distorted fashion. What we perceive to be right and wrong becomes confused. Our perceptions of reality become blurred. We get out of sync with society's norms and ignore the proper boundaries for governing our behavior.

The books of Exodus, Leviticus, Numbers, and Deuteronomy are filled with laws and rules of conduct that were to govern every facet of Jewish life. They form the basis for our laws in the Judeo/Christian tradition. There were laws regarding diet, proper hygiene, relationships, business dealings, livestock, worship, marriage, sexuality, crime, and punishment. These clearly defined boundaries were set up by God to protect everyone and to help them maintain good relationships with him and with each other. King David once wrote, "God's laws are perfect. They protect us, make us wise, and give us joy and light. God's laws are pure, eternal, just" (Psalm 19:7-9).

Making amends will bring us back into line with the protective norms our society has set up. We need to recognize where we've overstepped boundaries. Making amends while using God's laws as the standard for wise behavior should help us learn to respect the dignity of others. It should also give us a clear vision of reality and, ultimately, will allow us to have joy and success.

Aligning ourselves with God's laws for recovery will bring light to our paths.

DAY 20 Free from Sin's Penalty

Bible Reading: Colossians 2:13-15

We made direct amends to such people wherever possible, except when to do so would injure them or others.

Sometime during the recovery process we will probably notice that we've begun to grow spiritually. And with this growth, we may realize that we've hurt God through the things we've done to ourselves and others. We may feel an obligation to try to do something to make it up to him. But what can we do? How can we ever make up for the long list of sins we've committed?

In Jesus' day, a criminal's charges were set out on a list to be brought before the court. If the criminal was sentenced to crucifixion for his crimes, the list would be nailed to the cross where he was to be executed. The crimes on the list were then fully paid for by his death. The apostle Paul wrote, "You were dead in sins, and your sinful desires were not yet cut away. Then he gave you a share in the very life of Christ, for he forgave all your sins, and blotted out the charges proved against you, the list of his commandments which you had not obeyed. He took this list of sins and destroyed it by nailing it to Christ's cross. In this way God took away Satan's power to accuse you of sin, and God openly displayed to the whole world Christ's triumph at the cross where your sins were all taken away" (Colossians 2:13-15).

All the sins we would ever commit were listed and nailed to the cross of Christ. His blood covered them all; they were paid for in full. When it comes to making amends to God, there's nothing left to do!

Since we're already forgiven by God, we are free to seek forgiveness from others.

DAY 21 Good and Bad

Bible Reading: Galatians 3:10-13

We made direct amends to such people wherever possible, except when to do so would injure them or others.

We may still feel like we're basically good people. Yes, our lives may have gotten a bit out of control, but the good we've done surely outweighs the bad. Maybe we don't need to turn our lives over to Jesus Christ and accept him as our Savior. Perhaps we can just make amends for the wrongs we've done, and do our best to be good in the future. Then everything will be fine.

Maybe not! The Bible doesn't say that God weighs our good deeds out against our bad. Here's what God says: "And the person who keeps every law of God, but makes one little slip, is just as guilty as the person who has broken every law there is" (James 2:10). "'Cursed is everyone who at any time breaks a single one of these laws that are written in God's Book of the Law.' Consequently, it is clear that no one can ever win God's favor by trying to keep the Jewish laws, because God has said that the only way we can be right in his sight is by faith" (Galatians 3:10-11). "For the wages of sin is death, but the free gift of God is eternal life through Jesus Christ our Lord" (Romans 6:23).

The Bible makes it clear that if we reject Jesus Christ's payment for our sins, we will have to pay the debt ourselves. The only acceptable payment is death. Not even a lifetime of our good deeds is enough to make amends for the bad deeds we've done, no matter how few they may be.

The cross frees us from having to be "good" so we can freely admit we are bad.

DAY 22 Nothing Added

Bible Reading:
Galatians 2:17-19

We made direct amends to such people wherever possible, except when to do so would injure them or others.

As we think about making amends to God, it seems there must be something we can do beyond placing our faith in Christ. What if God does expect us to do good works to make up for our sins? All right, maybe the sins we committed before we became Christians have been covered. But what about all the sins we've committed since then? Wouldn't it be wise to be on the safe side? Why not figure out some sort of payment system—adding to what Christ did—just to be safe?

The Christians of Paul's day asked similar questions. They thought, "But what if we trust Christ to save us and then find that we are wrong, and that we cannot be saved without being circumcised and obeying all the other Jewish laws? Wouldn't we need to say that faith in Christ had ruined us?" Paul replied to this question, "God forbid that anyone should dare to think such things about our Lord. Rather, we are sinners if we start rebuilding the old systems I have been destroying, of trying to be saved by keeping Jewish laws, for it was through reading the Scripture that I came to realize that I could never find God's favor by trying—and failing—to obey the laws. I came to realize that acceptance with God comes by believing in Christ" (Galatians 2:17-19).

Christ paid in full for all our sins. We can trust him fully to make amends for us with God. We don't have to rely partly on our own ability to make amends to God. It's already done!

Jesus Christ has made direct and complete amends on our behalf.

DAY 23 A Clean Slate

Bible Reading: Ephesians 2:8-10

We made direct amends to such people wherever possible, except when to do so would injure them or others.

Recovery is hard work. Step Nine is one of the hardest. Notice, however, that this step focuses our attention on making amends to people, not God. Once we realize that our amends to God have already been settled, we are free to focus our attention on making amends to the people in our lives.

The apostle Paul wrote, "Yes, all have sinned; all fall short of God's glorious ideal; yet now God declares us 'not guilty' of offending him if we trust in Jesus Christ, who in his kindness freely takes away our sins" (Romans 3:23-24). "Because of his kindness, you have been saved through trusting Christ. And even trusting is not of yourselves; it too is a gift from God. Salvation is not a reward for the good we have done, so none of us can take any credit for it. It is God himself who has made us what we are and given us new lives from Christ Jesus; and long ages ago he planned that we should spend these lives in helping others" (Ephesians 2:8-10).

We don't need to give God anything to make amends for our sins. What we can do is turn our attention toward healing our relationships with the people close to us. God loves us all. Now that we have been freed up from having to worry about our forgiveness from God, we can spend our lives helping others. When we make amends for the harm we've caused, we are helping others. We are acknowledging the value of their lives, their feelings, and their property.

Since our slate is clean with God, we are free to make things right with others.

DAY 24 Proper Sensitivity

Bible Reading:
1 Corinthians
10:23-33

We made direct amends to such people wherever possible, except when to do so would injure them or others.

When we're making amends, we need to be wise in the way we go about it. We may be so anxious to get things off our chest that we may blurt things out without fully considering the people involved. We need to consider how our actions may injure them. We may feel so pressured by guilt and fear of exposure that we rush ahead and make mistakes we can't erase.

Many of the people in the apostle Paul's world worshiped idols. Part of their pagan worship included sacrificing an animal, and then cooking and eating the meat. The Christians of that day struggled with the rightness of eating this sacrificed meat. Paul explained that there was nothing wrong with eating the meat, but he advised them not to eat it if it would offend another Christian's conscience. Paul said, "Don't think only of yourself. Try to think of the other fellow, too, and what is best for him. . . . In this case *his* feeling about it is the important thing. . . . That is the plan I follow, too. I try to please everyone in everything I do, not doing what I like or what is best for me, but what is best for them" (1 Corinthians 10:24, 29, 33).

When making amends we need to weigh the feelings and needs of the people who will be exposed to what we say and do. Since we are not always the best judge of what needs to be disclosed and when, we can rely on our support group for help in these decisions. We need to make sure that no one will be hurt by our disclosures.

Recovery will bring with it renewed sensitivity in our relationships.

DAY 25 Sexual Boundaries

Bible Reading: Leviticus 18:6-26

We made direct amends to such people wherever possible, except when to do so would injure them or others.

While under the influence we may have violated someone's sexual boundaries. This may have involved some form of incest, molestation, rape, or other behavior that violated another person's privacy. Or we may have been taken advantage of in this way. In dealing with something so shameful and damaging, it's common to be in denial. Our denial continues the cycle of shame and devastation in the lives of everyone involved.

God made a long list of forbidden sexual practices including rape, incest, and molestation. Offenders of these laws were sentenced to death. God listed almost every conceivable sexual violation and set up definite boundaries to protect our sexuality. Here are a few: "None of you shall approach anyone who is near of kin to him, to uncover his nakedness: I am the Lord" (Leviticus 18:6, NKJV). "The nakedness of your son's daughter or your daughter's daughter, their nakedness you shall not uncover" (18:10, NKJV). "If a man has sexual intercourse with his sister . . . it is a shameful thing. . . . He shall bear his guilt" (20:17).

Our nakedness—our sexual identity—is precious. It's meant to be ours alone until it's given to a husband or wife. If we have violated another's sexual boundaries, we need to admit the devastation we've caused and get help. If we've been the victim, we need to acknowledge the violation and get help for ourselves.

By admitting our faults, we begin the process toward healing even the deepest of devastations.

DAY 26 Giving Something Back

Bible Reading: Romans 13:7-10

We made direct amends to such people wherever possible, except when to do so would injure them or others.

It's relatively easy to know how to make amends for the property we've damaged. It's much harder to know how to make amends when it comes to the intangible losses in our human relationships.

The apostle Paul wrote, "Pay everyone whatever he ought to have; . . . give honor and respect to all those to whom it is due. Pay all your debts except the debt of love for others—never finish paying that! For if you love them, you will be obeying all of God's laws, fulfilling all his requirements" (Romans 13:7-8). Regarding marriage he said, "The man should give his wife all that is her right as a married woman, and the wife should do the same for her husband: for a girl who marries no longer has full right to her own body, for her husband then has his rights to it, too; and in the same way the husband no longer has full right to his own body, for it belongs also to his wife. So do not refuse these rights to each other" (1 Corinthians 7:3-5).

When we were under the influence, we may have failed to show respect and honor to others. We can go back now and express our feelings of love and respect. Whenever we're not sure what to do, we can never go wrong by expressing love. This entails treating others as we would like to be treated. In marriage, it's not enough to stop giving ourselves to our addiction or to others. We need to give ourselves back to our spouses, devoting ourselves to them sexually and in every other appropriate way.

As Christ has loved us, so we ought to love others.

DAY 27 Trusting Again

Bible Reading:
Acts 5:1-11

We made direct amends to such people wherever possible, except when to do so would injure them or others.

Deception and addictions go hand in hand. We've probably lost the trust of others, if we've told lies and hidden the truth. Making amends includes reestablishing a healthy trust.

In the early church many people sold their possessions and donated the money to the poor. "There was a man named Ananias (with his wife Sapphira) who sold some property, and brought only part of the money, claiming it was the full price. (His wife had agreed to this deception.) But Peter said, ' . . . When you claimed this was the full price, you were lying to the Holy Spirit. The property was yours to sell or not, as you wished. And after selling it, it was yours to decide how much to give. How could you do a thing like this? You weren't lying to us but to God.' As soon as Ananias heard these words, he fell to the floor, dead! Everyone was terrified. . . . About three hours later his wife came in, not knowing what had happened. Peter asked her, 'Did you people sell your land for such and such a price?' 'Yes,' she replied, 'We did.' . . . Instantly she fell to the floor, dead" (Acts 5:1-5, 7-8, 10).

Ananias and Sapphira had a chance to make things right by being honest with Peter. Instead they chose to continue with the deception. Our recovery program will include making amends for the lies we've told and the truth we've hidden. We are making amends every time we choose to tell the truth. We're also allowing trust to be reestablished after a history of deception.

Trust can be recovered over time by means of truth and grace.

DAY 28 Testing the Water

Bible Reading: Genesis 32:13-21

We made direct amends to such people wherever possible, except when to do so would injure them or others.

When we've deeply hurt someone and are preparing to make amends, we may be hesitant. We may want to spend some time considering the best strategy for approaching them.

Jacob had deeply offended Esau. He was afraid as he approached Esau after a twenty-year separation. Before they were to meet, "Jacob stayed where he was for the night, and prepared a present for his brother Esau." The gift he prepared was a large herd of livestock. "He instructed his servants to drive them on ahead, each group of animals by itself, separated by a distance between. He told the men driving the first group that when they met Esau and he asked, 'Where are you going? Whose servants are you? Whose animals are these?'—they should reply: 'These belong to your servant Jacob. They are a present for his master Esau! He is coming right behind us!' Jacob gave the same instructions to each driver, with the same message. Jacob's strategy was to appease Esau with the presents before meeting him face to face! 'Perhaps,' Jacob hoped, 'he will be friendly to us'" (Genesis 32:13-20).

Notice that Jacob told the servants to call Esau "master." When Jacob left home he had stolen Esau's birthright to be master over him. The words and gift were designed to bring peace. There are times when it may be wise to send a gift and a pacifying message to test the waters before a face-to-face meeting.

We need to take precautions as we seek to make amends—it's OK to test the waters.

DAY 29 Long-Awaited Healing

Bible Reading: Genesis 33:1-11

We made direct amends to such people wherever possible, except when to do so would injure them or others.

Returning to someone we've hurt is a scary thing. The passing years, lack of communication, and memories of the anger and hateful exchanges of emotion can all create a tremendous weight of fear. Even though we may make some contact through a third party, there will still be tension until we see that person face to face.

This was the case for Jacob upon returning to see Esau. "Then, far in the distance, Jacob saw Esau coming with his 400 men. . . . Then Jacob went on ahead. . . . And then Esau ran to meet him and embraced him affectionately and kissed him; and both of them were in tears!" After being introduced to Jacob's family, Esau asked, "'And what were all the flocks and herds I met as I came?' . . . Jacob replied, 'They are my gifts, to curry your favor!' 'Brother, I have plenty,' Esau laughed. 'Keep what you have.' 'No, but please accept them,' Jacob said, 'for what a relief it is to see your friendly smile! I was as frightened of you as though approaching God! Please take my gifts. For God has been very generous to me and I have enough.' So Jacob insisted, and finally Esau accepted them" (Genesis 33:1, 3-4, 8-11).

Jacob's tremendous fear gave way to relief. The last time Jacob had seen Esau, he was being restrained to keep him from killing Jacob. With the passing of time, both of them had changed. When Jacob faced his brother, he found that there was still affection, even though they both remembered the pain.

Time can heal only those hurts we've brought out into the open.

DAY 30 A Time for Mending

Bible Reading: Hosea 3:1-3

We made direct amends to such people wherever possible, except when to do so would injure them or others.

If we have broken trust with a spouse, especially if we've violated our marriage vows, making amends will take time. Perhaps we've made so many false promises in the past that our spouse will need time before fully resuming the relationship.

The prophet Hosea was told by God to marry a prostitute. His marriage was to be a living example to the nation of Israel of her infidelity toward God. It had to hurt Hosea deeply when she returned to her life of prostitution. Hosea said, "Then the Lord said to me, 'Go, and get your wife again and bring her back to you and love her, even though she loves adultery. For the Lord still loves Israel though she has turned to other gods and offered them choice gifts.' So I bought her [back from her slavery] for a couple of dollars and eight bushels of barley, and I said to her, 'You must live alone for many days; do not go out with other men nor be a prostitute, and I will wait for you'" (Hosea 3:1-3).

Hosea needed some time before he could be close to her again. Sometimes the best way we can make amends with our mate is to allow time to go by. During that time, we need to prove to our spouse that there is no reason to fear that our wrong behavior has continued. If a time of separation is needed to see that our commitment is real, we need to give our spouse that time and focus on our own recovery.

As God has bought us back, we need to restore our most important relationships.

STEP TEN

We continued to take personal inventory and when we were wrong promptly admitted it.

"*Keep putting into practice all you learned from me and saw me doing, and the God of peace will be with you*" (Philippians 4:9).

STEP TEN

DAY 1 Looking in the Mirror

Bible Reading: James 1:21-25

We continued to take personal inventory and when we were wrong promptly admitted it.

How many times do we look in the mirror each day? Suppose we saw someone looking in the mirror who found that he had mustard smeared around his mouth. We would find it very strange if he didn't immediately wash his face and clear up the problem. In the same way, we need to routinely look at ourselves in a spiritual mirror. Then if anything is wrong, we can make the proper adjustments.

James used a similar illustration to show how God's Word should be like a spiritual mirror in our lives. He said, "And remember, it is a message to obey, not just to listen to. So, don't fool yourselves. For if a person just listens and doesn't obey, . . . as soon as he walks away, he can't see himself anymore or remember what he looks like. But if anyone keeps looking steadily into God's law for free men, he will not only remember it but he will do what it says, and God will greatly bless him in everything he does" (James 1:22-25).

We can use this illustration to support the sensibility of doing routine personal inventories. As we examine ourselves, we need to respond with immediate action if something has changed since we last looked. If we put off taking care of a problem that we see, it may soon slip our minds. Just as we would think it foolish to go all day with mustard on our face, it's absurd to notice a problem that could lead to a fall and not correct it promptly.

The mirror of God's Word helps us to see what we should become.

DAY 2 Dealing with Anger

Bible Reading: Ephesians 4:26-27

We continued to take personal inventory and when we were wrong promptly admitted it.

Many of us have a hard time dealing with anger. Some of us have a history of rage, so we try to stifle our feelings. Others of us stuff down the feelings of anger; we pretend they don't exist because we were never allowed to express them in the past. If some of our problems stem from not knowing how to express anger properly, we may try to avoid dealing with it altogether. We may try to just "put it off" and hope it goes away. Evaluating how to deal with anger appropriately is an important part of our daily inventory.

The apostle Paul once said, "If you are angry, don't sin by nursing your grudge. Don't let the sun go down with you still angry—get over it quickly; for when you are angry you give a mighty foothold to the devil" (Ephesians 4:26-27). One key is to have a daily time limit for handling our feelings of anger—a time to find a way to express the feelings and then let them go.

Dealing with anger promptly is important because when it is left to fester, it becomes bitterness. Bitterness is anger that has been buried and given time to grow. The Bible warns us, "Watch out that no bitterness takes root among you, for as it springs up it causes deep trouble, hurting many in their spiritual lives" (Hebrews 12:15).

AA teaches that we should never allow ourselves to become too Hungry, Angry, Lonely, or Tired. We can accomplish this by promptly dealing with our anger as it occurs.

We need to deal with short-term anger before it causes long-term destruction.

DAY 3 Preventing Relapse

Bible Reading: Hebrews 4:12-13

We continued to take personal inventory and when we were wrong promptly admitted it.

Who among us takes a fall without a preceding thought, a flirtation with desire, or a season of being enticed? Who among us falls into a pit without walking near the edge? Relapse doesn't appear from nowhere to grab us by the throat. There are warning signs of complacency, confusion, and compromise that we can watch for as a precaution.

In order to safeguard against relapse, we must ask God to help us keep a close watch on our motives, desires, and thoughts. He has the power to do this. "For whatever God says to us is full of living power: it is sharper than the sharpest dagger, cutting swift and deep into our innermost thoughts and desires with all their parts, exposing us for what we really are" (Hebrews 4:12). As God shines his light into the darkness of our souls, we are enabled to see the problems lurking there. Then we can ask for God's help in dealing with them.

Temptation is progressive. James wrote, "Each one is tempted when he is drawn away by his own desires and enticed. Then, when desire has conceived, it gives birth to sin; and sin, when it is full-grown, brings forth death" (James 1:14-15, NKJV).

As we continue to take personal inventory, we can't afford to wait for harmful behaviors to surface before dealing with them. We need to look at the attitudes in our hearts that cause those behaviors. In this way, we can be alerted to problem areas and deal with our temptations before they become full-grown and overpowering.

God's Word will help us to continue in recovery and avoid the devastation of a relapse.

DAY 4 Dangerous Pride

Bible Reading: 1 Corinthians 10:12-13

We continued to take personal inventory and when we were wrong promptly admitted it.

When we begin to experience the benefits of recovery, it's easy to forget the power of our addictions. When we grow comfortable in our sobriety, we may begin to trust ourselves more than we should. We need to stay on the lookout for pride; it is a danger each of us must seek to crush.

King Solomon wisely noted, "Pride goes before destruction and haughtiness before a fall" (Proverbs 16:18). The apostle Paul also cautioned us, "So be careful. If you are thinking, 'Oh, I would never behave like that'—let this be a warning to you. For you too may fall into sin. But remember this—the wrong desires that come into your life aren't anything new and different. Many others have faced exactly the same problems before you. And no temptation is irresistible. You can trust God to keep the temptation from becoming so strong that you can't stand up against it, for he has promised this and will do what he says" (1 Corinthians 10:12-13).

Pride whispers to us, "Don't worry, you can handle this one; you're not like those addicts anymore." It is pride that pushes us to take foolish chances by walking into situations that support our addictions. We will never be able to "handle" making provisions for our compulsive inclinations. When we start to tell ourselves that we can, we're entertaining pride, which will only lead to our downfall. Pride often masquerades behind progress. We must be vigilant to reveal and abandon it whenever it tiptoes into our lives.

Even the pride we feel in our recovery can set us up for temptation and relapse.

DAY 5 Spiritual Exercises

Bible Reading:
1 Timothy 4:7-8

We continued to take personal inventory and when we were wrong promptly admitted it.

It is amazing to behold what a human being can achieve through a consistent disciplined effort. How many times have we watched seasoned gymnasts or other athletes and marveled at the ease with which they performed their sport? We realize that they developed that ability through rigorous training, which is what sets the true athlete apart from the spectator. There are parallels to the discipline of continuing our inventories.

Paul wrote to Timothy, "Spend your time and energy in the exercise of keeping spiritually fit. Bodily exercise is all right, but spiritual exercise is much more important" (1 Timothy 4:7-8). The word translated *exercise* specifically referred to the disciplined training done by gymnasts in Paul's day.

Spiritual strength and agility only come through practice. We need to develop our spiritual muscles through consistent effort and daily discipline. Continuing to take personal inventory is one of the disciplines we can develop. The Bible describes it as having our "senses exercised to discern both good and evil" (Hebrews 5:14, NKJV). Like the athlete, we can motivate ourselves to continue in a disciplined routine by looking to our reward. This kind of discipline "will help you not only now in this life, but in the next life too" (1 Timothy 4:8). We must not expect overnight results. As we continue practicing these disciplines each day, we'll eventually grow to enjoy the benefits.

Our continued inventory will keep us spiritually fit and strong in the face of temptation.

DAY 6 Personal Boundaries

Bible Reading: Genesis 31:45-55

We continued to take personal inventory and when we were wrong promptly admitted it.

We all have particular weaknesses and it is often helpful to establish personal boundary lines to support these weaker areas. We may need to clearly define our commitments to others; we may need to agree on certain limitations in order to maintain peace. Once the boundaries have been established, honesty is needed to maintain them. An assessment of our honesty in keeping our commitments needs to be part of our regular inventory.

Jacob and his father-in-law, Laban, had some conflicts. As they were working them out, they entered into an agreement by drawing a clearly defined boundary line and setting up a monument to remind them of that commitment. "'May the Lord see to it that we keep this bargain when we are out of each other's sight. . . . This heap [of stones],' Laban continued, 'stands between us as a witness of our vows. . . .' So Jacob took oath before the mighty God of his father, Isaac, to respect the boundary line" (Genesis 31:49, 51-53).

Restoring trust in our relationships is part of recovery. To do this we should define our expectations and cautiously enter into commitments. We are not merely responsible for what the other person knows about. We are personally responsible for our own honesty before the watchful eyes of God. These relational commitments are not to be entered into lightly. But when we make them, they must be vigilantly maintained.

Honest inventories help us maintain boundaries important to our recovery.

DAY 7 Positive Thoughts

Bible Reading: Philippians 4:8-9

We continued to take personal inventory and when we were wrong promptly admitted it.

As we take personal inventory, we will probably be inclined to focus on the bad things in our lives. Early on in recovery it's hard to see much that's very good. It's easy to get our perspective out of focus, allowing pessimism to grow. We may even feel awkward about taking inventory of the good things in our lives.

The apostle Paul advised, "Fix your thoughts on what is true and good and right. Think about things that are pure and lovely, and dwell on the fine, good things in others. Think about all you can praise God for and be glad about. Keep putting into practice all you learned from me and saw me doing, and the God of peace will be with you" (Philippians 4:8-9).

Balance is an important part of our recovery. Our daily balance sheet needs to have two sides, since there is both good and bad in all of us. We'll make choices that are right and choices that are wrong. We may take a step back now and again, but we should also take into account the two steps we took forward. Let's not get overwhelmed by focusing on the failure in ourselves and others. It is good to confess our wrongs and receive God's forgiveness on a daily basis. But once we've done this, it's time to stop and consider what remains in our lives. We should look for everything that is fine and pure, the things that are wonderful and lovely. Let's take some time during our continuing inventory to count our blessings. Let's take note of everything we can praise God for in our lives!

What we keep in our minds and hearts often determines what we do and say.

DAY 8 Perseverance

Bible Reading:
2 Timothy 2:3-7

We continued to take personal inventory and when we were wrong promptly admitted it.

Recovery is a lifelong process. There will be times when we grow tired and weary, times when we want to throw in the towel. We'll experience pain, fear, and a host of other emotions. We'll win some battles but lose others in our war to gain wholeness. We may get discouraged at times when we can't see any progress, even though we've been working hard. But through it all, we must persevere or lose the ground we've gained.

The apostle Paul used three illustrations to teach about perseverance. He wrote to Timothy, "Take your share of suffering as a good soldier of Jesus Christ, just as I do; and as Christ's soldier do not let yourself become tied up in worldly affairs, for then you cannot satisfy the one who enlisted you in his army. Follow the Lord's rules for doing his work, just as an athlete either follows the rules or is disqualified and wins no prize. Work hard, like a farmer who gets paid well if he raises a large crop. Think over these three illustrations, and may the Lord help you to understand how they apply to you" (2 Timothy 2:3-7).

Like the soldier, we're in a war that we can only win if we fight to the end. Like the athlete, we must train for a new way of life and follow the steps of recovery to the finish line. Like the farmer, we must do our work in every season and then wait patiently until we see the growth. If we stop working our program before reaching our aim, we may lose everything we've fought for, trained ourselves for, and worked hard for.

You cannot win the race for recovery by going just part of the way.

DAY 9 Our Defender

Bible Reading:
1 John 2:1-2

We continued to take personal inventory and when we were wrong promptly admitted it.

At times we may feel like we're the worst sinner in the whole world. We just seem to keep doing the same things over and over again. We feel guilty! Can God just wink at our sin and pretend that it's all right? How can he repeatedly forgive us for committing the same wrongs?

The apostle John said, "My little children, I am telling you this so that you will stay away from sin. But if you sin, there is someone to plead for you before the Father. His name is Jesus Christ, the one who is all that is good and who pleases God completely. He is the one who took God's wrath against our sins upon himself, and brought us into fellowship with God; and he is the forgiveness for our sins, and not only ours but all the world's" (1 John 2:1-2).

God takes sin very seriously. As a righteous Judge, he can't just ignore sin and act like it doesn't matter. But we can be forgiven completely and repeatedly. The words used here are legal terms. Jesus is our advocate, a defense attorney in a court of law, who intercedes for us, the lawbreakers. But he is not only the defense attorney; he's also "the one who took God's wrath against our sins upon himself." This means that his death has been accepted by the court as admissible payment for all of our sins. We're all guilty. The sentence is death! But our sentence has already been paid by Jesus, if we've trusted in him. When we bring our sin to Jesus, he goes back to the Judge on our behalf, reminding him that the sentence has already been paid.

There is nothing in our lives that Jesus can't handle.

DAY 10 No Shortcuts

Bible Reading: Matthew 4:1-11

We continued to take personal inventory and when we were wrong promptly admitted it.

We may be searching for a shortcut to happiness. The road of life often takes us through painful places we'd rather avoid. Some of us have gotten off the right track, lured away by hopes of a faster and easier way to "the good life."

Jesus faced this same temptation. He was destined to become the King of all the earth. The plan was that he would come to earth as a man, live a sinless life, die to pay for our sins, rise from the dead, and go back to heaven to wait for those who would be his. Then he would return to earth to claim his people and his rightful place as King of kings. Satan offered him a shortcut. "Satan . . . showed him [Jesus] the nations of the world and all their glory. 'I'll give it all to you,' he said, 'if you will only kneel and worship me.' 'Get out of here, Satan,' Jesus told him. 'The Scriptures say, "Worship only the Lord God. Obey only him"'" (Matthew 4:8-10). If Jesus had fallen for this trick, he would have sinned and lost everything.

We need to beware of "shortcuts" that take us even one step outside of God's will. We're warned, "Resist the devil and he will flee from you" (James 4:7). This resistance is sometimes shown by ignoring offers that are "too good to be true." There are really no quick fixes in life. The path of recovery can be long and hard, but many have gone before us and made it. As we stay on the path, taking one step at a time, we'll find the good things in life.

On our journey toward recovery, shortcuts are only stepping-stones to a relapse.

DAY 11 Daily Recovery

Bible Reading: Romans 7:18-25

We continued to take personal inventory and when we were wrong promptly admitted it.

We may feel like we're just no good. Deep down inside there is a sense of brokenness that is a constant reminder of our humanity. Hopefully, we'll get to a place where our behavior is under control and we'll be able to maintain sobriety. But we should always be aware that as long as we're in this human body, we'll have to contend with our lower nature.

Paul said of himself, "I know I am rotten through and through so far as my old sinful nature is concerned. No matter which way I turn I can't make myself do right. I want to but I can't. . . . There is something else deep within me, in my lower nature, that is at war with my mind and wins the fight and makes me a slave to the sin that is still within me" (Romans 7:18, 23). King David described God's tenderness toward us because of our human condition: "He is like a father to us, tender and sympathetic to those who reverence him. For he knows we are but dust, and that our days are few and brief" (Psalm 103:13-16).

No matter how far we progress, our lower nature will always be inclined toward and susceptible to the lure of our addictions. We can't afford to forget this or let down our guard. Paul wrote, "Make no provision for the flesh, to fulfill its lusts" (Romans 13:14, NKJV). It is this realization that should convince us that maintaining sobriety is something we will need to nurture for the rest of our lives, one day at a time.

We will always be tempted by our old lives; but we need not always fall prey to them.

DAY 12 Self-Nourishment

Bible Reading: 1 Samuel 14:20-45

We continued to take personal inventory and when we were wrong promptly admitted it.

We once used our addictions to find comfort and to help us cope with life's daily battles. In recovery, we may have become so focused on the battle at hand that we've neglected our basic physical needs. We may have forgotten our need to enjoy some of the sweet things of life. Failure to take care of ourselves can leave us weak and vulnerable.

During a difficult battle, King Saul had declared, "'A curse upon anyone who eats anything before evening—before I have full revenge on my enemies.' . . . Jonathan, however, had not heard his father's command; so he dipped a stick into a honeycomb, and when he had eaten the honey he felt much better. Then someone told him that his father had laid a curse upon anyone who ate food that day, and everyone was weary and faint as a result. 'That's ridiculous!' Jonathan exclaimed. 'A command like that only hurts us. See how much better I feel now'" (1 Samuel 14:24, 27-29).

When we're in recovery, we already feel deprived. We need to make sure that we're being good to ourselves in healthy ways, eating good food and tasting some of the sweet things that life naturally provides. Recovery isn't a time for unnecessary deprivation. If we allow ourselves to become too hungry, physically or emotionally, we'll find ourselves weary and less able to fight the battles we face each day.

We should be more interested in what is right than in looking good.

DAY 13 True Wisdom

Bible Reading:
James 3:17-18

We continued to take personal inventory and when we were wrong promptly admitted it.

Many of us in recovery are learning to think and act in new ways. So we may find it hard to recognize true wisdom, even when it's staring us in the face. We may need some guidelines to help us identify wisdom in our thoughts and choices of action.

According to the Bible, there are two aspects of wisdom: the spiritual and the practical. Spiritual wisdom gives insight into the true nature of things. It includes things like "asking God to help you understand what he wants you to do; asking him to make you wise about spiritual things; . . . learning to know God better and better" (Colossians 1:9-10). Special wisdom is also sometimes given "that your hearts will be flooded with light so that you can see something of the future he has called you to share" (Ephesians 1:18).

Wisdom can be evaluated by its qualities. The Bible tells us that God's wisdom is "first of all pure and full of quiet gentleness. Then it is peace-loving and courteous. It allows discussion and is willing to yield to others; it is full of mercy and good deeds. It is wholehearted and straightforward and sincere" (James 3:17).

On the practical level, our wisdom can be judged by whether our actions conform to God's instructions or not. God's instructions were given to us because they naturally lead to healthy living. Using them, we can find the wisdom we need to walk progressively toward wholeness. This can be one of the standards we use in our continuing daily inventory.

True wisdom will always lead those who follow it toward peace and wholeness.

DAY 14 Moderation in Everything

Bible Reading:
Hebrews 12:16-17

We continued to take personal inventory and when we were wrong promptly admitted it.

Our appetites can overtake us and make us their slaves. Perfectly good activities can get us into trouble when we fail to practice them in moderation. Or there may be times when we don't feed our appetites in a balanced way. Then we find ourselves so starved that we fall to our addictions at the first opportunity.

This happened to Esau. One day he came home so hungry that he promised his birthright to his younger brother in exchange for a bowl of porridge. We're warned, "Watch out that no one becomes involved in sexual sin or becomes careless about God as Esau did: he traded his rights as the oldest son for a single meal. And afterwards, when he wanted those rights back again, it was too late, even though he wept bitter tears of repentance. So remember, and be careful" (Hebrews 12:16-17). The apostle Paul wrote, "I can do anything I want to if Christ has not said no, but some of these things aren't good for me. Even if I am allowed to do them, I'll refuse to if I think they might get such a grip on me that I can't easily stop when I want to" (1 Corinthians 6:12).

We need to satisfy our appetites in appropriate ways, so we don't become starved and become more susceptible to temptation. There may be some good things that have such control over us that it's best to avoid them altogether. If we allow the demands of our appetites to become overpowering, we risk losing things (or people) that we might never get back.

We must learn to evaluate the long-range effects of our choices and actions.

DAY 15 Softened Hearts

Bible Reading: Matthew 13:1-9, 18-23

We continued to take personal inventory and when we were wrong promptly admitted it.

As we move through our recovery, our attitudes can change. We long to live a productive life. We may be exposing ourselves to new ideas, even to the Bible, much more than we ever did before. Yet as we examine ourselves in our personal inventory, we may not see the kind of growth we had hoped for. If this is true, we may need to ask whether our minds and emotions are really receptive to the new thoughts and truths we're hearing.

Jesus told a story to illustrate four ways that the human heart responds to God's Word. Describing the first way, he said, "A farmer was sowing grain in his fields. As he scattered the seed across the ground, some fell beside a path, and the birds came and ate it. . . . The hard path where some of the seeds fell represents the heart of a person who hears the Good News about the Kingdom and doesn't understand it; then Satan comes and snatches away the seeds from his heart" (Matthew 13:3-4, 19).

We may find the Bible to be confusing. Maybe we're not able to understand because we are defensive toward God, still feeling that he's rejected us. Perhaps we're angry because of the pain he's allowed in our lives. It won't do us any good, however, if God's Word is getting into our minds, but not our hearts. We can ask God to help us understand and overcome whatever is causing our resistance toward him. As our hearts grow softer, we will begin to see positive spiritual growth.

We don't need to understand everything; God will open our minds and soften our hearts.

DAY 16 Dealing with Disappointment

Bible Reading: Matthew 13:1-9, 18-23	**We continued to take personal inventory and when we were wrong promptly admitted it.**

When we first began our recovery, we may have been surprised to find that God wasn't the enemy we'd thought him to be. Perhaps we were enthusiastic about our new relationship with God. We may have expected that when we turned our will and our life over to God, the struggle with our addictions would miraculously disappear. That sounded great! Finally there was an escape from the pain! But as we progressed in our recovery, we discovered that we still had to live life in the real world. We had access to God and his power, but we still had to fight the battles. This may have caused us to get discouraged about our relationship with God, causing our spiritual life to wilt.

Jesus described a similar condition using a farming illustration: "And some [seeds] fell on rocky soil where there was little depth of earth; the plants sprang up quickly enough in the shallow soil, but the hot sun soon scorched them and they withered and died, for they had so little root" (Matthew 13:5-6). Jesus explained, "The shallow, rocky soil represents the heart of a man who hears the message and receives it with real joy, but he doesn't have much depth in his life, and the seeds don't root very deeply, and after a while when trouble comes, or persecution begins because of his beliefs, his enthusiasm fades, and he drops out" (Matthew 13:20-21).

God never promised an easy life. If we're disappointed, it's because our expectations were unrealistic. Have we allowed life's troubles to destroy our budding faith?

By continuing with our personal inventories, we allow the seeds of recovery to take root.

DAY 17 Weeding the Garden

Bible Reading: Matthew 13:1-9, 18-23

We continued to take personal inventory and when we were wrong promptly admitted it.

While growing in our recovery we may find that weeds crop up in our lives, threatening to choke out the good. We may find ourselves cynical and mistrusting; we become so self-centered that our relationships with others suffer. We may learn to take care of our own needs, which is healthy, but we may go beyond that to where we become greedy and demanding. We may be caught up with worries and fears of various kinds or lapse back into bouts of self-pity. These types of weeds can choke out the good that's growing out of our recovery.

Jesus described this danger in his illustration about the four types of soil. He said, "Other seeds fell among thorns, and the thorns choked out the tender blades" (Matthew 13:7). Then he explained, "The ground covered with thistles represents a man who hears the message, but the cares of this life and his longing for money choke out God's Word" (Matthew 13:22).

As we continue to take personal inventory, we need to watch for the weeds that spring up in our lives. We may have had the chance to taste a better way of life. But once the crisis of confronting our addiction is past, there are new types of distractions that can choke out our spiritual life. We need to take a few moments each day to weed out all the greed, worry, fear, selfishness, cynicism, self-pity, and other negative tendencies that may take root in our hearts. Our support group can help us see when these "weeds" start inhibiting our growth.

Continuing our personal inventory is like weeding a garden; it allows the good things to grow.

DAY 18 Open to Growth

Bible Reading: Matthew 13:1-9, 18-23

We continued to take personal inventory and when we were wrong promptly admitted it.

Our initial goal was to stop the addictions that made our lives unmanageable. Once that was done, we may have experienced some confusion about what should come next. We may now wonder what life should be like with our addictions out of the way. Being free from our addictions may produce opportunites for us to put our talents and abilities to work. If we don't find worthwhile outlets for the new life growing in us, we may become frustrated.

One of Jesus' parables relates to this. He said, "Some [seeds] fell on good soil, and produced a crop that was thirty, sixty, and even a hundred times as much as he had planted" (Matthew 13:8). He explained, "The good ground represents the heart of a man who listens to the message and understands it and goes out and produces a crop many times greater than the amount planted—thirty, sixty, or even a hundred times as much" (Matthew 13:23).

Jesus described how God's Word, received and understood, can take root in people's lives. Its growth there will cause them to develop into the productive people God created them to be. There's great potential within each of us! As we accept God's perspective on our lives and respond openly to him, new life will sprout in us. This new life will then find expression in our talents and abilities. There's a world of opportunities for growth. As we take our inventory, we need to check for signs of frustration about not using our talents and look for ways to develop them.

As we admit our wrongs, the seeds of God's goodness and love blossom in our lives.

DAY 19 New Life

Bible Reading: 1 Peter 2:1-3

We continued to take personal inventory and when we were wrong promptly admitted it.

Recovery often brings us into a new life. Everything may seem so new to us! We may feel like a little child, somewhat helpless and not yet able to take care of ourselves the way other people do. A new life is great, but we still need to grow up. As we continue to take personal inventory we can monitor how regularly we are feeding ourselves on God's Word, which will help us grow. We can also keep our eyes open for the feelings and behavior patterns that characterized our old life. It's not unusual for some of them to crop up again.

The apostle Peter wrote, "So get rid of your feelings of hatred. Don't just pretend to be good! Be done with dishonesty and jealousy and talking about others behind their backs. Now that you realize how kind the Lord has been to you, put away all evil, deception, envy, and fraud. Long to grow up into the fullness of your salvation; cry for this as a baby cries for his milk" (1 Peter 2:1-3). Here is another rendering of Peter's words: "If you have tasted the Lord's goodness and kindness, cry for more, as a baby cries for milk. Eat God's Word—read it, think about it—and grow strong in the Lord and be saved."

Our old patterns of hatred, pretending, dishonesty, jealousy, gossip, and the like have to be dealt with as they arise. They will show up! But as they do, we need to get rid of them, one by one. We also need to feed on God's Word every day so that we can continue in to grow in our new life.

The longer we continue in recovery, the more we want to recover.

DAY 20 A Sensitive Conscience

Bible Reading:
1 Timothy
1:18-20

We continued to take personal inventory and when we were wrong promptly admitted it.

We've probably experienced the feelings that result when we do something our conscience has warned us against. We've felt the shame, and we may have distanced ourselves from God as a result. We may find that our conscience has been revived as we've worked through recovery. A healthy conscience is a necessary tool for recognizing wrong and taking a personal inventory. There are things we can do to help reactivate a conscience that has been damaged or put to sleep.

Paul told Timothy, "Cling tightly to your faith in Christ and always keep your conscience clear, doing what you know is right" (1 Timothy 1:19). The word *conscience* literally means "having a co-perception." It describes the act of perceiving our will and the will of God simultaneously. As we learn what the will of God is, we can set that perception alongside our own, thus strengthening our conscience. As we exercise our choice to do what is right (i.e., God's will), our conscience will be clear.

One way to strengthen our conscience is to apply ourselves to study the Bible. Paul said, "Work hard so God can say to you, 'Well done.' Be a good workman, one who does not need to be ashamed when God examines your work. Know what his Word says and means" (2 Timothy 2:15). Doing these things will help us become better able to recognize the sin in our lives, so we can promptly deal with it.

When we've discovered what God wants of us, we've also discovered the shortest road to inner peace.

DAY 25 Healing Hunger

Bible Reading: John 6:32-35

We continued to take personal inventory and when we were wrong promptly admitted it.

There is a hunger in every human soul—a hunger for true love, a hunger to be understood, a hunger to be valued. There's a hunger for God. He created that hunger to drive us to himself. We may have fed our hunger with the stuff that tasted good emotionally, but it was never satisfied.

The Lord spoke through the prophet Isaiah asking, "Say there! Is anyone thirsty? Come and drink—even if you have no money! Come, take your choice of wine and milk—it's all free! Why spend your money on food that doesn't give you strength? Why pay for groceries that do you no good? Listen and I'll tell you where to get good food that fattens up the soul!" (Isaiah 55:1-2).

Jesus said, "'And now he [my Father] offers you true Bread from heaven. The true Bread is a Person—the one sent by God from heaven, and he gives life to the world. . . . I am the Bread of Life. No one coming to me will ever be hungry again. Those believing in me will never thirst'" (John 6:32-33, 35).

Jesus Christ claimed to be the Person we're all really hungry for. We could be just filling ourselves up on meetings and even religious rituals without nourishing ourselves on a relationship with him. We may not be using our previous addictions to deal with our hunger, but are we really finding satisfaction? What are we doing to make sure that we're taking in the "true Bread," which can satisfy the deepest of needs?

Our dependencies cannot fill the void that only God was meant to fill.

DAY 26 Opening Up

Bible Reading: Acts 13:21-23

We continued to take personal inventory and when we were wrong promptly admitted it.

We may be inclined to cover up our wrongs or insist that our way is right, even though it's contrary to what God says in the Bible. This attitude may have played a significant role in our past problems. We may not yet believe that it's better to honestly and repeatedly admit our wrongs than to work hard at covering them up.

In recounting the history of Israel, the apostle Paul said, "The people begged for a king, and God gave them Saul . . . who reigned for forty years. But God removed him and replaced him with David as king, a man about whom God said, 'David . . . is a man after my own heart, for he will obey me'" (Acts 13:21-22).

King Saul looked great on the outside. He was tall and handsome. He seemed to always have an answer to cover up his wrongdoing. But God finally removed him from the kingship because whenever he was wrong, he refused to admit it! (See 1 Samuel 15.) God replaced him with David. We might assume that David was an exemplary man. But actually, David was a man who committed many terrible sins, including adultery and murder. The one quality that distinguished him from Saul was that he always agreed with God's view of morality. He immediately admitted his sins when he knew he had violated God's commands.

God isn't looking for someone who looks good on the surface. God has unfailing mercies and love for us when we agree with his commands and admit our faults when we don't measure up.

A spring cleaning is only possible after the dirty rooms have been opened.

DAY 27 Repeated Forgiveness

Bible Reading: Romans 5:3-5

We continued to take personal inventory and when we were wrong promptly admitted it.

We may grow impatient with ourselves when we continue to run into the same sins over and over again. This may cause us to get discouraged, or we may be afraid that we are doomed to relapse.

Peter asked Jesus, "'Sir, how often should I forgive a brother who sins against me? Seven times?' 'No,' Jesus replied, 'seventy times seven!'" (Matthew 18:21-22). If this is to be our attitude toward others, doesn't it make sense that we should extend the same grace to ourselves? We need to be patient with ourselves.

Paul wrote, "We can rejoice, too, when we run into problems and trials, for we know that they are good for us—they help us learn to be patient. And patience develops strength of character in us and helps us trust God more each time we use it until finally our hope and faith are strong and steady. Then when that happens . . . we know how dearly God loves us, and we feel this warm love everywhere within us because God has given us the Holy Spirit to fill our hearts with his love" (Romans 5:3-5).

Learning to wait patiently is an important characteristic for us to develop. Each time we admit wrong and accept God's forgiveness, our hope and faith have a chance to be exercised and to grow stronger. We no longer have to hide in shame every time we slip. We can admit our wrongs and move on. God's love is reaffirmed every time we rely on it. In this way, God helps us to hold our heads high no matter what happens.

Our repeated failures afford us repeated opportunies for healing and growth.

DAY 28 Recurrent Sins

Bible Reading: 1 John 1:8-10

We continued to take personal inventory and when we were wrong promptly admitted it.

We may feel awkward about bringing our recurrent sins before God. We may be embarrassed by the number of times we've had to deal with the same issues—issues that stubbornly refuse to be washed away. We may imagine that God is collecting a long list to be used against us.

The apostle John wrote, "If we say that we have no sin, we are only fooling ourselves, and refusing to accept the truth. But if we confess our sins to him, he can be depended on to forgive us and to cleanse us from every wrong. [And it is perfectly proper for God to do this for us because Christ died to wash away our sins.] If we claim we have not sinned, we are lying and calling God a liar" (1 John 1:8-10).

To confess means to agree with God that what he declares to be wrong really is. To do this, we need to recognize our wrongs when they occur. Notice that he says he will forgive us and cleanse of from *every* wrong. Each time we confess a sin it is washed away. Our lives are like slates that have been wiped clean. Our sins are not recorded on some celestial list. They're gone forever! And each time we confess a sin we've dealt with before, it's forgiven all over again. Some areas of our lives need more cleaning than others! God doesn't get angry when we come back to him again and again. This is the process he set up to cleanse the areas in our lives that cause the most trouble. There's no need to feel awkward. God wants us to come every time we sin.

Confession opens up our hearts to God's cleansing power.

DAY 29 Healing Fellowship

Bible Reading: 1 Thessalonians 5:12-13

We continued to take personal inventory and when we were wrong promptly admitted it.

We've all had different experiences at the churches we've attended. Some of us may have felt condemned and shamed at a church when we desperately needed its help. We may fear rejection. We may wish we were part of a church but don't know how to find a good one. Or we may feel out of place in the church we presently attend. Some of us may think that we don't need a church, that we can do fine on our own.

The Bible makes it clear that no church is perfect, but we're still told to join with a group of Christians. It is through our relationships in the church that God molds us. The apostle Paul once wrote, "Honor the officers of your church who work hard among you and warn you against all that is wrong. Think highly of them and give them your wholehearted love because they are straining to help you" (1 Thessalonians 5:12-13).

The Bible also says, "Let us not neglect our church meetings, as some people do, but encourage and warn each other" (Hebrews 10:25). The church should be a place where believers can encourage and warn each other. They should urge each other to pursue a godly course of conduct. Notice that Paul's advice looks to the future rather than looking back. In the church context, God can raise up people to encourage us to keep moving ahead in our spiritual development. Their perspective can help us to continue taking stock of our lives as we recover.

The church community should provide help, encouragement, and direction.

DAY 30 Human Weakness

Bible Reading: Zechariah 4:6-7

We continued to take personal inventory and when we were wrong promptly admitted it.

As we continue to take personal inventory, we will be reminded that we are human. We are powerless in ourselves, weak and constantly in need of God's mighty power.

Just before Jesus ascended into heaven, he told his disciples, "And now I will send the Holy Spirit upon you, just as my Father promised. Don't begin telling others yet—stay here in the city until the Holy Spirit comes and fills you with power from heaven" (Luke 24:49). When Zerubbabel was given the responsibility for rebuilding the Jewish Temple, God sent him this message: "Not by might, nor by power, but by my Spirit, says the Lord Almighty—you will succeed because of my Spirit, though you are few and weak. Therefore no mountain, however high, can stand before Zerubbabel. For it will flatten out before him! And Zerubbabel will finish building this Temple with mighty shouts of thanksgiving for God's mercy, declaring that all was done by grace alone" (Zechariah 4:6-7).

Every day we need to rely on God's Spirit to fill us with the power we need to live our new life. Just as Zerubbabel could not rely on his own might and power, we cannot trust in our own strength. But we can see our admitted weaknesses swallowed up in the power of God. We can succeed and scale whatever mountains we face by the power of God's Spirit. When we learn to live this way, we will be full of thanksgiving for God's mercy. We'll be able to tell everyone that it is the grace of God that keeps us.

Our weaknesses provide endless opportunities for God to prove his power.

STEP ELEVEN

We sought through prayer and meditation to improve our conscious contact with God, as we understood him, praying only for knowledge of his will for us and the power to carry that out.

"*They that wait upon the Lord shall renew their strength. They shall mount up with wings like eagles; they shall run and not be weary; they shall walk and not faint*" (Isaiah 40:31).

STEP ELEVEN

DAY 1 Joy in God's Presence

Bible Reading: Psalm 65:1-4

We sought through prayer and meditation to improve our conscious contact with God, as we understood him, praying only for knowledge of his will for us and the power to carry that out.

Most of us need to desire something before we will wholeheartedly seek after it. Until we realize how much God loves us and cares about the details of our lives, we won't want to pray to him. Until we sincerely believe that he has completely forgiven us, we will be ashamed to face him. If we hold to our misconceptions about God, this step will be a formidable chore rather than a joy.

The life of King David gives us hope. Long after he had come face to face with his own sinfulness, he was able to sing, "O God in Zion, we wait before you in silent praise, and thus fulfill our vow. And because you answer prayer, all mankind will come to you with their requests. Though sins fill our hearts, you forgive them all. How greatly to be envied are those you have chosen to come and live with you within the holy tabernacle courts! What joys await us among all the good things there" (Psalm 65:1-4). God wants us to be like those who live and serve in his temple, walking freely into his presence. He wants us to know that we are welcome and valued before him. (See also Matthew 10:29-31.)

The place where God lives can be a place of joy and happiness for us now. We can look forward to spending time with him and living in his presence every day.

It is essential for our recovery that we draw close to God.

DAY 2 Pools of Blessing

Bible Reading: Psalm 84:5-11

We sought through prayer and meditation to improve our conscious contact with God, as we understood him, praying only for knowledge of his will for us and the power to carry that out.

Where do we find the desire to seek after the knowledge of his will for us and the power to carry it out? We probably realize that seeking after our own will only brought us misery. Instead of happiness we found sorrow; instead of power we found that we became powerless. In following our own will we ended up depressed and exhausted, on a road leading nowhere.

The desire to seek after the knowledge of God's will comes from realizing that God's plan for us is good. The psalmist wrote, "Happy are those who are strong in the Lord, who want above all else to follow your steps. When they walk through the Valley of Weeping it will become a place of springs where pools of blessing and refreshment collect after rains! They will grow constantly in strength and each of them is invited to meet with the Lord in Zion" (Psalm 84:5-7).

Those who long and pray for God's will are on a road that leads to happiness. We may still walk through the "Valley of Weeping," but out of the sorrow will spring new life. Instead of depression, exhaustion, and a road to nowhere, we will find joy, strength, and a road that leads to heaven and the presence of a loving God.

We are not alone in the Valley of Weeping; God walks there with us.

DAY 3 Meditation

Bible Reading:
Psalm 1:1-3

We sought through prayer and meditation to improve our conscious contact with God, as we understood him, praying only for knowledge of his will for us and the power to carry that out.

Imagination exerts amazing power! Many of us struggle with obsessive thoughts. Our imaginations are haunted by images of doing the things we crave. No matter how hard we try to exert willpower over our imaginations, our willpower loses the battle sooner or later. Instead of trying to summon up more willpower, perhaps we should try a different tactic.

The Lord told Joshua, "Constantly remind the people about these laws, and you yourself must think about them every day and every night so that you will be sure to obey all of them. For only then will you succeed" (Joshua 1:8). When the psalmist described people not caught up in evil, he said, "They . . . are always meditating on his laws and thinking about ways to follow him more closely" (Psalm 1:2). Each of these passages describes meditating as a key to success in following God's will for our lives.

The word *meditate* in the Bible means "to imagine" and "to ponder repeatedly." The key to winning the battle over obsessive thoughts is to fill our imaginations with images of a life lived according to God's plan. There's a better way of life for us. When we begin to "delight in" imagining what that would be like, we will find that we begin to win more of our inner battles.

The more we bask in the joy of God's presence, the more we will discover joy within.

DAY 4 Powerful Secrets

Bible Reading:
Psalm 119:9-11

We sought through prayer and meditation to improve our conscious contact with God, as we understood him, praying only for knowledge of his will for us and the power to carry that out.

The secrets we hide away have enormous power over our lives. How many of our addictive/compulsive behaviors were hidden or covered up? When we took the step to admit the exact nature of our wrongs to another human being, we were amazed at the way the addiction lost power as it was exposed. The power of hidden behaviors and secrets can work for us as well as against us.

David said, "I have thought much about your [God's] words, and stored them in my heart so that they would hold me back from sin" (Psalm 119:9-11). The word rendered *stored* can be translated "to hide by covering over" or "to hoard secretly." If we "hide" God's Word in our hearts by memorizing and imagining it, we will find new power to keep our minds and hearts clean.

The power of secrets also will work to our advantage in our prayer lives. Jesus taught us, "But when you pray, go away by yourself, all alone, and shut the door behind you and pray to your Father secretly, and your Father, who knows your secrets, will reward you" (Matthew 6:6). Secrets have a way of being exposed. When we begin to use our ability to keep secrets for prayer and meditation, we'll find that power working for us. And if these secrets are "exposed," it will be God's rewards that people see.

Special secrets with God can overpower the destructive secrets that hide within us.

DAY 5 Finding God

Bible Reading: Psalm 105:1-9

We sought through prayer and meditation to improve our conscious contact with God, as we understood him, praying only for knowledge of his will for us and the power to carry that out.

As we work the Twelve Steps, we spend a lot of time looking back. We often think about the wrong things we've done in the past. As we proceed in our recovery, we will need strength to move along the path God wants us to follow. Part of this strength will come as we visualize God's constant presence with us.

The psalmist wrote, "Thank the Lord for all the glorious things he does; proclaim them to the nations. Think of the mighty deeds he did for us. . . . Remember how he destroyed our enemies. He is the Lord our God. His goodness is seen everywhere throughout the land. Though a thousand generations pass he never forgets his promise" (Psalm 105:1, 6-9).

From now on when we look back we will see the "mighty deeds he did for us" and "remember how he destroyed our enemies." We will look around to find his goodness "everywhere throughout the land" and look forward to the fulfillment of his promises. In prayer we thank him for what he's done; we seek him for the strength we need today; and we ask him to fulfill his promises for tomorrow. In meditation we remember our victories, ponder his presence with us today, and consider his faithfulness and the hope that gives us for tomorrow.

When we look, we will find God in the past, the future, and the present.

DAY 6 Seeking and Finding

Bible Reading: John 14:15-24

We sought through prayer and meditation to improve our conscious contact with God, as we understood him, praying only for knowledge of his will for us and the power to carry that out.

We can only get to know people to the degree they allow us to do so. We cannot get close to people who choose not to reveal themselves. In most of our human relationships we find that love can open up the door to the heart of the one we seek to know. It is the same way with God.

God reached out to us through the person of Jesus Christ. When we genuinely seek after a love relationship with God, he will then reveal himself to us. Jesus said, "If you love me, obey me; and I will ask the Father and he will give you another Comforter, and he will never leave you. He is the Holy Spirit, the Spirit who leads into all truth. . . . No, I will not abandon you or leave you as orphans in the storm—I will come to you. . . . I will only reveal myself to those who love me and obey me. The Father will love them too, and we will come to them and live with them" (John 14:15-18, 23).

The way to find the knowledge of God's will is through the person of the Holy Spirit who leads us into all truth. We find the power through our relationship with the person of Jesus Christ. As we seek God with a desire to know him and a willingness to obey, he will reveal himself: Father, Son, and Holy Spirit.

As we reach out toward God, we will find his hand already waiting.

DAY 7 Patient Waiting

Bible Reading: Isaiah 40:28-31

We sought through prayer and meditation to improve our conscious contact with God, as we understood him, praying only for knowledge of his will for us and the power to carry that out.

We all want to recover as quickly as possible. It's hard to be patient as we wait for the process to work. Sure, we realize that we didn't get to the difficult spot we're in overnight. We understand that we can't undo a lifetime of damage in a moment. But still, it is a challenge to wait patiently. Every part of recovery requires time and patience with ourselves. This step also requires that we learn to wait for God.

The prophet Isaiah gave us this promise: "They that wait upon the Lord shall renew their strength. They shall mount up with wings like eagles; they shall run and not be weary; they shall walk and not faint" (Isaiah 40:31). Jeremiah said, "The Lord is wonderfully good to those who wait for him, to those who seek for him. It is good both to hope and wait quietly for the salvation of the Lord" (Lamentations 3:25-26).

Waiting for the Lord has its rewards. We can remain calm when it appears that nothing is happening in our recovery. As we learn to respond to life in new ways, the winds of adversity will lift us up, like wind beneath the wings of an eagle, instead of immediately knocking us down. As we develop a patient faith in God we will be able to endure to the end of the race—and win.

Even the strongest of people tire, but God's power never diminishes.

DAY 8 Paralyzed by Perfectionism

Bible Reading: Matthew 25:14-30

We sought through prayer and meditation to improve our conscious contact with God, as we understood him, praying only for knowledge of his will for us and the power to carry that out.

Perfectionism can paralyze us. Perhaps we've been shamed for not being exactly what others wanted us to be. Now the shadow of their unrealistic expectations is cast over how we see ourselves, creating unrealistic expectations for our progress.

Jesus told a story of a man who loaned three servants money to invest for him while he was away. The first two men invested and doubled the money; the third hid his money in a hole. The third servant saw the master through the eyes of fear. He "came and said, 'Sir, I knew you were a hard man, and I was afraid you would rob me of what I earned, so I hid your money in the earth and here it is!' But his master replied, ' . . . Since you knew I would demand your profit, you should at least have put my money into the bank so I could have some interest'" (Matthew 25:24-27).

When we measure ourselves by others' expectations or by our own need to be perfect, we may not even try. All God asks is that we try to do something with our abilities and resources. When we allow ourselves the option of just making modest progress, we'll find courage to try. Even the least improvement is better than being doomed to complete failure by our perfectionism.

Being willing to try will open the door to new aspects of our recovery.

DAY 9 Antidote to Depression

Bible Reading: Psalm 42:4-11

We sought through prayer and meditation to improve our conscious contact with God, as we understood him, praying only for knowledge of his will for us and the power to carry that out.

In bad times we may get lost in our memories of the "good old days." We may find ourselves struggling with conflicting emotions, teetering between the extremes of depression and hope.

The psalmist reflected these emotions, saying to himself, "Take courage, my soul! Do you remember those times (but how could you ever forget them!) when you led a great procession to the Temple on festival days, singing with joy, praising the Lord? Why then be downcast? Why be discouraged and sad? Hope in God! I shall yet praise him again. Yes, I shall again praise him for his help. Yet I am standing here depressed and gloomy, but I will meditate upon your kindness. . . . For I know that I shall again have plenty of reason to praise him for all that he will do. He is my help! He is my God!" (Psalm 42:4-6, 11).

Look how the psalmist improved his conscious contact with God. He talked to himself, commanding his emotions to "hope in God!" He repeated, "I shall yet praise him again," even though he didn't feel that way right then. In the dark times he sang songs, thought about God's steadfast love, and prayed. We can do these things, too.

We will discover hope when we discard our inabilities for God's infinite ability.

DAY 10 Enjoying the "Calm"

Bible Reading: Matthew 16:24-26

We sought through prayer and meditation to improve our conscious contact with God, as we understood him, praying only for knowledge of his will for us and the power to carry that out.

Some of us are addicted to chaos. We may be so used to crisis that we don't know how to enjoy the calm. Life in recovery may seem boring in comparison to our old ways. We may miss the excitement and danger. The rewards may seem too slow in coming.

The apostle Paul said, "And let us not get tired of doing what is right, for after a while we will reap a harvest of blessing if we don't get discouraged and give up" (Galatians 6:9). Weeds spring up immediately. The good crops must be tended steadily even before we can see anything growing. It's only in time that we'll enjoy the fruit.

Jesus suggested that we expand our perspective even further, with a view toward eternity. "Jesus said to the disciples, 'If anyone wants to be a follower of mine, let him deny himself and take up his cross and follow me. For anyone who keeps his life for himself shall lose it; and anyone who loses his life for me shall find it again. What profit is there if you gain the whole world—and lose eternal life?'" (Matthew 16:24-26).

It is God's will for us to have a rewarding and fulfilled life. It may be easier to adjust to our new way of life if we remember that denying ourselves immediate pleasures will bring a harvest of rich rewards, in this life and the life to come.

Immediate pleasures usually have razor blades planted in them.

DAY 11 Showing Love

Bible Reading:
1 Corinthians 13:1-7

We sought through prayer and meditation to improve our conscious contact with God, as we understood him, praying only for knowledge of his will for us and the power to carry that out.

We may have given up on love. Perhaps we've waited for love to find us, only to be disappointed. Maybe our loved ones have hurt us so badly that we needed to numb ourselves from the pain. Our addictions helped to keep us numb. Now that we're in recovery we have to find a way to deal with the issue of love once again.

It's God's will that we love; without love nothing else matters (see 1 Corinthians 13:1-3). Love is more than a feeling. It's a choice of behavior that grows in our lives; it's a fruit of the Holy Spirit, produced in our lives as we yield to God. The Bible defines it this way, "Love is very patient and kind, never jealous or envious, never boastful or proud, never haughty or selfish or rude. . . . If you love someone you will be loyal to him no matter what the cost. You will always believe in him, always expect the best of him, and always stand your ground in defending him" (1 Corinthians 13:4-7).

No one loves perfectly, but we must not give up on loving. We can accept the responsibility to love others and stop playing the victim by waiting for them to love us. We can be patient with ourselves while love grows. When we choose to act lovingly, the emotions will follow. We'll also find that love comes back to us.

The better we know God, the more we'll find ourselves showing love.

DAY 12 Love Is Waiting

Bible Reading:
1 John 4:7-10

We sought through prayer and meditation to improve our conscious contact with God, as we understood him, praying only for knowledge of his will for us and the power to carry that out.

We may feel like love just doesn't seem to work for us. We may wonder if we're doing something wrong. Perhaps we have problems loving because we're disconnected from the source of true love.

The apostle John wrote, "Dear friends, let us practice loving each other, for love comes from God. . . . But if a person isn't loving and kind, it shows that he doesn't know God—for God is love" (1 John 4:7-8).

Jesus said, "I am giving a new commandment to you now—love each other just as much as I love you" (John 13:34). Trying to love without first receiving God's love is like trying to water something with a hose that's disconnected from the faucet. When we receive God's unconditional love for us we can begin to love ourselves. We are then told to love others as we love ourselves and as Jesus has loved us. There is a boundless reservoir of love available to us; but without receiving the love of God in Christ we will run dry.

Jesus is waiting for us to open up and receive his love. He said, "Look! . . . I am constantly knocking. If anyone hears me calling him and opens the door, I will come in and fellowship with him and he with me" (Revelation 3:20). Love is waiting. All we have to do is to open up to the love God offers us.

The more contact we have with God, the more we're aware of his love for us.

DAY 13 Loved by God

Bible Reading: Psalm 8:1-6

We sought through prayer and meditation to improve our conscious contact with God, as we understood him, praying only for knowledge of his will for us and the power to carry that out.

We develop our self-perception by noticing how the important people in our lives see us. If we grew up in a dysfunctional family, their skewed view of us probably warped our ability to see ourselves as we truly are in God's eyes.

King David was amazed at the place God has made for us in his plan. He said, "I cannot understand how you can bother with mere puny man, to pay any attention to him! And yet you have made him only a little lower than the angels, and placed a crown of glory and honor upon his head. You have put him in charge of everything you made; everything is put under his authority" (Psalm 8:4-6). "How precious it is, Lord, to realize that you are thinking about me constantly! I can't even count how many times a day your thoughts turn toward me. And when I waken in the morning, you are still thinking of me!" (Psalm 139:17-18). The greatest demonstration of how precious we are in God's sight is that Jesus gave his life for us.

God wants us to realize how precious we are to him and to begin to see ourselves in the light of his love. Consider this: If we were worth God's giving up the most precious thing he had (his only Son), what does that say about our value?

It is overwhelming when we begin to realize how much God really loves us.

DAY 14 A New Hiding Place

Bible Reading:
2 Samuel 22:1-33

We sought through prayer and meditation to improve our conscious contact with God, as we understood him, praying only for knowledge of his will for us and the power to carry that out.

In the past we used our addictions as a hiding place when life became overwhelming. Now that we are in recovery, life can at times feel even more overwhelming. We'll need a new place of refuge to escape the storms and find protection.

King David experienced many battles. He said of God, "Jehovah [God] is my rock, my fortress and my Savior. I will hide in God, who is my rock and my refuge. He is my shield and my salvation, my refuge and high tower. . . . I will call upon the Lord, who is worthy to be praised; he will save me from all my enemies. The waves of death surrounded me; floods of evil burst upon me; I was trapped, and bound by hell and death; but I called upon the Lord in my distress, and he heard me from his Temple. My cry reached his ears. . . . He shields all who hide behind him. Our Lord alone is God; we have no other Savior. God is my strong fortress; he has made me safe" (2 Samuel 22:2-7, 31-33).

There will always be times when we feel the need for a safe place to run and hide. God can be that hiding place. When we were in distress, "trapped and bound by hell and death," we called to God and he brought us to where we are today. He's always there, ready to shield and protect us whenever we call on him.

When our lives are shaky, God is the only safe place for us to hide.

DAY 15 A Time to Rest

Bible Reading: Exodus 20:8-11

We sought through prayer and meditation to improve our conscious contact with God, as we understood him, praying only for knowledge of his will for us and the power to carry that out.

We need to have all our faculties about us as we seek to maintain our sobriety. If we allow ourselves to get overtired we'll be less able to cope with the demands of life and more susceptible to relapse.

Rest is essential to the maintenance of any kind of balanced life. Weekly rest was included as one of the Ten Commandments. God declared, "Six days a week are for your daily duties and your regular work, but the seventh day is a day of Sabbath rest before the Lord your God. On that day you are to do no work of any kind. . . . For in six days the Lord made the heaven, earth, and sea, and everything in them, and rested the seventh day; so he blessed the Sabbath day and set it aside for rest" (Exodus 20:9-11). The Sabbath is described as "a weekly reminder forever of my promises to the people of Israel" (31:17).

God wants us to have rest and balance. A weekly "Sabbath" or intermission is a time to relax from our regular duties and allow our bodies to rest. It is also a time of spiritual refreshment, a time to reflect on God's promises. It is a day of renewing our contact with God and remembering that he sustains us in our sobriety.

We all need a day to draw close to God, his power, and his promises.

DAY 16 God Is for Me!

Bible Reading: Job 19:8-27

We sought through prayer and meditation to improve our conscious contact with God, as we understood him, praying only for knowledge of his will for us and the power to carry that out.

When we experience pain and loss because of something that seems out of our control, we may feel like God is our enemy. We may never grasp why God allows such torment, but we can have faith that a time will come when we will understand his will for us.

Job felt this way, too. He said, "God has blocked my path and turned my light to darkness. He has stripped me of my glory and removed the crown from my head. He has broken me down on every side, and I am done for. He has destroyed all hope. His fury burns against me; he counts me as an enemy. He sends his troops to surround my tent. . . . My best friends abhor me. Those I loved have turned against me. I am skin and bones and have escaped death by the skin of my teeth. . . . Oh, that I could write my plea with an iron pen in the rock forever. But as for me, I know that my Redeemer lives, and that he will stand upon the earth at last. And I know that after this body has decayed, this body shall see God! Then he will be on *my* side! Yes, I shall see him, not as a stranger, but as a friend! What a glorious hope!" (Job 19:8-27).

God is on our side, even if we can't see it now.

We can be sure that God is on our side, even when life lets us down.

DAY 17 Running to Win

Bible Reading: Hebrews 11:1–12:1

We sought through prayer and meditation to improve our conscious contact with God, as we understood him, praying only for knowledge of his will for us and the power to carry that out.

Many of us feel like losers that have dropped out of the race of life. Faith in God can give us the motivation to run the race, with a real chance at life's rewards.

Chapter 11 of Hebrews has been called faith's "Hall of Fame." It refers to people whose lives were used by God because of their faith. The following chapter begins this way: "Since we have such a huge crowd of men of faith watching us from the grandstands, let us strip off anything that slows us down or holds us back, and especially those sins that wrap themselves so tightly around our feet and trip us up; and let us run with patience the particular race that God has set before us" (12:1).

This illustration referred to the Olympic games. In Bible times, men wore flowing robes. At the time of an event the athletes would strip off their robes and lay them aside to run without encumbrance. If someone tried to compete in his robes, he would get tangled up, losing both the race and the prize.

It is God's will for us to win the race of life. The robes of our recurrent sins need to be laid aside. There will be pain from the exertion, but we're told to pace ourselves and to bear it with patience. And remember, others who have run the same race and finished well are cheering us on!

The closer we come to God, the simpler our lives become.

DAY 18 Rebuilding Our Faith

Bible Reading: Luke 22:31-34

We sought through prayer and meditation to improve our conscious contact with God, as we understood him, praying only for knowledge of his will for us and the power to carry that out.

It is easy to lose faith when we're troubled. As we're buffeted about by life, we may feel like the faith we once had has slipped away. We may begin to feel anger toward God.

Simon Peter had his ups and downs with God. On the night Simon Peter would deny him, Jesus said to him, "Simon, Simon, Satan has asked to have you, to sift you like wheat, but I have pleaded in prayer for you that your faith should not completely fail. So when you have repented and turned to me again, strengthen and build up the faith of your brothers" (Luke 22:31-32).

Jesus pointed out that Simon had an assailant in the spiritual realm. Jesus knew Peter would be attacked and "sifted," but he also was confident that afterwards Peter would return to God. Wheat is sifted by throwing it repeatedly into the air and catching it. The kernels are separated from the chaff as the lighter chaff is carried away by the wind. All that remain are the solid wheat kernels, which are good.

We should not be surprised that we face times when our faith seems to disappear. We may feel like we are being ripped open and our faith is being blown away. But we needn't worry. We'll find the core of our faith again. And when we do, we'll be all the better for it—and better able to encourage others, too.

With God's help, even our failures can be useful in our recovery.

DAY 19 A New Life

Bible Reading: 1 Chronicles 28:19-21

We sought through prayer and meditation to improve our conscious contact with God, as we understood him, praying only for knowledge of his will for us and the power to carry that out.

Full recovery doesn't stop with repairing our brokenness. It includes building a new life that's free, full, and rich. It takes courage to let ourselves dream of the life we truly desire. What if we allow ourselves to hope only to be disappointed again? What if we start and fail, suffering public humiliation? These fears can paralyze us and keep us from life in all its fullness.

David dreamed of building a magnificent temple. In commissioning his son Solomon to do the work he said, "Every part of this blueprint . . . was given to me in writing from the hand of the Lord. . . . Be strong and courageous and get to work. Don't be frightened by the size of the task, for the Lord my God is with you; he will not forsake you" (1 Chronicles 28:19-20). The apostle Paul said, "We who believe are carefully joined together with Christ as parts of a beautiful, constantly growing temple for God" (Ephesians 2:21).

Just as David dreamed of building a magnificent temple, we can dare to dream of building a magnificent new life. We need not be frightened by the size of the task, for "God who began the good work within you will keep right on helping you grow in his grace until his task within you is finally finished" (Philippians 1:6).

Our knowing God will provide the courage we need to build a new life.

DAY 20 Common Sense

Bible Reading: Proverbs 4:1-10

We sought through prayer and meditation to improve our conscious contact with God, as we understood him, praying only for knowledge of his will for us and the power to carry that out.

We're learning to think in new ways. As we develop new thought processes we may lack confidence in our own wisdom and common sense. We may hesitate to carry out God's will if we are afraid of the criticism of the people around us.

Common sense could be defined as our ability to figure out in advance what the likely consequences of our choices and actions will be. We're told, "Getting wisdom is the most important thing you can do! And with your wisdom, develop common sense and good judgment" (Proverbs 4:7). We can exercise our common sense by thinking about what we can do and then doing the things that we can.

A woman wanted to do something to display her love for Jesus. So she poured some expensive perfume on him. When she did this she was criticized by the disciples. Jesus came to her defense with these words, "Let her alone; why berate her for doing a good thing? . . . She has done what she could" (Mark 14:6-8). These are words we also can cling to.

God wants to renew our minds and help us develop wisdom and common sense. As we try to sort out our choices and develop common sense, people may criticize us. But we can trust that God will come to our defense as long as we do what we can.

God will bring about our recovery as we seek to do what we can.

STEP ELEVEN

DAY 21 A Listening God

Bible Reading: Genesis 18:20-33

We sought through prayer and meditation to improve our conscious contact with God, as we understood him, praying only for knowledge of his will for us and the power to carry that out.

Sometimes we become involved in extremely touchy situations. We may wonder if it's possible to change the circumstances while staying within God's will.

Here's what Abraham did in such a situation. "The Lord told Abraham, 'I have heard that the people of Sodom and Gomorrah are utterly evil, and that everything they do is wicked. I am going down to see whether these reports are true or not.' . . . Then Abraham approached him and said, 'Will you kill good and bad alike? Suppose you find fifty godly people there within the city—will you destroy it, and not spare it for their sakes?. . . Why, you would be treating the godly and wicked exactly the same! Surely you wouldn't do that! Should not the Judge of all the earth be fair?' And God replied, 'If I find fifty godly people there, I will spare the entire city for their sake'" (Genesis 18:20-26). The bargaining went on: Suppose there are only forty-five . . . forty . . . thirty . . . twenty . . . ten? And God said, "Then for the sake of the ten, I will not destroy it" (18:32).

Abraham wasn't sure what God's will was in this case; so he talked it over with him. When we don't know how much of a change we can—or even should—make, we can talk it over with God and then try to do as much as we feel confident doing.

God is interested in us and will support our desires for change.

DAY 22 Selfishness

Bible Reading:
Isaiah 14:12-15

We sought through prayer and meditation to improve our conscious contact with God, as we understood him, praying only for knowledge of his will for us and the power to carry that out.

When we were following after our addictions, we were powerfully directed by our desires. We were driven. We didn't think about the effect this had on others. Our selfishness was in control and cut us off from life as it should have been.

Selfishness is at the heart of destructive behavior. The Bible indicates that Satan was once a high-ranking angel in service of the Lord. Isaiah gives us a glimpse of Satan's fall, writing: "How you are fallen from heaven, O Lucifer, son of the morning! How you are cut down to the ground. . . . For you said to yourself, 'I will ascend to heaven and rule the angels. . . . I will climb to the highest heavens and be like the Most High.' But instead, you will be brought down to the pit of hell, down to its lowest depths" (Isaiah 14:12-15).

The same kind of selfishness that brought Satan down resides in the hearts of all people on earth. No one is exempt. Addicts are no worse in nature than anyone else. It's just that the ways we've chosen to meet our needs have led us to hit bottom and go through our own personal hell. When we are free enough to focus on God's will and his power to work in our lives, he will show us a way to fulfill the needs we were trying to satisfy in vain.

When our recovery becomes selfish, a relapse is just around the corner.

DAY 23 The Highest Power

Bible Reading: John 14:6-10

We sought through prayer and meditation to improve our conscious contact with God, as we understood him, praying only for knowledge of his will for us and the power to carry that out.

Christian people may have condemned us to the point that now we associate Jesus Christ with rejection and disapproval. These images may make us shy away from Jesus as a distinct representative of God. We may feel more comfortable with a nameless higher Power, whose nature is rather vague.

"Jesus shouted to the crowds, 'If you trust me, you are really trusting God. For when you see me, you are seeing the one who sent me. I have come as a Light to shine in this dark world, so that all who put their trust in me will no longer wander in the darkness'" (John 12:44-46). Then he told his disciples, "I am the Way—yes, and the Truth, and the Life. No one can get to the Father except by means of me. If you had known who I am, then you would have known who my Father is. From now on you know him—and have seen him! . . . The words I say are not my own but are from my Father who lives in me. And he does his work through me" (14:7, 10).

Jesus said clearly, "This is the will of God, that you believe in the one he has sent" (John 6:29). If we accept the Bible at all, we will see that the knowledge of God's will isn't vague and mysterious. It starts with believing in Jesus.

Following God's will starts by believing that Jesus is the highest power.

DAY 24 Friends of the Light

Bible Reading:
John 3:18-21

We sought through prayer and meditation to improve our conscious contact with God, as we understood him, praying only for knowledge of his will for us and the power to carry that out.

Sometimes we don't want to know God's will because there are areas in our lives that we aren't ready to deal with yet. Recovery is a process for us. We may be ready to pray for God's will in some areas but feel uncomfortable with having God's light shine into the areas that are still hidden in shame.

When talking about those who refuse to trust him with their lives, Jesus said, "The Light from heaven came into the world, but they loved the darkness more than the Light, for their deeds were evil. . . . They stayed away from that Light for fear their sins would be exposed and they would be punished" (John 3:19-20). "Later in one of his talks, Jesus said to the people, 'I am the Light of the world. So if you follow me, you won't be stumbling through the darkness, for living light will flood your path'" (John 8:12).

Darkness is great when we're trying to hide something; but light is needed when we're trying to walk without stumbling. When we were hiding the shameful issues of our lives and holding on to our addictions, the darkness seemed like our friend. Now that we're trying to walk in the steps of recovery, we need the light to keep us from stumbling. We don't have to be afraid of God's light anymore. He wants to safely guide us on the right path.

The better we know God, the closer we will walk to the light of his will.

DAY 25 Persistent Prayer

Bible Reading: Luke 11:5-10

We sought through prayer and meditation to improve our conscious contact with God, as we understood him, praying only for knowledge of his will for us and the power to carry that out.

We may not pray because when we prayed in the past, it didn't seem to work. We may even have prayed for things that are promised in the Bible, but didn't get a response. This can be discouraging and make us want to give up on prayer.

While teaching about prayer, Jesus used this example: "Suppose you went to a friend's house at midnight, wanting to borrow three loaves of bread. . . . I'll tell you this—though he won't do it as a friend, if you keep knocking long enough he will get up and give you everything you want—just because of your persistence" (Luke 11:5-8).

In Old Testament times God had given promises to Israel regarding Jerusalem. Then he told them, "I have set intercessors on your walls who shall cry to God all day and all night for the fulfillment of his promises. Take no rest, all you who pray, and give God no rest until he establishes Jerusalem" (Isaiah 62:6-7).

Prayer takes persistence. It's not a magic button we push to make God move. We can be confident that if we persistently pray for the things that are God's will and don't rest from prayer until he fulfills his promises, we will see results.

When we ask persistently of a generous God, we will receive a generous share.

DAY 26 God's Peace

Bible Reading: Philippians 4:4-7

We sought through prayer and meditation to improve our conscious contact with God, as we understood him, praying only for knowledge of his will for us and the power to carry that out.

There are times when we're caught off guard by life. We are suddenly faced with problems that can wipe out our joy in an instant. Our hearts are disquieted and our minds begin to race. When we are grappling with unsettling problems that come our way and cause us to worry, it's time to run to God in prayer.

From his prison cell, Paul wrote this message, "Don't worry about anything; instead, pray about everything; tell God your needs and don't forget to thank him for his answers. If you do this you will experience God's peace, which is far more wonderful than the human mind can understand" (Philippians 4:6-7).

The psalmist wrote, "Go through his open gates with great thanksgiving; enter his courts with praise. Give thanks to him and bless his name. For the Lord is always good. He is always loving and kind, and his faithfulness goes on and on to each succeeding generation" (Psalm 100:4-5).

God's gates are always open to us. He's waiting for us, whenever we're upset and in need of a friend. We'll still feel the painful emotions. We don't just hand them over to God and expect them to disappear. Prayer is a useful tool to help us work through our problems. He will give us his peace, reminding us that he's there with us. For this, we can be thankful.

A life bathed in prayer is the best antidote for worry.

DAY 27 Knowing and Being Known

Bible Reading: Hosea 6:1-3

We sought through prayer and meditation to improve our conscious contact with God, as we understood him, praying only for knowledge of his will for us and the power to carry that out.

Intimacy issues can be intimidating, especially for those of us who grew up in dysfunctional families. We may not feel safe to reveal our true selves to anyone. We may be afraid that if we were deeply intimate with others, if we let them into our hearts, they would reject us once they really knew us. We may find prayer intimidating for some of the same reasons.

Hosea once said, "Oh, that we might know the Lord! Let us press on to know him, and he will respond to us as surely as the coming of dawn or the rain of early spring" (Hosea 6:3).

God wants us to know him; but he wants an intimate relationship with us, not just a surface one. The biblical word translated *know* is also used to describe sexual intimacy. It's the same word used in Genesis to describe the sexual intimacy between Adam and Eve (Genesis 4:1, NKJV). Coming to know God is an act of growing and deep intimacy. It is more than knowing him with our heads; it is a knowing that takes place in our hearts as well.

If we are afraid of knowing or being known deeply by God, we will want to avoid prayer. And yet Daniel reminds us that it is those of us who are intimate with God who will have the strength to do great things. We are safe to reveal our true selves to God. As we dare to do so, he will surely respond.

As our knowledge of God grows, so will our strength for recovery.

DAY 28 Resting in God

Bible Reading:
John 14:12-14

We sought through prayer and meditation to improve our conscious contact with God, as we understood him, praying only for knowledge of his will for us and the power to carry that out.

We may have lived most of our lives trying to take care of our own needs. Our addictive behaviors may have been misplaced attempts to accomplish this very thing. Once we've given up our addictions, it's still hard to rely on others to do things for us, even when we don't have the power to handle them ourselves. This tendency to avoid reliance on others may come into play in our prayer lives, making it hard for us to depend on God.

Jesus told his disciples, "In solemn truth I tell you, anyone believing in me shall do the same miracles I have done, and even greater ones, because I am going to be with the Father. You can ask him for *anything*, using my name, and I will do it, for this will bring praise to the Father because of what I, the Son, will do for you. Yes, ask *anything*, using my name, and I will do it!" (John 14:12-14).

Jesus has been given all authority in heaven and earth to do anything. He demonstrated this throughout his life by the mighty miracles he performed. We may feel that it would take a miracle to deal with some of our unresolved issues. But we may also be afraid of being disappointed if we rely on God to meet our needs. Jesus has given us an open door and strong assurances that there's no need too big or too small. We really can rely on him for anything!

When our requests are in line with God's will, he promises to answer.

DAY 29 A Trustworthy God

Bible Reading: Mark 11:22-24

We sought through prayer and meditation to improve our conscious contact with God, as we understood him, praying only for knowledge of his will for us and the power to carry that out.

We may have avoided prayer before we entered recovery and now find that we have questions about it. Maybe we find that our prayers go unanswered and wonder why. We may lack faith because we're not sure the things we're asking for are in God's will. Our faith may also be weak because of all the broken promises we've experienced with others. All of these things can discourage.

There are a few basic guidelines to follow when asking God for something in prayer. First, we need to ask: "The reason you don't have what you want is that you don't ask God for it" (James 4:2). Second, we need to ask in accordance with God's will: "Even when you do ask you don't get it because your whole aim is wrong—you want only what will give *you* pleasure" (James 4:3). God won't give us the things that feed our lusts and addictions.

"Jesus said to the disciples, . . . 'All that's required is that you really believe and have no doubt! Listen to me! You can pray for *anything*, and *if you believe, you have it;* it's yours!" (Mark 11:22-24). The way we develop a faith without doubt is to become sure about what is in God's will. This assurance comes from knowing what he has promised us in the Bible.

The better we know God, the more we will discover how trustworthy he is.

DAY 30 Thirst for God

Bible Reading: Psalm 27:1-6

We sought through prayer and meditation to improve our conscious contact with God, as we understood him, praying only for knowledge of his will for us and the power to carry that out.

We may have started out going to God for the sake of what he could do for us, namely, freeing us from the power and effects of addiction. Now we may be surprised to find that we're going to God out of a desire to be near someone who is wonderful, who loves us completely.

King David gave us a glimpse into his relationship with God, saying, "The one thing I want from God, the thing I seek most of all, is the privilege of meditating in his Temple, living in his presence every day of my life, delighting in his incomparable perfections and glory. There I'll be when troubles come. He will hide me. He will set me on a high rock out of reach of all my enemies. Then I will bring him sacrifices and sing his praises with much joy" (Psalm 27:4-6).

David found great joy by improving his conscious contact with God. God is always there, but we're not always aware of his presence. When we began to go to God to get what we needed, we grew more and more attracted to him. But when we begin to focus on getting to know God as an end in itself, we will discover that he will slowly and surely give us our hearts' desires. Then we will see that he can be trusted with every area of our lives.

We should run to God every day—even on the best of days!

STEP TWELVE

Having had a spiritual awakening as the result of these steps, we tried to carry this message to others and to practice these principles in all our affairs.

***"The Spirit of the Lord God is upon me, because the Lord has anointed me to bring good news to the suffering and afflicted"* (Isaiah 61:1).**

STEP TWELVE

DAY 1 Our Stories

Bible Reading: Mark 16:14-18

Having had a spiritual awakening as the result of these steps, we tried to carry this message to others and to practice these principles in all our affairs.

Each one of us has a valuable story to tell. We may be shy and feel awkward about speaking. We may wonder if what we have to share is trivial. Is it actually going to help anyone else? We may struggle to get beyond the shame of our past. But our recovery story can help others who are trapped back where we were. Are we willing to allow God to use us to help free others?

Jesus left us with this vital task, "You are to go into all the world and preach the Good News [of salvation from the bondage and penalty of sin] to everyone, everywhere" (Mark 16:15).

Paul traveled the world over telling everyone the story of his conversion. He ended up in chains, but his spirit was free. He presented his defense (and his own story of redemption) before kings. King Agrippa interrupted him to say, "'With trivial proofs like these, you expect me to become a Christian?' And Paul replied, 'Would to God that whether my arguments are trivial or strong, both you and everyone here in this audience might become the same as I am, except for these chains'" (Acts 26:28-29).

Within each personal story of the journey from bondage to freedom is a microcosm of the gospel. When people hear our story, even if it seems trivial, we are offering them the chance to loosen their chains and begin a recovery story of their own.

All of our recovery stories are custom designed for another person's encouragement.

DAY 2 Never Forget

Bible Reading: Titus 3:1-5

Having had a spiritual awakening as the result of these steps, we tried to carry this message to others and to practice these principles in all our affairs.

As we get further along in our recovery, the memory of how bad it really was may begin to fade. Do we vividly remember what we once were? Can we recall the dark emotions that filled our souls? Do we have true compassion and humble sympathy for those to whom we try to carry the message?

When we take the message of recovery to others it is vital that we never forget where we came from and how we got where we are. Paul told Titus: "Once we, too, were foolish and disobedient; we were misled by others and became slaves to many evil pleasures and wicked desires. . . . But when the time came for the kindness and love of God our Savior to appear, then he saved us—not because we were good enough to be saved, but because of his kindness and pity—by washing away our sins and giving us the new joy of the indwelling Holy Spirit" (Titus 3:3-5).

As we share our message, let us never forget the following truths. We, too, were slaves just like they now are. Our hearts were filled with the confusion and painful emotions that others still feel. We were saved only because of the love and kindness of God, not because we became good enough. We must also remember that we are only able to stay free because God is with us, upholding us every step of the way.

Sharing our recovery will remind us of how far we've come and how much God loves us.

DAY 3 Sharing Together

Bible Reading: Galatians 6:1-3

Having had a spiritual awakening as the result of these steps, we tried to carry this message to others and to practice these principles in all our affairs.

Since we have worked through the Twelve Steps, we are in a special position to carry the message to others. We can recognize the warning signs of addictive/compulsive tendencies in those around us, as well as in ourselves. When touching on such deep and sensitive issues it's important to speak in the language of love, not condemnation.

The Bible tells us that if someone "is overcome by some sin, you who are godly should gently and humbly help him back onto the right path, remembering that next time it might be one of you who is in the wrong. Share each other's troubles and problems, and so obey our Lord's command" (Galatians 6:1-2). The command was the one Jesus taught his disciples, "And so I am giving a new commandment to you now—love each other just as much as I love you" (John 13:34). "I demand that you love each other as much as I love you. And here is how to measure it—the greatest love is shown when a person lays down his life for his friends" (15:12-13).

We are not the Savior, but we can love others as he has loved us. Love goes beyond mere words. Sometimes it is spoken in silence, when we don't condemn someone who's looking for help. Love doesn't just tell them what the problem is. It helps carry the weight of their burdens. We can be a part of a support network to help carry our friends until they are able to take steps toward recovery on their own initiative.

Sharing our own recovery will remind us of our need for others.

DAY 4 Our Mission

Bible Reading:
Isaiah 61:1-3

Having had a spiritual awakening as the result of these steps, we tried to carry this message to others and to practice these principles in all our affairs.

A life that has been set free from addiction is a beautiful sight to behold. When we practice these principles, people will gain hope and see the glory of God in our lives. We know from experience the depths of suffering, affliction, and brokenness. We know the pain of being enslaved to our passions and blinded by our denial. We have endured our season of grieving. We can relate to those who struggle to be free. We also know that there is more to life than bondage. There is healing and freedom; there is clarity and mercy; there is beauty and joy; there is heaven as well as hell.

When Jesus came to earth he had a mission, which was expressed in these words, "The Spirit of the Lord God is upon me, because the Lord has anointed me to bring good news to the suffering and afflicted. He has sent me to comfort the brokenhearted, to announce liberty to captives, and to open the eyes of the blind. He has sent me to tell those who mourn that the time of God's favor to them has come. . . . To all who mourn . . . he will give: beauty for ashes; joy instead of mourning; praise instead of heaviness" (Isaiah 61:1-3).

This mission has been passed on to us. Some people talk about "preaching the gospel" but may alienate those who need the Good News the most. We're in a unique position to share our experience, strength, and hope in a way that broken people can receive it.

Our mission is to share the "good news" of our recovery.

DAY 5 Celebrating Success

Bible Reading: Hebrews 10:25

Having had a spiritual awakening as the result of these steps, we tried to carry this message to others and to practice these principles in all our affairs.

Life flows in seasons. We all deal with life in terms of days and weeks, months and years. Special events, both personal and spiritual, are commemorated throughout the calendars of our lives. Birthdays, anniversaries, and holidays are woven into the fabric of our days to help keep us connected to God. They also remind us where we've come from and where we're headed.

The Bible is full of examples that show the importance of integrating the spiritual with the "practice of the principles" in our everyday life. Daniel prayed three times a day, every day. The disciples of Jesus went to the Temple regularly for worship and prayer, "as was their custom." Christians are told, "Let us not neglect our church meetings, as some people do, but encourage and warn each other" (Hebrews 10:25). All faithful Jews were required to celebrate the sacred feasts three times each year.

God knows that we easily forget the deep truths of the spirit if we disconnect the spiritual from our daily lives. We need to take care to commemorate the victories we've had. We need to attend regular meetings, to encourage one another, to celebrate each year of our sobriety, to tell our story over and over again "to our children and our children's children." That way, we will never forget and we will bring hope to others.

Celebrating our past victories can bring encouragement to ourselves and others.

DAY 6 The Narrow Road

Bible Reading: 1 Peter 4:1-4

Having had a spiritual awakening as the result of these steps, we tried to carry this message to others and to practice these principles in all our affairs.

We probably came into recovery because we'd had enough! We'd had enough of the pain, the lies, and the destruction that addictive/compulsive behaviors bring with them. One day at a time, we learned the principles on the road to recovery. Now we're at a place we weren't sure we could ever reach—Step Twelve. Now we're told to share the message with others. We mustn't be discouraged when we find that not everyone will welcome the message.

Peter pointed out, "You have had enough in the past of the evil things the godless enjoy—sex sin, lust, getting drunk, wild parties, drinking bouts. . . . Your former friends will be very surprised when you don't eagerly join them anymore in the wicked things they do, and they will laugh at you in contempt and scorn" (1 Peter 4:3-4).

Jesus said, "Heaven can be entered only through the narrow gate! The highway to hell is broad, and its gate is wide enough for all the multitudes who choose its easy way. But the Gateway to Life is small, and the road is narrow, and only a few ever find it" (Matthew 7:13-14).

Our message won't be accepted by the masses. The people on the "highway to hell" won't eagerly restrict themselves to the clearly defined steps on the road to recovery.

As we share our recovery with others, we bring new strength to our own recovery journey.

DAY 7 Talking the Walk

Bible Reading:
1 Timothy
4:14-16

Having had a spiritual awakening as the result of these steps, we tried to carry this message to others and to practice these principles in all our affairs.

When we wake up to realize everything we've gained by following the Twelve Steps, it will be natural to want to share this life-giving message with others. If we think back to the time before we entered recovery we'll probably recall that we didn't respond very well to "preaching." And yet, we also realize that there are people in our lives who our message could help. We are right in our estimation of how vital our message is to their lives. This is why we need to communicate in a way that they can receive.

The apostle Paul taught Timothy that to get the message across, we need to combine the practice of our beliefs with the telling of them. He said, "Throw yourself into your tasks so that everyone may notice your improvement and progress. Keep a close watch on all you do and think. Stay true to what is right and God will . . . use you to help others" (1 Timothy 4:15-16). When we practice the principles of the Twelve Steps, others will be watching and will notice the changes. This will open the door for us to be able to tell them our story as well.

We must never let ourselves forget that every addict is a precious lost soul whom God loves and wants to rescue. "If anyone has slipped away . . . that person who brings him back to God will have saved a wandering soul from death, bringing about the forgiveness of his many sins" (James 5:19-20).

Talking about our recovery helps us to keep ourselves on track.

DAY 8 Ready to Help

Bible Reading: Romans 12:1-5

Having had a spiritual awakening as the result of these steps, we tried to carry this message to others and to practice these principles in all our affairs.

We may feel like we're not good enough to be an example for others. We may realize that we need other people, but find it hard to believe that our story could help anyone else.

The apostle Paul said, "Just as there are many parts to our bodies, so it is with Christ's body. We are all parts of it, and it takes every one of us to make it complete, for we each have different work to do. So we belong to each other, and each needs all the others" (Romans 12:4-5).

To have a true view of where we fit in the scheme of things, we need to see that God has a purpose for our lives. God created each of us with abilities and talents. He likens us to a part of a body where every part is needed for the proper working of the whole. If you isolate any one part of a body and examine it, apart from its proper place among the other members, it may seem odd and useless. It is only when it is connected to the body and doing its appointed job that it realizes its usefulness. And so it is with us.

We need to find a place where our talents and abilities can be used to help others. Doing this will show that we have gained an honest understanding of whom God created us to be. He loves us and wants to help us realize our place in the body of Christ and our purpose in life.

We're ready to help others when we've taken the step they're about to take.

DAY 9 A Shield of Protection

Bible Reading:
Ephesians 6:13-17

Having had a spiritual awakening as the result of these steps, we tried to carry this message to others and to practice these principles in all our affairs.

Recovery is not a battle anyone wins alone. We help each other to think and live in new ways. Alone we're vulnerable. Together we form a shield of protection for one another.

The apostle Paul wrote, "In every battle you will need faith as your shield to stop the fiery arrows aimed at you by Satan" (Ephesians 6:16). Faith here refers to trust in Christ for salvation. In general terms, it also means having constancy in our convictions. This can apply to our convictions about the Twelve Step principles. The shield of faith was likened to the shields carried by Roman soldiers, which were able to cover the entire body. To advance in battle, a group of soldiers would assemble together, making a wall of shields for protection as they moved.

In like manner, we are told to stick together, "not forsaking the assembling of ourselves together, as is the manner of some, but exhorting one another" (Hebrews 10:25, NKJV). We are to take our place in the unity that helps protect us and those with whom our lives are connected.

We need to assemble with others who share the common beliefs helpful in our recovery. Our encouragement of one another, our shared faith, and the principles of the Twelve Steps will be a form of protection as we continue to advance in recovery.

By standing together, we form a shield against a relapse and other dangers.

DAY 10 Listening First

Bible Reading:
Acts 8:26-40

Having had a spiritual awakening as the result of these steps, we tried to carry this message to others and to practice these principles in all our affairs.

We may be so excited about what God has done for us or so concerned for those in need of recovery that we want to rush right out and tell everyone our story. Or we may be very shy and hesitate to tell anyone, especially if we think they are better than us. We all have a valuable story to tell; we just need to learn how best to communicate it.

The apostle Philip was led to meet an influential traveler. "He had gone to Jerusalem to worship and was now returning . . . reading aloud from the book of the prophet Isaiah. The Holy Spirit said to Philip, 'Go over and walk along beside the chariot.' Philip ran over and heard what he was reading and asked, 'Do you understand it?' 'Of course not!' the man replied. 'How can I when there is no one to instruct me?' . . . So Philip began with this same Scripture and then used many others to tell him about Jesus" (Acts 8:27-31, 35).

The way Philip communicated can be a model for us. He was sensitive to allow God to lead him to someone who was ready. He wasn't so intimidated by the man's status that he hesitated in sharing his story. Philip began by listening carefully. He led the man's need and interests into the message he was prepared to share. Whether we are zealous or shy, following this model can help us communicate in a way that people can understand and receive.

We'll tell our own stories best, after we've listened first.

DAY 11 Raindrops of Truth

Bible Reading: Isaiah 55:10-11

Having had a spiritual awakening as the result of these steps, we tried to carry this message to others and to practice these principles in all our affairs.

As we've practiced the principles of the Twelve Steps, we've seen growth in our lives. We have experienced a spiritual awakening, even if we weren't looking for one when we started. As the seasons passed, we worked at applying each step. We noticed that some of the hunger that used to drive us began to subside. We realized more of our human dignity.

God tells us that his Word in our lives has this kind of impact. He says, "As the rain and snow come down from heaven and stay upon the ground to water the earth, and cause the grain to grow and to produce seed for the farmer and bread for the hungry, so also is my Word. I send it out and it always produces fruit. It shall accomplish all I want it to, and prosper everywhere I send it" (Isaiah 55:10-11).

The principles of the Twelve Steps are tremendously powerful to change lives. One reason is that they incorporate and apply many powerful truths from the Word of God. Sometimes they come to us in gentle showers or flurries. Sometimes the truth drenches us like a sudden downpour. The principles settle into our lives and seep down into our hearts. In time, they produce fruit in our lives that nourishes our souls. As we continue to soak in the godly principles found in the Twelve Steps we will prosper as God intended.

Our recovery stories can soak into the lives of others, like rain into parched ground.

DAY 12 Fir Trees from Thorns

Bible Reading: Isaiah 55:12-13

Having had a spiritual awakening as the result of these steps, we tried to carry this message to others and to practice these principles in all our affairs.

Once we've been free from our addictions for a while we start to feel great! So many people in our lives are relieved of the pain and worry they used to suffer when we were in bondage. The places in our lives that used to be wasted and overgrown with thorns have been cleaned up. There's more joy and peace in our lives.

A promise in the book of Isaiah can be applied to us. God said, "You will live in joy and peace. The mountains and hills, the trees of the field—all the world around you—will rejoice. Where once were thorns, fir trees will grow; where briars grew, the myrtle trees will sprout up. This miracle will make the Lord's name very great and be an everlasting sign [of God's power and love]" (Isaiah 55:12-13).

As time passes and we continue to practice the principles of the Twelve Steps, we will see good things developing in areas of our lives that used to be thorny and wasted. The people around us will happily get used to the new us, and there will be a lot more joy in living. But we still need to look back and remember the "thorns" of our addiction now and again. We need to be willing to talk about our recovery at appropriate times. There are people whose lives are still filled with "thorns," who need to hear our story so they can receive the hope our recovery can offer.

By remembering our thorny past, we will give hope to others of a glorious future.

DAY 13 Suffering That Heals

Bible Reading:
Isaiah 53:1-12

Having had a spiritual awakening as the result of these steps, we tried to carry this message to others and to practice these principles in all our affairs.

Those of us who have worked through the Twelve Steps will see life from a distinctive viewpoint. We'll see things differently from those who haven't acknowledged and dealt with their own pain. We've processed the depth of suffering that comes from growing up in this broken world. We're well acquainted with our own grief, and compassionate toward others who are hurting. The things we've suffered have helped us learn valuable lessons about life that can't be learned any other way. We have a message of hope for those still held prisoner by their addictions.

Even the Savior of the world learned from the things he'd suffered. Jesus spoke of himself by quoting Isaiah, "The Spirit of the Lord God is upon me, because the Lord has anointed me to bring good news to the suffering and afflicted. He has sent me to comfort the brokenhearted, to announce liberty to captives, and to open the eyes of the blind. He has sent me to tell those who mourn that the time of God's favor to them has come" (Isaiah 61:1-2). Isaiah told us that Christ would be, "a man of sorrows, acquainted with bitterest grief" (53:3).

We're not the Savior of the world, but like him, we've learned through the things we've suffered. And we have good news for those who are brokenhearted, blind, and imprisoned.

We have learned much through our painful steps toward recovery; we will learn even more as we share it with others.

DAY 14 God's Faithfulness

Bible Reading: Isaiah 38:1-20

Having had a spiritual awakening as the result of these steps, we tried to carry this message to others and to practice these principles in all our affairs.

We may not have been on the verge of death, but something devastated our lives enough to lead us into recovery.

Once, King Hezekiah became deathly sick and was told to set his affairs in order because he was going to die. He broke down sobbing and prayed for God to heal him. God heard and spared his life. Here's part of a poem he wrote about his experience: "All night I moaned; it was like being torn apart by lions. . . . All my sleep has fled because of my soul's bitterness. O Lord, your discipline is good and leads to life and health. Oh, heal me and make me live! Yes, now I see it all—it was good for me to undergo this bitterness, for you have lovingly delivered me from death; you have forgiven all my sins. . . . Think of it! The Lord healed me! Every day of my life from now on I will sing my songs of praise" (Isaiah 38:13, 15-17, 20).

We, too, can look back on the painful process of our recovery and say, "It was good for me to undergo this bitterness, for you have lovingly delivered me." We need to make God's faithfulness known to the next generation. We can do this by talking about our experiences and singing his praises every day we live.

When our recovery is centered on God, his transforming power can turn our pain into gladness.

DAY 15 Known but Not Rejected

Bible Reading: John 4:28-42

Having had a spiritual awakening as the result of these steps, we tried to carry this message to others and to practice these principles in all our affairs.

One thing we gain through recovery groups is the support of people who love and accept us, even though they know all about us. This kind of support is well worth telling others about.

Jesus met a Samaritan woman by a well in the middle of a hot day. She didn't have the best reputation. He knew she was thirsty for more than just water. She was thirsty for acceptance and love, something that Jesus gave her. After their talk, "the woman left her waterpot beside the well and went back to the village and told everyone, 'Come and meet a man who told me everything I ever did! Can this be the Messiah?' So the people came streaming from the village to see him. . . . Many from the Samaritan village believed he was the Messiah because of the woman's report: 'He told me everything I ever did!'" (John 4:28-30, 39).

This woman had gone through five broken marriages and was living with a man who wasn't her husband. She was despised in her community and rejected. When she met someone who knew all of this but accepted her anyway, she spread the news. We, too, can find God's love and acceptance in recovery groups, and tell others about the support available. Then they can come and find recovery for themselves.

We will find new courage when we discover that we are known by God, but not rejected.

DAY 16 Qualified to Encourage

Bible Reading: Luke 10:30-37

Having had a spiritual awakening as the result of these steps, we tried to carry this message to others and to practice these principles in all our affairs.

Maybe we've been treated like we're subhuman. Perhaps we've been despised and rejected because of the shameful effects of our addictions. We may feel like we aren't educated enough to help anyone recover. Don't they need a professional trained to deal with these issues? What do we have to offer that could really help?

The Samaritans of Jesus' day were a mixed race. They worshiped the Lord, but worshiped pagan gods as well (see 2 Kings 17:24-41). For these two reasons, they were hated and persecuted. Jesus tells a story about a Jew who was attacked and left bleeding on a roadside. "By chance a Jewish priest came along; and when he saw the man lying there, he crossed to the other side of the road and passed him by. A Jewish Temple-assistant walked over and looked at him lying there, but then went on. But a despised Samaritan came along, and when he saw him, he felt deep pity" (Luke 10:31-33). It was the Samaritan who helped the man recover.

The two spiritual professionals looked on the man's injuries but weren't moved to do anything. Perhaps they had never really suffered themelves! The despised Samaritan could feel deep pity because he knew what suffering and rejection were like. Who is better equipped to help a hurting person than someone who has been hurt himself and is able to display sincere compassion?

There is no one better qualified to help than someone who's already been there.

DAY 17 Extending the Invitation

Bible Reading: Luke 14:16-24

Having had a spiritual awakening as the result of these steps, we tried to carry this message to others and to practice these principles in all our affairs.

Some of us entered recovery or a relationship with God because someone encouraged us. Others of us had to find our own way because no one took an interest in us. Perhaps people thought we were too far gone to be worth their time; maybe they disqualified us for some other reason.

Jesus told this story about inviting people into the Kingdom of God. "A man prepared a great feast and sent out many invitations. When all was ready, he sent his servant around to notify the guests that it was time for them to arrive. But they all began making excuses. . . . The servant returned and reported to his master what they had said. His master was angry and told him to go quickly into the streets and alleys of the city and to invite the beggars, crippled, lame, and blind. But even then there was still room. 'Well, then,' said his master, 'go out into the country lanes and out behind the hedges and urge anyone you find to come, so that the house will be full'" (Luke 14:16-18, 21-23).

Step Twelve says to "carry this message to others." "You are to go into all the world and preach the Good News to everyone, everywhere" (Mark 16:15). In both regards, we should be careful not to prejudge and disqualify anyone from hearing the message. Our job is just to extend the invitation.

Our part is to share our journey; God's part is to help others listen.

DAY 18 Small Beginnings

Bible Reading: Matthew 13:31-32

Having had a spiritual awakening as the result of these steps, we tried to carry this message to others and to practice these principles in all our affairs.

When we first decided to admit we were powerless and that our lives had become unmanageable, we took a tiny step. We probably had a hard time believing that we could go even one day without relapsing into our old ways. Now we're amazed to see how working the steps has caused a new life to grow and has positively impacted every area of our lives. We may shake our heads in wonder to realize how many days have passed (one day at a time) since we last fell.

Jesus gave this illustration: "The Kingdom of Heaven is like a tiny mustard seed planted in a field. It is the smallest of all seeds, but becomes the largest of plants, and grows into a tree where birds can come and find shelter" (Matthew 13:31-32). The phrase "Kingdom of Heaven" refers to a realm or sphere in which, at any given time, God's rule is acknowledged.

When we turned our lives over to the care of God, we opened up our lives to becoming part of the sphere of God's rule. From such small beginnings we have seen a whole new life grow, and beyond our wildest expectations! The tiny seed of our being that was dwarfed by our addictions has now burst open with our spiritual awakening.

When sharing, remember how God made great things happen from small beginnings.

DAY 19 A Gradual Miracle

Bible Reading: Mark 8:22-26

Having had a spiritual awakening as the result of these steps, we tried to carry this message to others and to practice these principles in all our affairs.

Some of us have a spiritual awakening that's sudden. We're jolted to our senses—like being awakened by a splash of ice-cold water. For others of us the change is more gradual. We have a hard time shaking loose the darkness of our past. But whether we awoke in an instant or gradually, we have a valid message to take to others.

"Jesus took [a] blind man by the hand and led him out of the village, and spat upon his eyes, and laid his hands over them. 'Can you see anything now?' Jesus asked him. The man looked around. 'Yes!' he said, 'I see men! But I can't see them very clearly; they look like tree trunks walking around!' Then Jesus placed his hands over the man's eyes again and as the man stared intently, his sight was completely restored, and he saw everything clearly, drinking in the sights around him. Jesus sent him home to his family" (Mark 8:22-26).

This miracle sounds like a messy process. It didn't all happen in an instant, but this doesn't make the story any less important. It's in the Bible right along with all the stories of instantaneous healing (see Matthew 9:27-31). If our awakening and recovery has been a long and messy process, we still need to tell others. There are those who think there's something wrong with them because their recovery isn't a "sudden miracle." By hearing our stories of gradual recovery, they will be encouraged.

A gradual miracle is no less a miracle than an instant one.

DAY 20 A Light of Hope

Bible Reading:
1 Thessalonians 5:5-8

Having had a spiritual awakening as the result of these steps, we tried to carry this message to others and to practice these principles in all our affairs.

Now that we've had a spiritual awakening, we can see how a daily practice of the principles in all our affairs is important. We can't just do things now and again, here and there, and hope to stay alert.

Paul warned all believers to be alert and ready for the return of Christ at any moment. "For you are all children of the light and of the day, and do not belong to the darkness and night. So be on your guard, not asleep like the others. Watch for his return and stay sober. Night is the time for sleep and the time when people get drunk. But let us who live in the light keep sober, protected by the armor of faith and love, and wearing as our helmet the happy hope of salvation" (1 Thessalonians 5:5-8).

Just as we need sleep on a regular basis to keep us alert during the daytime, we need regular application of the Twelve Steps to keep us sober. Jesus told his disciples, "You are the world's light—a city on a hill, glowing in the night for all to see. Don't hide your light! Let it shine for all . . . to see, so that they will praise your heavenly Father" (Matthew 5:14-16).

Light makes itself evident by contrast. As we practice the Twelve Steps in all of our affairs, we'll shine in a dark world. We can be a light of hope for people still searching for answers. Let's not hide our light, but let it shine!

As our lives brighten through recovery, we can bring hope to others by letting the light shine out.

DAY 21 A Solid Foundation

Bible Reading:
Matthew 7:24-27

Having had a spiritual awakening as the result of these steps, we tried to carry this message to others and to practice these principles in all our affairs.

At this point in our recovery we've started to rebuild our lives. We came to realize that our past lives weren't able to hold up under the pressure of life's storms. Now we're trying to do things differently so we don't repeat past mistakes and see it all come crashing down again.

Jesus told a story that relates to this. "All who listen to my instructions and follow them are wise, like a man who builds his house on solid rock. Though the rain comes in torrents, and the floods rise and the storm winds beat against his house, it won't collapse, for it is built on rock. But those who hear my instructions and ignore them are foolish, like a man who builds his house on sand. For when the rains and floods come, and storm winds beat against his house, it will fall with a mighty crash" (Matthew 7:24-27).

The instructions Jesus gave are integrated into the principles of the Twelve Steps. By practicing them we will be following Jesus' instructions. Life will always have storms and floods! We will face challenging problems and hurts in the future, as we have in the past. Practicing the principles of the Twelve Steps—honesty, humility, accountability, reliance upon God, self-evaluation, interdependence with others, openness to transformation, consideration, prayer, and diligence—will create a firm foundation for the new life we're working to build.

Our recovery takes time, but should reach and transform the very roots of our being.

DAY 22 Transformation

Bible Reading: Romans 12:1-2

Having had a spiritual awakening as the result of these steps, we tried to carry this message to others and to practice these principles in all our affairs.

Those of us who have sincerely practiced the Twelve Steps will begin to experience a transformation. The way we think and live will grow more and more in line with the satisfying life God intends for us. We're growing away from our old ways and experiencing more and more freedom.

Paul said, "Don't copy the behavior and customs of this world, but be a new and different person with a fresh newness in all you do and think. Then you will learn from your own experience how his ways will really satisfy you" (Romans 12:2). He also said, "The Lord is the Spirit who gives . . . life, and where he is there is freedom. . . . We can be mirrors that brightly reflect the glory of the Lord. And as the Spirit of the Lord works within us, we become more and more like him" (2 Corinthians 3:17-18).

By turning our lives over to the care of God, preparing for him to remove our defects of character, humbly asking him to remove our shortcomings, and seeking through prayer and meditation to improve our conscious contact with God, we have opened our lives up to the Holy Spirit. As he continues to work within us, and we continue to remain open to God, our transformation will continue. Our growing freedom is a reflection to others of the freedom they can have, too.

Only a recovery that shares itself with others will be a transforming one.

DAY 23 Hanging On

Bible Reading: Genesis 32:24-31

Having had a spiritual awakening as the result of these steps, we tried to carry this message to others and to practice these principles in all our affairs.

For some of us our relationship with God has seemed like a wrestling match at times. We almost see him as an opponent who's fighting against us. And yet we don't dare let him go because we know that without God's help we're lost.

Jacob had a strange experience. He was in camp alone "and a Man wrestled with him until dawn. And when the Man saw that he couldn't win the match, he struck Jacob's hip and knocked it out of joint at the socket. Then the Man said, 'Let me go, for it is dawn.' But Jacob panted, 'I will not let you go until you bless me.' 'What is your name?' the Man asked. 'Jacob.' . . . 'It isn't anymore!' the Man told him. 'It is Israel—one who has power with God. Because you have been strong with God, you shall prevail with men.' 'What is *your* name?' Jacob asked him. 'No, you mustn't ask,' the Man told him. And he blessed him there. Jacob named the place 'Peniel' ('The Face of God'), for he said, 'I have seen God face to face, and yet my life is spared.'" (Genesis 32:24-31).

Jacob had a real wrestling match with God. He went away with a new name and God's blessing, but he also was limping. We may have to wrestle with God as he changes who we are. But if we refuse to let go of God, he will bless us. Those of us who wrestle with God may also come away with a "limp" to remind us of the intensity of the struggle which led to our new identity.

Holding on to God is always rewarded by his blessing.

DAY 24 Sharing Our Hope

Bible Reading: Acts 9:36-43

Having had a spiritual awakening as the result of these steps, we tried to carry this message to others and to practice these principles in all our affairs.

Our spiritual awakening and recovery may seem to us like a resurrection from the dead. We have seen what the power of God can do. Now we're in a position to share that powerful message.

Jesus once referred to himself as "Petra," a massive rock. He renamed Simon "Petros," meaning a stone detached from the rock. Jesus was calling Simon a "chip off the old block"! One day Peter was brought in to see the body of a woman who had recently died. "The room was filled with weeping widows who were showing one another the coats and other garments Dorcas had made for them. But Peter asked them all to leave the room; then he knelt and prayed. Turning to the body he said, 'Get up, Dorcas,' and she opened her eyes!" (Acts 9:39-40).

We may wonder how Peter knew what to do in this situation. In Mark 5:22-43, we read about a time when Peter saw Jesus raise a girl from the dead in similar circumstances. Peter had been with Jesus when death was raised to new life. So later, Peter was able to take the power of God and the hope of renewed life to others.

We have seen how God can use the Twelve Steps to awaken us spiritually from lives that were killing us. We can recall what we saw God do for us. Then we can extend the life and the message of hope to others who are living lives that are killing them.

We don't need eloquent words; we need only share what God has done in our lives.

DAY 25 Freedom from Shame

Bible Reading:
2 Samuel 6:14-21

Having had a spiritual awakening as the result of these steps, we tried to carry this message to others and to practice these principles in all our affairs.

When God does great things in our lives we may well be overjoyed. We may feel like dancing and singing! We might want to tell the whole world! But we may get some negative reactions.

David knew the feeling! "David danced before the Lord with all his might, and was wearing priests' clothing. So Israel brought home the Ark of the Lord with much shouting and blowing of trumpets. (But as the procession came into the city, Michal, Saul's daughter [and David's wife], watched . . . and she was filled with contempt for him.) . . . When it was all over, and everyone had gone home, David returned to bless his family. But Michal came out to meet him and exclaimed in disgust, 'How glorious the king of Israel looked today! He exposed himself to the girls along the street like a common pervert!' David retorted, 'I was dancing before the Lord. . . . So I am willing to act like a fool in order to show my joy in the Lord'" (2 Samuel 6:14-16, 19-21).

Michal wasn't a part of the celebration. She stayed back and fumed, rehearsing her criticisms, attempting to shame David. When we begin to express our joy over the great things God is doing for us, those who aren't in on the celebration will resent our display. They may try to shame us into being quiet. We don't have to be ashamed anymore! It's sad that they won't celebrate with us, but that's no reason for our party to stop.

God is able to remove our shame and replace it with joy.

DAY 26 Something to Boast about

Bible Reading: Psalm 107:1-32

Having had a spiritual awakening as the result of these steps, we tried to carry this message to others and to practice these principles in all our affairs.

Those of us who have worked through the Twelve Steps come from many different backgrounds. We could be categorized or labeled in many different ways. But we share a common past of imprisonment to the powerful effects of an addiction or compulsion. We can also share the common experience of having been rescued by God and set free from our peculiar prisons.

Psalm 107 is addressed to various groups of people who have been rescued by God. It says, "He satisfies the thirsty soul and fills the hungry soul with good. . . . They cried to the Lord in their troubles and he rescued them! He led them from the darkness and shadow of death and snapped their chains. Oh, that these men would praise the Lord for his loving-kindness and for all of his wonderful deeds! For he broke down their prison gates of brass and cut apart their iron bars. . . . Let them praise him publicly before the congregation, and before the leaders of the nation" (Psalm 107:9, 13-16, 32).

King David sang, "I will boast of all his [God's] kindness to me. Let all who are discouraged take heart. Let us praise the Lord together, and exalt his name" (Psalm 34:2).

Those of us who have been set free have something to boast about. We're called to praise God and to exalt him publicly.

Our natural response to recovery should be to shout our story from the rooftops!

DAY 27 Never Too Late

Bible Reading: John 3:1-8

Having had a spiritual awakening as the result of these steps, we tried to carry this message to others and to practice these principles in all our affairs.

Perhaps we thought we were too old and set in our ways to start all over again—but we found a new life anyway! In working the Twelve Steps we had a spiritual awakening. This may not be something we feel comfortable talking about openly, but we do want to carry the message to others.

"After dark one night a Jewish religious leader named Nicodemus . . . came for an interview with Jesus. 'Sir,' he said, 'we all know that God has sent you to teach us. Your miracles are proof enough of this.' Jesus replied, 'With all the earnestness I possess. I tell you this: Unless you are born again, you can never get into the Kingdom of God.' 'Born again!' exclaimed Nicodemus. 'What do you mean? How can an old man go back into his mother's womb and be born again?' Jesus replied, '. . . Men can only reproduce human life, but the Holy Spirit gives new life from heaven'" (John 3:1-6).

Nicodemus had spent many years working his way up in the religious and social hierarchy. He thought he was too old to change, but he experienced a spiritual awakening in his encounter with Jesus. There was at least one person with whom he shared his faith. After the crucifixion, he and another secret disciple, an influential Jew like himself, buried the body of Jesus. We may feel uncomfortable telling our story to the world, but there are other people like us who may be receptive, one on one.

God often works in the hearts of the people we least expect him to.

DAY 28 Remembering the Lost

Bible Reading:
Luke 15:1-7

Having had a spiritual awakening as the result of these steps, we tried to carry this message to others and to practice these principles in all our affairs.

As time goes by in our recovery we may find that some of our friends look down on us for attending meetings with "addicts and sinners." We may hear complaints about associating with this "kind of people." Or we may find that we forget about those who are still lost in the wilderness of addiction.

"Dishonest tax collectors and other notorious sinners often came to listen to Jesus' sermons; but this caused complaints from the Jewish religious leaders and the experts on Jewish law because he was associating with such despicable people—even eating with them! So Jesus used this illustration: 'If you had a hundred sheep and one of them strayed away and was lost in the wilderness, wouldn't you leave the ninety-nine others to go and search for the lost one until you found it? And then you would joyfully carry it home on your shoulders. When you arrived you would call together your friends and neighbors to rejoice with you because your lost sheep was found. Well, in the same way heaven will be happier over one lost sinner who returns to God than over ninety-nine others who haven't strayed away!'" (Luke 15:1-7).

God doesn't see people as either despicable or good. He sees them all as precious, whether they are lost or found. Now that we have been found, we must not forget those who are still lost.

God loves us so much that he seeks each one of us out and rejoices when we are found.

DAY 29 A Spiritual Recovery

Bible Reading: Luke 12:16-21

Having had a spiritual awakening as the result of these steps, we tried to carry this message to others and to practice these principles in all our affairs.

Being free from our addictions and compulsions is wonderful! We have the chance to build a life that's rich in every way. We may know people who have used the Twelve Steps to find freedom from their addictions, but who have never accepted Jesus Christ as the Savior of their souls. Perhaps, we are in this situation. We've found a better life, but our eternal life is still in jeopardy.

Jesus gave this illustration: "A rich man had a fertile farm that produced fine crops. In fact, his barns were full to overflowing—he couldn't get everything in. He thought about his problem, and finally exclaimed, 'I know—I'll tear down my barns and build bigger ones! Then I'll have room enough. And I'll sit back and say to myself, "Friend, you have enough stored away for years to come. Now take it easy!"' . . . But God said to him, 'Fool! Tonight you die. Then who will get it all?' Yes, every man is a fool who gets rich on earth but not in heaven" (Luke 12:16-21). Another time Jesus said, "What profit is there if you gain the whole world—and lose eternal life? What can be compared with the value of eternal life?" (Matthew 16:26).

Our earthly life may be wonderful now that our addictions are under control. But, God's "kindness is meant to lead [us] to repentance" (Romans 2:4). In the final evaluation, recovery is wasted if we lose our eternal souls. We need to keep this in mind for ourselves and those with whom we share our message.

What is the use of recovery in this life if we are still eternally lost?

DAY 30 We Will Make It!

Bible Reading: Philippians 1:3-11

Having had a spiritual awakening as the result of these steps, we tried to carry this message to others and to practice these principles in all our affairs.

We may have gotten through the Twelve Steps (for the first time or for the tenth time), but we are all still in process. God began a work within us which is continuing each day we live. His grace is at work within us, as we practice the principles we've learned, and as we carry the message of recovery to others.

The apostle Paul wrote a message for the Philippians which applies to us in many ways. He wrote, "I am sure that God who began the good work within you will keep right on helping you grow in his grace until his task within you is finally finished on that day when Jesus Christ returns. . . . My prayer for you is that you will overflow more and more with love for others, and at the same time keep on growing in spiritual knowledge and insight, for I want you always to see clearly the difference between right and wrong, and to be inwardly clean, no one being able to criticize you from now until our Lord returns" (Philippians 1:6, 9-10).

Grace is the gift of God's unearned favor. God favored us when we were still held in bondage by our addictions. He took us in his arms when no one else would touch us. He bought us when no one else was sure we were worth much. He is the author and finisher of our faith. We can be sure we will make it, because he has lavished his grace on us and committed himself to our recovery.

When God starts a project, he finishes it!

STARTING OVER

"For I am convinced that nothing can ever separate us from his love. Death can't, and life can't. The angels won't, and all the powers of hell itself cannot keep God's love away. Our fears for today, our worries about tomorrow, or where we are—high above the sky, or in the deepest ocean—nothing will ever be able to separate us from the love of God demonstrated by our Lord Jesus Christ when he died for us" (Romans 8:38-39).

Starting Over

Day 1 The Morning After

Bible Reading:
Matthew
26:33-35, 74-75

Yesterday we may have sworn there was no way we were going to fall again. Things were going well. But what happened? Now we're sitting here, aching inside, and cursing ourselves. Maybe we allowed ourselves to be lured into a risky situation. We convinced ourselves there was good reason—that it would be all right. Maybe we just felt like we could handle it—but we couldn't—or at least we didn't. And now we're miserable!

Peter had his own "morning after" experience. Peter had sworn to Jesus, "If everyone else deserts you, I won't." Jesus replied "The truth is that this very night, before the cock crows at dawn, you will deny me three times!" Peter responded, "I would die first!" (Matthew 26:33-35). Jesus had been right, as always! Jesus was betrayed, arrested, tried, and beaten. It was more than Peter could bear; but he couldn't walk away. So he followed. He was suspected of being a collaborator. Each time he lied to protect himself. The third time, he "began to curse and swear. 'I don't even know the man,' he said. And immediately the cock crowed. Then Peter remembered what Jesus had said, 'Before the cock crows, you will deny me three times.' And he went away, crying bitterly" (Matthew 26:74-75).

Jesus knew Peter was going to fall in advance; and his love didn't skip a beat! God doesn't hate us on the morning after. He loves us every bit as much today as he did before we fell.

God's love for us never changes, even when we've failed.

Day 2 Not Disqualified

Bible Reading:
Matthew 4:18-20

We may accept God's forgiveness, but feel that our fall has disqualified us from serving God or aspiring to great things. We may conclude that we're only fit for the kind of position in life we had before we began to hope and work for something better.

The apostle Peter started out as a fisherman named Simon. That was all he was qualified for, at least before Jesus came along. "One day as he [Jesus] was walking along the beach beside the Lake of Galilee, he saw two brothers—Simon, also called Peter, and Andrew—out in a boat fishing with a net, for they were commercial fishermen. Jesus called out, 'Come along with me and I will show you how to fish for the souls of men!' And they left their nets at once and went with him" (Matthew 4:18-20). For the next three years Jesus trained him to "fish for souls," and during that time Peter witnessed many miracles. But then he blew it! In the end he denied Jesus. He went through three days of utter hell, and then the greatest miracle of all happened. Jesus was alive again! But Peter still thought of himself as disqualified. He started up his fishing business again. That's where Jesus found him, back in his old life. It was on that same shore that Jesus reaffirmed his call. Again he said to Peter, "Follow me" (John 21:19).

We may consider ourselves disqualified after a fall, but God doesn't. The apostle Paul said, "For God's gifts and his call can never be withdrawn; he will never go back on his promises" (Romans 11:29). Just because we've blown it doesn't mean that we should give up and go back to our old lives. God still has a wonderful future for us.

We only really fail when we refuse to get up and start again.

Day 3 God Still Loves Us

Bible Reading: Romans 8:38-39

We may feel like God hates us. We may hate ourselves right now. We wonder how God's love can continue when we've disappointed him so. It's a wonder that God doesn't just throw us away! It's a wonder that he keeps us at all!

This may be how we feel, but it isn't true! The apostle Paul once wrote: "For I am convinced that nothing can ever separate us from his love. Death can't, and life can't. The angels won't, and all the powers of hell itself cannot keep God's love away. Our fears for today, our worries about tomorrow, or where we are—high above the sky, or in the deepest ocean—nothing will ever be able to separate us from the love of God demonstrated by our Lord Jesus Christ when he died for us" (Romans 8:38-39). King David prayed, "O Lord, you have examined my heart and know everything about me. . . . You know what I am going to say before I even say it. You both precede and follow me, and place your hand of blessing on my head. This is too glorious, too wonderful to believe! I can *never* be lost to your Spirit! I can *never* get away from my God!" (Psalm 139:1, 4-7).

Once we've accepted Christ's death as payment for our sins, there's absolutely nothing we can do to escape the love of God! God knows everything we've done—every thought, word, and deed. In fact, he knew things would happen as they did before they ever happened. He is determined to bless us, to love us, and to keep us. He'll never throw us away!

There is absolutely nothing we can do to make God love us any less.

Day 4 Wanting to Die

Bible Reading: 1 Kings 19:3-7

When we fall, we may wish we could just die. We may feel like the struggle is just too much for us. We've tried but failed again; now we're exhausted! When we feel this way we may withdraw from those who could help us. Our shame over the failure makes us want to hide. We feel like the journey is over. The last thing we want to do is start back on the steps of recovery.

Elijah, the great prophet, had similar feelings. Almost immediately after winning one of his greatest victories for God, he became overwhelmed by a threat from wicked Queen Jezebel. "So, Elijah fled for his life. . . . He went on alone into the wilderness . . . and prayed that he might die. 'I've had enough,' he told the Lord. 'Take away my life. I've got to die sometime, and it might as well be now.' Then he lay down and slept beneath the broom bush. But as he was sleeping, an angel touched him and told him to get up and eat! He looked around and saw some bread baking on hot stones, and a jar of water! So he ate and drank and lay down again. Then the angel of the Lord came again and touched him and said, 'Get up and eat some more, for there is a long journey ahead of you'" (1 Kings 19:3-7).

After this dark moment, Elijah lived to experience many more great victories. We will too! We probably are exhausted. Right now we need to give ourselves some rest and nourishment. We need someone by our side who will encourage us to get up and get going again. There's still a long journey ahead of us.

When we want to quit we need to look for loving people who will encourage and nourish us.

Day 5 No Condemnation

Bible Reading: Romans 7:15–8:1

We may be punishing ourselves. We certainly feel like we deserve it! We don't just feel guilty; we feel like this last fall proves that we're rotten to the core. Our feelings of self-condemnation may go beyond guilt for the wrong behavior, convincing us of our worthlessness. It seems futile to keep trying.

The apostle Paul talked about how frustrating it can be to fall back into the very things we hate (see Romans 7). But then he concludes, "So there is now no condemnation awaiting those who belong to Christ Jesus. For the power of the life-giving Spirit—and this power is mine through Christ Jesus—has freed me from the vicious circle of sin and death" (Romans 8:1-2).

Our feelings of condemnation come from ourselves and Satan, not from God. The Bible calls Satan the Accuser. Looking to a future day, it says, "It has happened at last! God's salvation and the power and the rule, and the authority of his Christ are finally here; for the Accuser of our brothers has been thrown down from heaven onto earth—he accused them day and night before our God" (Revelation 12:10).

God will convict us of the wrong of our behavior, so we can confess it and receive cleansing forgiveness. Remember, "If we confess our sins to him, he can be depended on to forgive us and to cleanse us from every wrong" (1 John 1:9). Let's not give in to the condemnation. We're not hopeless and worthless! We just fell. God wants to dust us off and set us back on the path to a better life.

God never condemns those who look to him for forgiveness, even after the greatest of failures.